FROM
BASIC
TO
PASCAL

No. 1466
$18.95

FROM
BASIC
TO
PASCAL

BY RONALD W. ANDERSON

TAB BOOKS Inc.
BLUE RIDGE SUMMIT, PA. 17214

FIRST EDITION

SIXTH PRINTING

Printed in the United States of America

Library of Congress Cataloging in Publication Data

Anderson, Ronald W.
    From Basic To Pascal.

    Includes index.
     1. Basic (Computer program language)
2. PASCAL (Computer program language) I. Title.
QA76.73.B3A35   001.64′24   82-5671
ISBN 0-8306-2466-X   AACR2
ISBN 0-8306-1466-4 (pbk.)

Basic
RIP

Contents

Note: Comments in the complete listings are enclosed in brackets ({ }). These comments are enclosed in parentheses in the fragments of programs that have been typeset.

List of Programs

Preface

Before you read this book, it makes sense for you to know something of my background. I've written several articles for popular computer magazines, and I currently write a monthly column for '68' *Micro Journal,* a small publication that specializes in articles and information for users of the Motorola 6800 and 6809 microprocessors.

I use microprocessors in my work and in addition I am an avid hobbyist. The manuscript for this book was prepared entirely on my 6809-based system. I tried all of the programs and program fragments on my system with at least two versions of Pascal. The BASIC programs have been run with Technical Systems Consultants Extended BASIC. I've used Programma's PIE Editor and TSC's text processor for formatting the text.

I write this not as an expert in computer science. I have a B.S. in electrical engineering and about 20 years of hardware experience. When microcomputers first became available (about 4 years ago), I saw applications in my work and began to study their use. The applications in which I am most interested are so-called "dedicated computer systems" in which a single program is installed in Read Only Memory at the factory. The computer is used to run a machine. The applications in which I am involved include measurement of unbalance in such diverse parts as grinding wheels, automobile wheels and brake drums, crankshafts, clutch parts, flywheels, pulleys, fans, transmission parts, etc. I am presently involved in a multi-axis machine control for a grinding machine.

Because of my needs, I am particularly conscious of the need for efficient code generation by compilers. I was involved in a great deal of assembler programming when compilers for microprocessor-based computers existed only in the minds of their programmer originators. Assembler is the most efficient code in terms of memory usage and speed for most applications. However, it is not cost effective in applications where production quantity of the product is to be small. In my search for the most usable compiler, I've found Pascal to be suitable and efficient. The code generated (for a large program) is 2 to 3 times that generated using assembler. The execution speed is reduced by a factor that varies greatly among the various compiler implementations. Perhaps 10 to 30 would be a good estimate. In many applications, speed is not critical, and the savings in programming time are immense.

Pascal really "shines," however, when a program is finished and a change is found to be necessary or desirable. Some time ago I was involved in a control for a large machine with CRT display and operator input keypad. I found that changes requested at the end of the project always took about a day to implement. Even something as simple as moving a word or two on the CRT display took this long. The listing for the whole program in assembler was about 120 pages. It, therefore, took in the neighborhood of two hours to get a fresh listing from our line printer. My estimate now is that about 18 pages of Pascal could have done the same thing. Changes in a Pascal program to do the same job are vastly easier to handle.

I would like to thank my friend, Art Weller of El Paso, Texas, for his careful review of my manuscript and for his innumerable suggestions, which made vast improvements in the clarity of the presentation. Of course, I must thank my family who have put up with my disappearing for nights into my "dungeon" to sit in front of the terminal and work on this book. I sincerely hope that you have as much fun and learn as much reading this as I did writing it.

Introduction

Learning is the process of proceeding in small steps from what you know to what you don't know. If you have picked up some of the currently available books on programming, you might have been discouraged because they assume that you already know the language. This book starts with the assumption that you have some facility with BASIC. It will take you through gradual and easy steps to an understanding of Pascal. If your BASIC is a little shaky, you will find yourself gaining proficiency in that language too. If you have ever studied a foreign language, you may remember that you learned a great deal about your native language in the process. I believe you will find the same thing to be true of learning a second computer language.

Many of the implementations of BASIC and nearly all of those of Pascal will allow you to use both upper- and lowercase letters, (though they may or may not be recognized as different). The standard will be adopted here to use uppercase only in programs or parts of them when they are referred to in the text. This is simply to make the distinction between text and program language commands more clear.

In proceeding from the known to the unknown, there is usually a point where things suddenly get very confusing. Until you reach that point, proceed through this text more or less as you would read a novel. When the "difficult part" comes, and that will be different for different people, slow down and re-read any point that is not clear. If it doesn't make sense after a few attempts, make a note of it and continue reading. Perhaps a later portion of the text will clarify it. Sometimes new ideas have to "soak" for a few days. A reading several days later might show that you now understand the point.

If you have a computer or access to one that runs BASIC and Pascal, you should type in the sample programs and fragments and experiment with them. There is no substitute for hands-on experience in learning programming with any language.

Chapter 1

What Are Programming Languages?

Programming languages are the interface between the programmer and the machine. They may be "low-level" interfaces similar to and including assembler, in which the programmer must be familiar with the intricacies of the particular processor being used, or they may be "high-level," machine-independent languages that are virtually the same regardless of the size or brand name of the computer on which they are being run. This machine independence may be achieved in different ways. One of the most used is to simulate a hypothetical computing machine and then write a set of instructions for that machine. The simulation program will then vary for different processors, but the instruction set will remain constant. When this approach is used, frequently the compiler will generate "pseudo code" instructions for the "simulated machine," and these will be interpreted by a program called a pseudo code (or P code) interpreter, which will be different for each different processor.

All programming languages must have certain basic elements or features to make them usable. At first glance, it may seem that these common elements would make all programming languages very much alike. After all, the end result of using most languages is the same: a running program. I have one of the programs used as an example in this book (Reverse) in running versions for BASIC, Pascal, FORTH, and assembler. I would defy anyone running the program to tell me which version is currently running.

All languages have variables, storage places to keep the starting data and the results as well as the intermediate calculations.

They direct the flow of the program execution by means of jumps, subroutines, loops, etc. This control of program flow, in all languages, is based on decision statements such as IF . . . THEN. Many have similar data structures such as arrays and files.

If they all produce the same results, why so many different languages, you may ask. The question is a valid one. A language will, to a large degree, reflect the goals of its creator(s). Since we are concerned here mainly with the two languages BASIC and Pascal, you might ask specifically, why are BASIC and Pascal so different?

Actually, BASIC and Pascal are not so different. They certainly appear to be so, but appearances are sometimes deceiving. The differences that you see result largely from the philosophy of their design. BASIC was designed to be a very easy language to learn. That is, why it is so popular as a "first language." Virtually all home computers are equipped to run BASIC. It purposely avoids some of the "complications" that make other languages more useful for complex applications. The designers of BASIC started out to create a language for beginners. Niklaus Wirth, in writing Pascal, had the goal of designing a language that could be used to teach structured programming. Computer languages generally reflect the specific objectives of the designer but may be awkward and inconvenient when used for an application not consistent with those objectives. All languages, therefore, have advantages and disadvantages. Many have simply disappeared, and others have grown in popularity, reflecting their usefulness in the eyes of the users. There is no perfect language that does everything for everyone.

Several years ago, Edsger Dijkstra wrote a technical paper for a computer journal, the premise of which was that the quality of a given computer program is inversely proportional to the number of GOTO statements it contains. (In other words, the more GOTO statements, the poorer the program.) That now-famous paper was the beginning of the formalization of a concept called "structured programming." At that time, FORTRAN was the language of computing. It has a GOTO statement similar to the one in BASIC. Dijkstra argued that with the proper program design and explicit features in the programming language to allow control of looping and branching, the GOTO is not necessary. Without it, it is much easier to follow the flow of a program (particularly someone else's).

Pascal, was designed as a tool to teach "structured programming" to computer science students. As computer languages go, it is toward the "simple" end of the spectrum, and it is relatively easy to learn. You might think Pascal requires you to go through a lot more "formality" than BASIC. You are correct. Pascal forces the programmer to plan a bit more than BASIC does. It forces you to think about how many variables you will need and what kinds of variables they will be. Generally, by the time you have gotten your Pascal program to compile without any detected errors, it is pretty close to running (though not necessarily correctly). If you don't like Pascal at first, please give it a chance. You will soon appreciate the clarity with which you can write a program. Your program will mean more to you in a week or a year than a program written in BASIC would after the same elapsed time, because Pascal is easier to read than BASIC. This is true partially because of the program structure forced on the programmer by Pascal and partly because Pascal allows the user to give variables and subroutines meaningful names.

Why write clear programs? We've passed the point where software is the larger cost in computer systems. Hardware costs are still falling rapidly. One of the main problems encountered by companies that write and maintain complex software is that a program must be understandable not only to the original author, but to someone else months or years later. That person has to modify it or perhaps find an obscure bug. Why not learn to do it clearly and increase your value as a programmer?

BASIC is usually implemented as an interpreter, and Pascal, as a compiler. Interpreters read the source program directly, line by line, and generate the machine codes necessary to carry out the instructions as they proceed through the program. If a loop in the program is executed 1000 times, each statement within the loop will be interpreted 1000 times. A compiler, on the other hand, reads the source code and generates machine code (called object code), usually saving it to a disk file. When the program is run, the object code is loaded to memory, and it is run. The source text file is not involved in the running of the program at all. It serves as the documentation of the program. Thus you can see that a compiler separates the source text and the actual running of the program by a step called the compiling operation. The act of programming is no longer interactive. With an interpreter, you can change a line of the program and run it immediately. It is easier to be a "sloppy" coder with an interpreter because it is easier to make a change and try again. The compiler has the advantage, on the other hand, of producing code that runs 10 to 80 times faster than interpreted code.

There is no inherent reason why Pascal cannot be implemented as an interpreter, and BASIC as a compiler. Several versions of BASIC compilers are, in fact, available for microcomputers. Though I don't know of one, it is highly likely that a Pascal interpreter also is available. The reason BASIC is usually implemented as an interpreter is that it is then more interactive with the user.

This book is not intended to be an exhaustive guide to every feature of the Jensen/Wirth Standard Pascal. Rather, it contains an introduction to the Pascal language on a practical basis with emphasis on those features implemented in most microcomputer versions. It has been prepared primarily for those with a knowledge of BASIC and little or no formal training in computer science. Many of us were educated long before the age of computers. This is an attempt to overcome that handicap. If I have succeeded to a degree, it is perhaps because I, too, lack that formal background, and I have not been involved in programming long enough to have forgotten what it was like to be a beginner.

Well, that is enough talk about BASIC and Pascal. Let's begin and see if we can make progress. The initial parts of this book may seem to approach Pascal on a piecemeal basis. All the pieces will, however, come together nicely in later chapters. The treatment of Pascal here will present (eventually) the complete Pascal as defined by the Jensen and Wirth standard. Emphasis will be on the subset of Pascal usually implemented in microcomputer versions.

As you work through the text, you will find that the emphasis switches gradually from BASIC to Pascal. Later chapters are primarily intended to be examples of Pascal programming. I've tried to choose areas that might be of interest and use to you. The example chapters are purposely diverse in subject matter so that perhaps there will be something of use to nearly everyone.

One more point must be made. I presently have four implementations of Pascal that I can run. Each has a few Standard Pascal features that are not implemented, and each has a few extensions to the standard. I've tried in the programs to use only standard features of Pascal. As a double check, where possible, I've run the programs in more than one implementation to insure that I've not done something illegal in standard Pascal that gets by one of the implementations. The likelihood that two or more versions would accept an illegal instruction is small, but not zero. Two implementations that I am using have most-useful but different extensions, and it has been difficult to resist using them here. Consequently, I've devoted the last chapter to a discussion and demonstration of those extensions.

4

Chapter 2

Variables

BASIC and Pascal use variables. A variable name is simply a "tag" or "label" that defines a place where a value may be stored in the computer memory. Variables may be of several types. Nearly all of the BASIC interpreters that are presently available for microcomputers allow *floating point arithmetic*. That is, numbers that are not "whole numbers" may be represented as whole numbers plus decimal fractions. For example, PI may be represented as 3.14159265.... The first digit, 3, is a whole number, and .14159265 is the decimal fraction part of the number. Though BASIC doesn't use the term, these floating point numbers are generally called *real* numbers. Whole numbers, are called *integer* numbers. Some BASIC's have only INTEGER arithmetic. Many of the larger BASIC's allow the user to specify whether a variable is an INTEGER or REAL type. Some mark integer variables by appending a "%" to the variable name. "A%" is therefore an INTEGER variable. The variable "A" on the other hand would be a REAL variable. Some BASIC's allow a DEFINT statement that defines the variables listed there as being INTEGER variables.

BASIC has another type of variable, called a *string*. BASIC universally uses "$" as a string identifier. A$ is, therefore, a string variable. In contrast, Pascal does not have built in string functions. It does have a type of variable for use to hold a character, however, called CHAR. Pascal's lack of STRING functions is a bit of a puzzle.

Perhaps it is because at the time Pascal was created, most computing was done on a "batch" basis with printed output, rather than having data input interactively from a terminal as is more prevalent today.

VARIABLE NAMES

BASIC generally allows the use of the letters A through Z for numeric variables and A$ through Z$ for strings. Most BASICs allow more variables by permitting a single digit after the letter. A1, Z9, V3, etc. are valid names. Many of the newer BASICs allow two-letter variable names such as PI, WT, etc. These may sometimes be used to advantage to impart an idea of the use of the variable in the program. If you have ever tried to write a long program in BASIC, you have probably wished for more meaningful variable names than A through Z.

Some of the currently available BASIC's have a companion *pre-compiler* that allows use of long variable names. These are an attempt to overcome the name limitation in BASIC and make it possible for a programmer to produce a more meaningful and readable program. The pre-compiler translates a more "wordy" version of the program with meaningful variable names and named subroutines into text that will be accepted by the BASIC interpreter. Using the pre-compiler has the disadvantage of adding a step between the writing and the running of the program. That is to say, the process of programming is no longer interactive and, therefore, a major advantage of the interpreter is lost.

Pascal refers to variable names, file names, and names of functions and procedures (any user generated names) as "identifiers." Identifiers in Pascal may be of any length (usually limited in most implementations, for practical reasons, to about 32 characters). They must be a single word. LENGTH, RADIUS, HYPOTENUSE and RATIO are all valid identifiers. Words that are concatenated by underlines such as DAYS_OF_WEEK may be valid too, but some implementations require only alphanumeric characters as in DAYSOFWEEK. Some implementations only use the first 8 characters internally, and you must use care to make these unique. That is, HYPOTENUSE_A and HYPOTENUSE_B would be regarded as the same variable in some Pascal versions since they only use HYPOTENU, the first 8 characters. Using A_HYPOTENUSE AND B_HYPOTENUSE would distinguish them nicely. You should therefore put the distinguishing part of a long variable name at the beginning if your version has this limitation.

STATEMENT PUNCTUATION AND SYNTAX

Pascal uses some punctuation that is different than you have seen in BASIC programs. This needs to be explained before presenting example programs in Pascal. In BASIC, the colon ':' is usually used to separate multiple program statements on one line. (Sometimes '/' is used.) In Pascal, the colon indicates an assignment of some sort. The example below shows one of its uses in the assignment of a TYPE to a variable.

B : INTEGER;

assigns the type INTEGER to variable B.

BASIC makes little distinction between a variable value assignment statement and an equality test. LET A=B assigns the value of B to the variable A. IF A=B tests the values of A and B to see if they are equal. Unfortunately, BASIC is too tolerant, and the LET is optional, so that the distinction between the two different actions is lost. In Pascal, however, the colon makes the distinction. A := B; assigns the value of B to the variable A. A=B without the colon is used for the equality test as in IF A = B THEN . . . .

BASIC and Pascal use a technique called parameter passing that will be discussed in some detail later. In order to distinguish between array subscripts and parameters, Pascal uses brackets [ ] to contain array subscripts as in NUMBER [3,7] := 17;. It uses parentheses for their normal mathematical function to override the precedence of multiplication and division over addition and subtraction and as delimiters for parameters. In the expression A := SIN(X+3),

X+3 is the parameter passed to the function SIN, the trigonometric SINE. Parameters are passed in BASIC only to functions. They are used more frequently in Pascal.

Remarks or *comments* are used in Pascal too. The use of the keyword REM in BASIC is rather annoying to me at least, for more than aesthetic reasons. In Pascal, a comment is set apart or delimited in either one or two ways. Braces are standard '{}', but since they are not available on all keyboards, a substitute is allowed '(* and *).' These double delimiters are less convenient, and the braces should be used if they are available. These symbols, at least, are more visually distinct from the program content and the comment that they delimit, than the word REM.

Pascal's use of the semicolon is rather more complex, and it will suffice here to say that it is used to end a statement, which may be longer or shorter than one line. Statements are not limited by line length.

VARIABLE DECLARATIONS

It should be understood that it is virtually impossible to present every feature of Pascal first. There will usually be some aspect of the example that has not yet been explained. Please don't worry about this. The part of the example dealing with the current topic should be clearly understandable. Here are some examples of variable declarations:

BASIC	PASCAL
DEFINT A,B (OR USES A%,B%)	(A,B : INTEGER;
(NO DECLARATION REQUIRED)	NUMBER : REAL;
DIM AR (4)	AR : ARRAY [1..4]
	OF REAL;

Here we have the first example of increased flexibility that brings about an increase in the complexity also. In Pascal, an array subscript range may be specified. In BASIC, the dimension 3 implies possible values of (0), 1,2, and 3. (Zero is used in some BASICs and not in others.) In Pascal, you must give both lower and upper limits. AR : ARRAY [3..7,9..12] would also be valid in Pascal. Why would you want to use subscripts 3 through 7? Pascal is good at "modeling" the real problem you are solving. Suppose you were writing a program for a junior high school that has grades 6 through 9. If you had an array that held the number of students enrolled in each grade level, you could define it as STUDENTS : ARRAY [6..9] OF INTEGER ; . The subscript would then match the grade. Space for the array values for subscripts, less than 6 in this case, is not reserved, and therefore not wasted.

FLEXIBLE ARRAY INDEX VARIABLES

Like BASIC, Pascal allows array subscripts of INTEGER, but in addition allows subscripts of type CHAR (for character). Suppose you were going to count frequency of occurrence of the 26 letters of the alphabet in a text. You could set up an array LETTER : ARRAY ['A'..'Z'] OF INTEGER; . The use of the letters A and Z automatically tells Pascal that the subscripts are to be of the type CHAR. The letters, however, must be in single quotes to distinguish them from variable names. The contents of the array are still defined as the INTEGER type. You may wonder why this feature would be of any value. This example is getting a little ahead of the story, but here is a BASIC program fragment to read a file of characters and count the number of times each letter occurs.

```
60 DIM LE(26) : REM THE ARRAY HOLDING COUNT OF
   EACH LETTER
```

```
100 READ C$ : REM READ A LINE FROM THE FILE
110 FOR N=1 TO LEN(C$)
120 A$=MID$(C$,N,1): REM GET CHARACTERS ONE AT A
    TIME
130 IF A$ > ="A" AND A$ < ="Z" THEN LE(ASC(A$)−
    64=LE(ASC(A$)−64)+1
140 NEXT N
150 IF NOT EOF THEN 100: REM READ ANOTHER LINE
    UNLESS END OF FILE
```

Caution, this is only part of a program. It will not run without other statements to support it. What is here illustrates the use of CHAR subscripts only. This program segment reads a previously opened text file and counts all the A's, B's etc. Note that the line referring to EOF is looking for the end of file condition. Your BASIC may implement this differently. In line 110, LEN(C$) returns the length of the line, or the character count. Line 120 uses the MID$ function to get one character at a time from the line. Line 130 tests the character to see if it is within the range of A to Z and then increments a count in the array corresponding to the letter. ASC(A$) gets the decimal value of the ASCII character. A has a value of 65. Subtracting 64 from this value, therefore, gets a number from 1 for A to 26 for Z. This number is used as an array index to increment a count in the LE array corresponding to the letter.

In Pascal, the program would look like this:

```
VAR
    CHARACTER : CHAR;
    LETTER : ARRAY ['A'..'Z'] OF INTEGER;
BEGIN
    REPEAT
        READ (CHARACTER);
        IF CHARACTER IN ['A'..'Z'] THEN LETTER
[CHARACTER] :=
            LETTER [CHARACTER] + 1;
    UNTIL EOF (DATA);
END.
```

This program is purposely oversimplified for illustrative purposes. There are a number of things we haven't discussed here. First of all, the variable "declarations" begin with the word VAR. The IN statement is a logical comparison, equivalent to BASIC's IF

C\$ > ="A" AND C\$ < ="Z". The Pascal program has no GOTO, and no line numbers are needed. There is a REPEAT UNTIL loop in the Pascal program. It starts at the REPEAT, and ends at the UNTIL. The UNTIL line gives the condition for ending the loop. If the condition is not fulfilled, the program resumes at the REPEAT line. The REPEAT UNTIL loop may be "nested" just like multiple FOR—NEXT loops in BASIC. As in BASIC, the first UNTIL terminates the innermost REPEAT. Indenting of the statements between a loop beginning and end is not mandatory, but it tremendously improves the readability of the program.

STRINGS IN PASCAL

I haven't said much at this point about strings in Pascal. String manipulations are BASIC's strength and Pascal's weakness. The standard Pascal has almost no features to make string handling easy. To define a string in Pascal, you must use an array of characters. The length must be given. RESPONSE : ARRAY [1..10] OF CHAR;. Since this is "weak" area of Pascal, many of the implementors have tried to patch it up. Most implementations of Pascal have "extensions" in this area. These are generally nonstandard and you will have to consult your manual for details.

BOOLEAN VARIABLES

Pascal allows other variable TYPES than those we have discussed so far. One of those is the TYPE BOOLEAN. A BOOLEAN variable has one of two possible logical values, TRUE or FALSE.

VAR
    ALPHA : BOOLEAN;
IF CHARACTER IN ['A'..'Z'] THEN ALPHA := TRUE;
IF ALPHA THEN LETTER [CHARACTER] := LETTER [CHARACTER]+1;

Notice specifically that it is not necessary to say IF ALPHA = TRUE. This of course is a handy feature for saving the result of a test for later use. It frequently speeds up the execution of a program, because testing the value of a Boolean variable is much faster than repeatedly evaluating a complex logical expression. Execution time is saved if the test is made once, setting the Boolean value and the result used again one or more times later in the program.

ENUMERATED VARIABLES

We come now to what Pascal calls SCALAR variable types. These are declared by the programmer. These types again allow the program to represent the real world in a better manner. SCALAR in the context of Pascal means enumerated or listed. The word SCALAR is not used in the TYPE declaration. All of the following are SCALAR types of variables. The word TYPE is used in describing a type of variable. INTEGER, REAL, and CHAR are variable types. The declarations below make DAYS_OF_WEEK, SIDE, and DIRECTION data TYPES on a par with the pre-declared types INTEGER, REAL, and CHAR.

TYPE
    DAYS_OF_WEEK = (MON,TUE,WED,THU,FRI,SAT,SUN);
    SIDE = (LEFT, RIGHT);
    DIRECTION = (NORTH, EAST, SOUTH, WEST);

The list in parentheses in each case enumerates all the possible values that a variable of that type may assume. These statements define data types, not variables. They must be followed by a variable declaration such as DAY : DAYS_OF_WEEK; In order to assign the type DAYS_OF_WEEK to the variable DAY. You may declare any number of variables of any TYPE, either standard or SCALAR. User-defined data types can also be used as array indices! TURNSIGNAL: ARRAY [LEFT..RIGHT] OF BOOLEAN; Now the statement in a program IF (TURNSIGNAL [LEFT]) AND (TURNSIGNAL [RIGHT]) THEN ERROR; may be used in a program, and it will be meaningful.

SUBRANGE TYPES

In addition to defining variables of any of the standard or SCALAR types in your program, you may use a subrange of one of the types. In fact you have already done this with array declarations. NUMBERS : [1..7] OF INTEGER; defines the index of the array as a subrange of the type INTEGER, which can take the values 1 through 7. WEEKDAY: [MON..FRI]; is a valid variable declaration if TYPE DAYS_OF_WEEK has been declared as above. In other words, you may use a subrange of any of the standard or user-declared types.

Perhaps you are beginning to see Wirth's philosophy here. The feature of allowing many data types may look like a bother initially. However, it not only makes the program easier to understand later, but it also makes debugging much easier. The compiler is able to catch much more than syntax errors. For example, if you had the assignment statement TURNSIGNAL [LEFT] := 17, though there is no syntax error, a BOOLEAN variable can't have the value 17, so the compiler will flag an error, probably indicating a TYPE MISMATCH.

Pascal allows a data type called FILE.

DATA : FILE OR CHAR;
NUMBERS : FILE OF REAL;

More will be said about these when we discuss input/output.

CONSTANTS

There is one other data type that is not a variable at all. BASIC has no mechanism for constants in the program. You must assign a value to a variable and then leave it alone. Pascal has a CONST section (like the VAR section) in which you may declare constant values.

```
CONST
    PI = 3.14159265;
    N = 17;
    NAME = 'PRIME NUMBERS';
```

Notice here that the type of the constant is understood by Pascal from the declaration. That is, if an integer is used (17) that constant is of type INTEGER. If a literal string is used, it is a string constant, etc.

STATEMENT LENGTH

Some BASICs allow continuation of a long statement on the next line or lines by the inclusion of some character such as "\". Pascal statements, as mentioned above, are terminated by ";", END, or one of the loop terminators to be discussed later. In my Pascal example above, the IF—THEN statement is longer than one line. While the use of the ";" may at first appear confusing, it is a real help as it allows the use of an indefinitely long statement or organization of a statement on separate lines for clarity.

Have you ever had trouble with an IF—THEN in BASIC when the true condition has to result in a number of actions? For example:
1000 IF A = B THEN C=0:D=0:E=0:A$="THE END" : PRINT
"THAT IS THE
END OF THE GAME"
That gets messy if only in appearance because the line overflows. You can split up the multiple actions by repeating the test as:
1000 IF A = B THEN C=0:D=0:E=0:A$="THE END"

1010 IF A = B THEN PRINT "THAT IS THE END OF THE GAME"

BASICs don't all work the same way. Some, in the case of line 1000 above will go directly to line 1010 if A < > B. That is, the multiple statements on line 1000 are only executed if A=B. Some BASICs will simply not execute the C=0 statement and continue on line 1000 executing D=0, E=0, and A$="THE END" regardless of the test. For these BASICs another approach works better:

1000 IF A < > B THEN 1100
1010 C=0:D=0:E=0:A$="THE END"
1020 PRINT "THAT IS THE END OF THE GAME"
1100 REM CONTINUE PROGRAM IF A < > B

In other words, a limitation BASIC forces you to use "reverse logic" and skip the consequences of a "TRUE" if the condition is "FALSE."

Pascal has a cleaner way of handling this situation. It is called the compound statement. A compound statement is a series of statements enclosed by a BEGIN and an END.

IF A = B THEN
BEGIN
    C=0; D=0; E=0;
    WRITELN ('THAT IS THE END OF THE GAME')
    [the string in the above statement is a parameter for the procedure WRITELN]
END;

The compound statement's END signals the end of the *previous* statement, so *that* statement doesn't need a ";", though most implementations don't object if one is there. Literal strings in Pascal are no problem. They are included in the WRITE statement in single quotes, just as in BASIC they are included in a PRINT statement in double quotes.

Chapter 3

Procedures and Subroutines

BASIC allows subroutines, though its structure doesn't encourage their use a great deal. You *call* a subroutine in BASIC and a GOSUB statement. GOSUB 1000, for example will send your program off to start execution at line 1000 and continue on succeeding lines until it reaches a RETURN statement. At that point it will return to the statement after the GOSUB and continue execution there. In Pascal a subroutine is called a *procedure*. Procedures have names that are considered identifiers just as variable names are. To call a procedure in Pascal, it is simply named. Suppose you have a procedure to output the control characters your terminal needs to clear the screen and put the cursor at the top left of the screen. It would look like this for a terminal using ASCII code 26.

```
PROCEDURE CLEARSCREEN:
BEGIN
      WRITE (CHR(26))
END;
```

To call this procedure from your main program you would simply use its name.

.

.

```
CLEARSCREEN;
WRITE ('THIS IS A CLEAN FRESH SCREEN');
```

Of course the main reason for using a PROCEDURE rather than just putting in the WRITE statement to clear the screen is that you might use the procedure in many places in a program. Another reason in Pascal is that the call tells the human reader of the program the purpose of the procedure without cluttering up the program with WRITE statements that require a comment each time in order to make their purpose clear. Of course this is only true if the programmer has used a name that describes what the PROCE-DURE will do. If, for example, the procedure were named DOITALL, the clarity would be lost. A third, and perhaps in the case of this example best, reason for using the procedure is that it may be changed easily to accommodate another terminal. By changing the 26 to a 12, for example, the program segment may be used in a system with a different terminal. Of course, if a certain PROCE-DURE is required in many places in the program and it is lengthy, the program code will be reduced considerably by making it a PROCEDURE. Don't forget, PROCEDURE = subroutine.

Compare the same code in BASIC

```
100  GOSUB 1000 : REM CLEAR SCREEN
110  PRINT "NOW THE SCREEN IS CLEARED"
990  REM THIS IS THE SUBROUTINE THAT CLEARS THE
     SCREEN
1000 PRINT CHR$(26)
1010 RETURN
```

While the Pascal code is almost self evident, comments must be used to make the BASIC version nearly as clear. Even without comments, a program in Pascal will be relatively easy to understand. Before that understanding comes, however, you must know enough of Pascal so that you can recognize the words that are not Pascal "commands" and realize that these are procedure or function calls.

PASSING PARAMETERS TO PROCEDURES

We've just touched on parameter passing. Now we come to the main use of this technique in Pascal. In BASIC its use is limited to functions as in the case of Y=SQR(A*B). Suppose in your BASIC program you want to have a subroutine that will calculate the hypotenuse of a right triangle, given the other two sides. You may remember Pythagoras' theorem that the hypotenuse is equal to the square root of the sum of the squares of the other two sides. Suppose we use A and B to represent the sides and H the hypotenuse. In BASIC:

```
100 A = 3: B = 4
110 GOSUB 1000
120 PRINT H
1000 H=SQR(A*A+B*B) : RETURN
```
You will see that the variables A, B, and H are used by the sub-routine. Also, it is necessary to assign the values of the dimensions of the two sides to A and B, and the result is "returned" in the variable H. Now suppose that somewhere else in the program, the dimensions of the sides of a triangle were contained in two other variables as the result of some other calculation. Suppose the variables are P and Q and that we want the result in variable R.
```
100 A = P: B = Q
110 GOSUB 1000
120 R = H
```
There are three assignment statements. If the subroutine could be made more general, they could be eliminated. Pascal handles this very nicely.
```
PROCEDURE HYPOTENUSE (A,B : REAL; VAR H : REAL);
BEGIN
        H := SQRT(SQR(A)+SQR(B));
END;
(MAIN PROGRAM BELOW)
BEGIN
        HYPOTENUSE (P,Q,R);(both input and output variables are
passed)
END.
```
Pascal uses SQR for the SQUARE function and SQRT for the SQUARE ROOT. The Pascal program assumes that P, Q, and R were declared as REAL variables at the beginning of the program (above the PROCEDURE HYPOTENUSE).

FORMAL PARAMETERS

The variables defined inside the parentheses in the procedure definition are called *formal parameters*. They have meaning only inside the procedure and may be thought of as "dummy variables for which the real ones will be substituted later in the program. Actually they are "copied from" the parameters passed to the procedure. In the above case, variables P and Q are not altered by the procedure.

The variables in the parentheses after the call (in the main program) may be variable names as in this case, expressions such as P+3.7, or numbers such as 5.3. There are three variables in the procedure definition, and three are passed to it by the call. The values of the three expressions that follow the call in the parentheses and separated by commas are passed to the three formal parameters in the procedure. Here comes the tricky part. The third parameter in the procedure definition (the variables in the parentheses in the procedure definition are called a "parameter list"), has the word VAR before it. This instructs the compiler not to pass to the procedure the value contained in the third parameter in the call, but to pass its location in memory, i.e., the place where the result is to be stored. It would therefore be wrong to make the third parameter anything but a variable name. VAR parameters in the procedure are used to return the results of the procedure. Of course this means that the contents of that third variable in the parameter list are changed as a result of the procedure.

Perhaps it is obvious, but for the sake of completeness, the formal parameters in the procedure parameter list take on the values of the parameters in the call in the order in which they are listed. That is, the parameters in the call must be in the same order and of the same number and type as the formal parameters.

The procedure receives two values (parameters of the non-VAR type are called value parameters) and an address at which to put the results of the calculation. The parameter names in the procedure HYPOTENUSE have meaning only within that procedure, and variables of the same name may appear elsewhere in the program without conflict. More on this later when the scope of variables is discussed. Just to clarify this a bit more, here are a few valid calls to the procedure HYPOTENUSE.

HYPOTENUSE (A+3,B−7,VALUE);
HYPOTENUSE (3,9,4,762,ANSWER);
HYPOTENUSE (SIN(X)+3, ARCTAN (2.7),H);

These are valid provided the proper variable declarations have been made previously. If brackets were not used to distinguish array subscripts, these parameters lists could easily be confused with them.

FUNCTIONS

BASIC has function definitions. So does Pascal. In BASIC the definition goes something like this.

10 DEF FNA(X)=SIN(X)*COS(X)

Later in the program:

150 Y=FNA(A−.3)

In Pascal, we could define a function to do the Hypotenuse procedure above.

```
FUNCTION HYPOTENUSE (A,B : REAL):REAL;
BEGIN
      HYPOTENUSE :=SQRT(SQR(A)+SQR(B));
END;
      R :=HYPOTENUSE (P,Q);
```

The above illustrates the definition of the function and a call to it. Functions may be used whenever the result is a single value. The function definition differs from the procedure definition only in that after the parameter list there is a declaration of the type of the value to be returned by the function, in this case REAL. Note that only two parameters are passed. Inside the FUNCTION block there must be one assignment statement that assigns the value calculated by the function to the identifier that is the name of the function. The call can't be just HYPOTENUSE(A,B), because no variable is specified for the result.

UNIFORM NOTATION

User-declared functions are called in exactly the same manner as those that are built into the Pascal. I have one implementation of Pascal that does not have the trigonometric functions. I wrote functions for them. To use these, the call is exactly the same as it would be if Pascal had implemented them, Y:=SIN(X), for example. The Pascal programs written using my functions may be compiled with a compiler that has them built in, simply by first deleting my added functions from the source text. The fact that user-supplied functions and built-in ones use the same calls is no accident. This feature is called *uniform notation*. Uniform notation makes Pascal an "extensible" language. This feature coupled with the fact that formal parameters in a procedure (and variables used internally to procedures) may have any name whatever and not conflict with names used in other places in the program allows Pascal users to build up a library of often-used procedures. These can be put together to generate other programs with virtually no changes (unless of course two procedures happen to have been given the same name).

A well-written Pascal program makes use of procedures and functions to a much greater extent than the average BASIC program. Though this is not a necessary consequence of the structure of BASIC or Pascal, it is usually true because the user of Pascal absorbs some of the spirit of the language's author. Most textbooks on Pascal also emphasize structured programming, stepwise refinement, and modularity of programs, all of which are facilitated by

Pascal, although they are certainly applicable to other languages, including BASIC.

LOGICAL OPERATORS

BASIC and Pascal are very similar in the choice of symbols for the logical comparison operators. The symbols $<$, $>$, and $=$ are used, and all the combinations that are valid in BASIC are also valid in Pascal. Only one difference arises when dealing with compound conditions, for example in an IF—THEN statement. In BASIC, the following would be allowed:

IF A $>$ B AND C $>$ D THEN . . .

In Pascal, each test must be enclosed in parentheses as in:

IF (A $>$ B) AND (C $>$ D) THEN . . .

However, if one of the tests is a BOOLEAN variable, (remember that naming a BOOLEAN variable implies the substitution of its value), it need not be enclosed:

IF ALPHA AND (C $>$ D) THEN . .

ARITHMETIC OPERATORS

All the standard math operators ($*$, $/$, $+$, and $-$) are used identically in Pascal and BASIC, and the operator precedence rules of BASIC apply in Pascal as well. That is to say that multiplication and division take precedence over addition and subtraction. Because Pascal makes better distinction between INTEGER and REAL variables, there are two other operators in Pascal. DIV is used for integer divide. The answer is not rounded, but truncated, in the same manner as the INT function works in BASIC. 3 DIV 4 yields 0, 4 DIV 3 yields 1. Associated with this integer division operator is an integer remainder operator. It is called MOD. 4 MOD 3 yields the remainder of the division or 1. 12 MOD 7 is 5. It might help to indicate that A DIV B $*$ B $+$ A MOD B $=$ A. For regular division the slash is used.

MIXED MODE ARITHMETIC

Since Pascal distinguishes REAL and INTEGER variables, you might expect some confusion over mixing the two types in an arithmetic expression. Pascal is very nice to you under these circumstances. Any combination for which no information is lost is allowed. That is, you may assign an integer value to a REAL variable or use an integer constant in an expression involving real variables. In Pascal, the number 2 appearing in an expression will be compiled as an INTEGER value, while 2.0 will be compiled as a REAL value. REAL/2 is a valid expression. Pascal will convert the INTEGER to a REAL and the result will be a REAL number. However, trying to assign a REAL value to an INTEGER variable, if it were successful, would lose the fractional part of the number. Pascal forces you to think about doing that and allows you two choices with regard to what to do with the fractional part. You may assign a REAL value to an INTEGER variable as:

INTEGERVARIABLE := TRUNC (REALVARIABLE);

or

INTEGERVARIABLE := ROUND (REALVARIABLE);

What each of these does should be fairly evident. TRUNC simply throws away the fractional part of the value of the REAL number, and ROUND rounds to the nearest INTEGER value. You have only the choice of which one to use. The compiler will flag an error if you forget to use one of these.

STANDARD FUNCTIONS

Pascal and BASIC share some standard functions. Since their names are slightly different in a few cases, they are shown below in tabular form.

BASIC	Pascal
ABS(X)	ABS(X)
ATN(X) or ATAN(X)	ARCTAN(X)
CHR$(X)	CHR(X)
COS(X)	COS(X)
LOG(X) (base 10 logarithm)	LN(X) (base e logarithm)
SIN(X)	SIN(X)
SQR(X) (square root)	SQRT(X) (square root
	SQR(X) (square BEWARE)
EXP(X)	EXP(X)

Pascal has a few functions of its own that need defining. EOF(X) is a test for an end of file condition. It returns a BOOLEAN TRUE or FALSE. EOLN(X) is a test for end of line. When reading input from a file or the terminal, EOLN will return TRUE if the last character read was a carriage return. ODD(X) will return TRUE if the argument (an integer value, expression or variable) is odd. ORD(X) is interesting. Remember our definition of the data type DAYS_OF_WEEK? The variable DAYS that was defined could have the values (SUN,MON,TUE,WED,THU,FRI,SAT). ORD(TUE) would return 2. TUE is the third value in the list, so that sounds peculiar at first, but ORD(SUN) will return 0. PRED (X) and SUCC (X) also deal with SCALAR variables. PRED (TUE) would return MON. PRED means predecessor. SUCC (TUE) would return WED. SUCC is for successor. Though there is no direct analogy in BASIC to these functions, perhaps it will help to envision a string array of the names of the days. Then if A$(X) happened to be 'TUE', the analog of PRED(X) would be A$(X–1) or 'MON' and the analog of SUCC(X) would be A$(X+1) or 'WED'. Note that PRED (SUN) will yield an error message, as will SUCC (SAT). Perhaps an example of how these might be used would help.

```
VAR
    SUNNY : ARRAY [SUN..SAT] OF BOOLEAN;
    DAY :=SUN;
    WHILE (DAY < =SAT) AND (MONTH = MARCH) DO
    BEGIN
        IF STATE = MICHIGAN THEN SUNNY [DAY]
        :=FALSE;
        IF STATE = ARIZONA THEN SUNNY [DAY]:=TRUE;
        DAY :=SUCC (DAY);
    END;
```

This loop would perform the operation for each day of the week. It will also produce an error message. Do you see why? When DAY gets to SAT and is incremented by DAY:=SUCC (DAY); there is no successor to SAT. How do we get around this problem? We will see later. Meanwhile, here is a way that will work correctly:

```
    FOR DAY := SUN TO SAT DO
    BEGIN
        PROGRAM STATEMENTS;
    END;
```

CONCLUSION

By now, you are getting the idea. Pascal has nearly everything that BASIC has, and (usually) more and better of it. You may be beginning to understand the comments made in Chapter 1. In fact, perhaps it would be a good time to go back and re-read that section. You probably now will see how BASIC was simplified to make it easy to learn. Many decisions were handled automatically by BASIC, mostly by not giving the user a choice, but this left the neophyte programmer free to concentrate on his program without having to spend long weeks learning all the detail. Pascal gives you many more ways to do things and allows the program to be a much better representation of the real world problem that you are solving. Because of this, the programmer faces many more decisions regarding variable types. Also because of this, the programmer may use more creativity in making his program understandable to others by using meaningful data types and variable names. You will see more of this in the chapters to come and will grow to appreciate the clarity of a properly written Pascal program.

Chapter 4

Loop and Branch Control Structures

In BASIC, there are two branch structures and one explicit loop structure. The branch structures are IF THEN ELSE and ON N GOTO. I hesitate to waste space here on examples, but for the sake of completeness, here are some.

```
100 IF A=B THEN PRINT "EQUAL" ELSE PRINT "NOT
    EQUAL"
200 IF A=-2 THEN N=1
210 IF A = 1 THEN N=2
220 IF A = 5 THEN N=3
230 REM
240 ON N GOTO 300, 400, 500
```

The IF THEN ELSE structure should be familiar to any BASIC user. Perhaps, though the ON N GOTO is not so widely used because it is awkward. The GOTO is followed by a list of line numbers. The branch is to one of these lines. If the variable (which need not be called N) has the value of 1, the first line number is the destination of the branch. If the variable has the value 2, the second, etc. Different BASICs handle the case in which the variable has a value outside of the range of the count of the line numbers somewhat differently. Some continue on the line after the ON N line, others default to the first line number given, etc. It is necessary to consult your BASIC manual to be certain. The difficulty here is of course that list of assignment statements that has to precede the ON N if the branch is to be made depending on some set of logical decisions.

In Pascal, the equivalent of the IF THEN ELSE statement is the IF THEN ELSE statement! Right, they are identical! Almost. Pascal allows the use of compound statements as we discussed earlier.

```
IF A = -2 THEN
    BEGIN
        P := 17;
        Q :=69
    END
ELSE
    BEGIN
        P := 69;
        Q := 17
    END;
```

This is a "stripped down" example, but you see the idea. Notice that the IF THEN ELSE is a single statement, either part of which may be compound. It is important that there be no semicolon after the END of the THEN portion, since the ELSE is part of the same statement. Within the compound statement, however, semicolons are required to separate the multiple statements. Note that the ELSE part is optional as it is in BASIC.

The equivalent in Pascal of the ON N GOTO, is the CASE statement. This structure is known as an "N WAY BRANCH". The CASE statement equivalent of the BASIC example used earlier is:

```
CASE A OF
    -2: NEGATIVE·
     1: UNITY;
     5: LARGE
END;
```

The identifiers NEGATIVE, UNITY, and LARGE are procedures to be executed in each of the three cases. After the execution of the selected procedure, the program continues on the line after the case statement. The Pascal standard has no provision for the "none of the above" situation. If none of the conditions in the CASE statement is fulfilled, Pascal reports an error. Some of the implementations have added an optional ELSE clause as a catch-all at the end of the CASE. Some implementations use the word OTHERWISE. If you have a standard version, the only way to prevent a "system error message" that will thoroughly confuse a nonprogrammer user, is to test to see that one of the conditions is fulfilled, and if not, provide an error message that makes sense to the user. In the present case, one could use an IN statement for the test:

```
IF A IN [-2, 1, 5] THEN
BEGIN
CASE A OF
    -2 : NEGATIVE;
     1 : UNITY;
     5 : LARGE
END
ELSE WRITE ('APPROPRIATE OPERATOR ERROR MES-
SAGE');
```

Pascal allows the same flexibility with the CASE statement as it does with array subscripts. It works with CHAR variables as well as SCALAR types. In fact, it is very useful with SCALAR types, because, although a variable of the type DAYS_OF_WEEK (DAY for example) can take on the values SUN, MON, TUE . . . (see the example earlier), it is not possible to use a write statement such as WRITE (DAY). A CASE statement must be used:

```
CASE DAY OF
MON : WRITE ('MONDAY');
TUE : WRITE ('TUESDAY');
WED : WRITE ('WEDNESDAY');
THU : WRITE ('THURSDAY');
FRI : WRITE ('FRIDAY');
SAT,SUN : WRITE ('WEEKEND')
    (multiple conditions can have the same result)
END;
```

A further example using the OTHERWISE extension available in some Pascals:

```
IF LETTER IN ['A'..'Z']THEN
BEGIN
    CASE LETTER OF
        'A','E','I','O','U' : WRITELN ('VOWEL');
        'S','T','N' : WRITELN ('FREQUENT')
    END; (CASE LETTER)
    OTHERWISE WRITELN ('ORDINARY');
    END;
```

Notice here that it is not necessary to call a procedure. The case condition (called a label) may be followed by a statement, even a compound one. Thus you can see, the CASE statement is rather powerful in Pascal.

LOOPING THE LOOP

BASIC has one basic (pardon the pun) loop control structure, the FOR NEXT loop. I hardly need to give an example of a FOR

NEXT loop here. Pascal has the exact equivalent (almost).

```
FOR I := 1 TO 10 DO ARRAY [I] := 0;
FOR N := 1 TO 15 DO
BEGIN
     REALVAL := REALVAL + N/10;
     WRITE (REALVAL)
END;
```

Notice that there is no NEXT required. The end of the statement marks the end of the loop. This is of course possible because of the compound statement feature of Pascal. Pascal doesn't allow a STEP specification like BASIC. The reason is that the loop index is an integer, thus making fractional values impossible. A loop with a step other than unity is better done a different way because of the inaccuracy of repeated additions and subtractions in floating point arithmetic anyway. It may be done in a FOR DO loop (and this is better practice in BASIC too), by the scheme shown in the example, of dividing or multiplying the INTEGER index value by a constant (N/10) in the example. Pascal has the capacity to step backwards. i.e., to use a negative unit step that is invoked by using the word DOWNTO rather than TO. For example, FOR K:= 10 DOWNTO 1 DO .... Negative integer numbers are allowed as index values but not as REAL numbers. The index variable must have been declared previously. Though REAL index variables are not allowed, other types are, specifically CHAR and SCALAR.

```
FOR DAY := MON TO SUN DO ...
FOR LETTER := 'A' TO 'Z' DO ...
```

PASCAL HAS MORE WAYS

Again here, you can see more flexibility at the expense of complexity. In Pascal, two other loop structures are allowed. BASIC has no direct counterpart, but they may be simulated using a GOTO statement in BASIC. These structures are the WHILE DO, and the REPEAT UNTIL.

```
WHILE A < B DO
BEGIN
     (SOME REPEATED FUNCTION)
     A := A + 0.15;
END;
REPEAT
     (SAME FUNCTION)
     A := A + 0.15;
UNTIL A > = B;
```

26

There is a difference between the two. In the WHILE DO structure, the condition is tested before the first time through the loop. If it is already fulfilled, the loop is not executed (not even once) and execution continues after the end of the loop. In the REPEAT UNTIL structure, on the other hand, the loop is executed before the condition is tested. Even if the condition is true before the loop is reached, the statements in the loop are executed at least once. The difference is subtle but useful. Just for fun, here's how you would do the same thing in BASIC:

```
100  IF A < B THEN 110 ELSE 200 : REM WHILE A < B DO
     BEGIN
110  REM STATEMENTS
120  A=A+.15
130  GOTO 100 : REM END
200  REM CONTINUE PROGRAM HERE
```

```
100  REM STATEMENTS : REM REPEAT
110  A = A+.15
120  IF A >= B THEN 200 ELSE 100 : REM UNTIL A >=B
200  REM CONTINUE PROGRAM HERE
```

That is the first example of learning BASIC with Pascal. We've seen a couple of useful structures in Pascal and shown how to simulate them in BASIC!

Note that in all the above examples, it is extremely important that the condition tested in the loop be modified somewhere within the loop in such a way that it will eventually become true. (The exception is if you are running Pascal on a computer that allows parallel processing.)

```
WHILE A < > B DO
BEGIN
     A := A + 1;
     (STATEMENTS)
END;
```

This loop will run 32,766 times and then give an INTEGER OVERFLOW error message if at the start B=1 and A=2. If B=1.5 at the start (which could only happen if it were a REAL), the loop will run "forever."

Chapter 5

Basic
RIP

Input/Output Functions

In a Pascal program, each file has an internal file name (i.e., within the program) that need not be the same as the "disk directory" file name. BASIC has, of course, a similar arrangement in that when a file is opened it is associated with a file number as in 100 OPEN 'DATAFILE' AS 1 or something similar. This associates the directory file name DATAFILE with the logical file number 1. Pascal for microcomputers has, in general, not implemented the opening and closing of files uniformly. However, once a file is open, it is handled by means of its internal file name and standard READ and WRITE statements.

To read the value of variable A from a file named DATA, for example, you would use READ (DATA,A);. In standard Pascal any files that are going to be used in the program must be listed by their internal file names as parameters in the first line of the program.

PROGRAM PROGRAMNAME (FILE1, FILE2);

These are the internal file names. In addition to appearing in the parameter list, the file names FILE1 and FILE2 must appear in a variable declaration. The above names FILE1 and FILE2 represents any descriptive names you care to give the files with the program. These names should reflect the function of the files.

VAR

FILE1 : FILE OF CHAR;
FILE2 : FILE OF INTEGER;

A file is associated with its directory name in one of two ways in different Pascal implementations. Some use the command line that causes the program to be run. The command line, by the order of the file names given, associates them with the internal file names in the first line of the program:

    RUN PROGNAME DIRFILE1 DIRFILE2
    (this is the command line to run the program)
PROGRAM PROGNAME (FILE1, FILE2);
(this is the first line of the program)
VAR (this is part of the variable declarations of the program)
    FILE1 : FILE OF CHAR;
    FILE2 : FILE OF INTEGER;
    RESET (FILE1);(this opens the file for read)
    RESET (FILE2);

Others allow the association to be made in the Pascal statement in which the file is opened. These still require declaration of the internal file names in the first line of the program and the declarations of the variables as above. Pascal uses the word RESET to open a file for read and REWRITE to open it for write or output. One implementation that I have seen would use the following:

    RESET (FILE1, 'DIRFILE1');

RESET will open the file as a read or input file. The association of the internal file name and the directory name is made here. Note that in this implementation, the directory file name is a string (in quotes). This particular implementation will accept a string variable name for the directory file name, and the program may be made to ask the user for the name of the file to be used.

COMMUNICATING WITH THE TERMINAL

The reason that I jumped off the deep end and introduced files before talking about input and output to the terminal is that the terminal input output is a special case of files. In fact INPUT is the internal name of a predeclared file of characters that is open for READ. OUTPUT is the internal name of a predeclared file of characters that is open for WRITE. The first line of a program, as in the examples above, if terminal input output is required in the program, would actually be:

    PROGRAM PROGNAME (INPUT, OUTPUT, FILE1, FILE2);

This is a comparison of BASIC and Pascal in reading the value of a variable A from a file. It is assumed that the file has been opened properly.

100 INPUT #1,A   READ (FILE1,A);

Some BASIC implementations use READ rather than INPUT. Now, let's compare the statements to read the value of variable A from the terminal.

100 INPUT A   READ (INPUT, A);

That's right, INPUT may be used just the same as FILE1 to specify a source for input. However, Pascal recognizes that INPUT and OUTPUT are probably the most used "files," and the words INPUT and OUTPUT are "understood." That is, they may be left out, and READ (A); will read the value of A from the terminal. If a file name is not given in the read statement, INPUT is understood. The same holds for OUTPUT in a WRITE statement. We've had to use the input/output statements in many of the previous examples, so, you have probably figured out how they work in part. The following examples illustrate how they differ from BASIC statements:

100 PRINT	WRITELN;
110 PRINT "HI THERE";	WRITE ('HI THERE');
120 PRINT "HI THERE"	WRITELN ('HI THERE');
130 PRINT "VALUE =";A	WRITELN ('VALUE =',A);

Don't confuse the special use of a semicolon in BASIC to inhibit the carriage return after a PRINT statement, with the "end of statement" function in Pascal. WRITE in Pascal inhibits the carriage return, and WRITELN includes it. Let's discuss the difference between READ and READLN.

Suppose we have a file of character called FILE open for read. The file consists of lines of data that are the values of variables A,B,C,D,X. If we now READ (FILE,A,B); we will get the first two values on the line of data into variables A and B. If we again use READ(FILE,A,B); however, all is not right, since there are three values left on our line of data. We will get the values of C and D. If we want to read, for example, only the first two values on each line of data, we may use READLN(FILE,A,B); repeatedly. The action of READLN is to find the start of the next line of the file and start reading there. BASIC automatically advances to the start of the next line on a READ or INPUT statement whether or not all the variables on the line are read. Pascal gives you a choice. READLN and WRITELN are only valid for a FILE or CHAR.

Just to review this usually confusing area of languages (confusing because there are large differences between implementations), we repeat that in BASIC, files are associated with "logical file numbers," and in Pascal, with "internal" file names (or if you like, "logical file names"). Have you noticed that Pascal allows the use of words that can give meaning to your program, whereas BASIC uses single letters and numbers? Standard Pascal, incidentally, insofar as I can determine, does not have a CLOSE statement (as does BASIC) for closing the files at the end of their use. All files are closed in an orderly manner at the end of a program. Of course files may be closed for write and re-opened for read by using RESET (FILENAME). Re-opening a file for write by using REWRITE (FILENAME) will destroy the contents of any existing file by the same name. If a file is re-opened with REWRITE and nothing is written into it, it will vanish when closed by reaching the end of the program, so the result is the same as deleting it. Some implementations of Pascal have a CLOSE (FILENAME) statement. You may expect to find that a particular implementation of Pascal may deviate considerably from the implementations described above, but you may be fairly certain that the concept of internal and directory file name association will be used.

OUTPUT FORMATTING

BASIC has little means to adjust the number of digits to be printed after the decimal point in numerical output. Some implementations have some form of a DIGITS command such as DIGITS=3 to set three places after the decimal point in the output. The more extended versions have a command called PRINT USING. This allows specifying a format in the form:

```
 10 F$="##.####"
100 PRINT USING F$,A,B,C
```

This would specify the form in which the value of the variables will be printed. The commas separating the variables call for printing in fields of 16 columns each. Print using format will "right justify" the output. Notice that values of the variables may be within the range of −9.9999 to 99.9999. That is, the minus sign uses one of the "places" reserved by the format definition. If you need numbers to −99, you must reserve three places before the decimal point. If a variable has a value such that it won't fit the format, an error will occur. Various BASICs handle these differently. Some will print *******. Others will revert to scientific notation; others will print the number anyway. The latter may overflow the 16-column field, resulting in all further columns of output being displaced by 16 spaces.

Pascal, too, has a way of specifying output formatting. A statement that would produce the format given above, is WRITE (A:7:4);. This means to print the variable in a field 7 columns wide (including the decimal point and sign if negative) with 4 digits after the decimal point. The above assumes that A is a REAL variable. Integer variables may be formatted with a single digit to specify the field width. Note that the field width may be larger than the number of digits that are printed. Numbers will always be "right justified" in the fields. This means that the decimal points will line up vertically if a constant format is used. By using field specifications you can do everything that can be done with PRINT USING, SPC, and TAB in BASIC. In the case of formatting, Pascal uses a method that is simpler than that of BASIC (or Fortran for that matter) unless only the simplest form of formatting is required. Field specifications work, incidentally, for strings as well, the string being right justified in the field. That is, WRITE ('HI THERE':40); would cause the last "E" of THERE to be in column 40. If a string is not given a format specification as in WRITE ('HI THERE');, the string is printed without leading or trailing spaces, i.e., wherever the cursor (print-head) happens to be when the WRITE statement is encountered. Again, notice the uniformity and regularity of the way it works in Pascal.

```
100 PRINT TAB(10);              WRITELN (N:19:5);
110 PRINT USING '###.#####',N
120 PRINT SPC(10);              WRITELN (Q:16:3);
130 PRINT USING '##.###',Q
```

The results of the above in BASIC and Pascal are identical. Note that in line 120, SPC(10) could be replaced by TAB(29). TAB(N) in BASIC always moves the next print position to column N COUNTING FROM THE FIRST PRINT POSITION ON THE LEFT OF THE PAGE. SPC(N) moves the print position N columns FROM ITS CURRENT LOCATION. Pascal format commands work more like SPC than TAB, in that each field begins where the last one ended. Spend some time trying various output formats for numbers in your Pascal implementation. You will find that if a format is not specified for a REAL variable, Pascal will use scientific notation for its output.

Chapter 6

A Program Outline and Example

A program in Pascal has a very definite structure (as you might guess from what you now know about Wirth's goals and philosophy). The order must be followed exactly, except that any part may be omitted if not needed. What follows is an outline:

PROGRAM NAME (INPUT,OUTPUT,FILE1,FILE2);

LABEL

    (LABELS ARE FOR USE WITH GOTO, WHICH IS IM-
    PLEMENTED BUT IS

    TO BE USED AS SPARINGLY AS POSSIBLE)

CONST

    PI = 3.14159265;

TYPE

    DAYS_OF_WEEK = (SUN,MON,TUE,WED, THU, FRI, SAT);

    (NOTE THAT THESE VALUES ARE NOT IN QUOTES
    AND ARE NOT STRINGS. THEY ARE MORE LIKE
    LABELS OR INDENTIFIERS. AS IN ALL PASCAL
    STATEMENTS, SPACES ARE IGNORED, NOTE THAT A
    COMMENT MAY BE SEVERAL LINES LONG)

VAR

    DAYS : DAYS_OF_WEEK;

    WEEKDAYS :[MON..FRI]; (THIS IS A SUBRANGE OF
    DAYS_OF_WEEK)

    N : INTEGER;

H,L,O : BOOLEAN; (MULTIPLE VARIABLES SEPA-
RATED BY COMMAS)
TIC_TAC_TOE : ARRAY [1..3,1..3] OF INTEGER;

(PROCEDURES AND FUNCTIONS ARE DEFINED NEXT.
THEY HAVE THE SAME FORM AS A PROGRAM)
PROCEDURE PROCNAME (PARAMETER LIST);
LABEL
CONST
TYPE
VAR
BEGIN
    (PROGRAM STATEMENTS THAT DEFINE THE PROCE-
    DURE)
END;
(OTHER PROCEDURES AND FUNCTIONS DEFINED AS RE-
QUIRED)

(MAIN PROGRAM FOLLOWS LAST PROCEDURE DEFINI-
TION. THE VARIOUS SECTIONS AT THE BEGINNING OF
THE PROGRAM (LABEL, CONST, TYPE, VAR) DEFINED THE
VARIABLES FOR THE MAIN PROGRAM. ALL OF THESE VAR-
IABLES ARE AVAILABLE TO THE PROCEDURES AND
FUNCTIONS AS WELL)
BEGIN
    (MAIN PROGRAM STATEMENTS, USUALLY A LIST OF
    CALLS TO THE PROCEDURES DEFINED PREVIOUSLY)
    PROCEDURE1;
    PROCEDURE2;
    WRITELN (RESULTS);
    PROCEDURE3 (PARAMETERS);
    VARIABLE := FUNCTION (PARAMETERS);
END. (MAIN PROGRAM ENDS WITH A PERIOD)

Before you get to the first full program listing, an explanation is
necessary. Because of the format of this book, the lines are limited
to 60 characters maximum. This limitation has caused a few problems most notably with WRITE statements for long literal strings.
It has also caused the listing to appear a bit "unstructured," which
the normal 96 character wide format would not. I had to do some
editing to minimize comment length or put comments on the next
line in many cases, but this doesn't detract seriously from the
information content and clarity. The fact that Pascal allows a state-

ment to be longer than a line was a definite help in this regard. I had considerably more trouble with the two BASIC listings of RE-VERSE, than with the Pascal listings. I mention this problem in order to avoid giving the impression that a "narrow" listing is desirable or necessary.

I can't keep the truth a secret any longer. Pascal does implement a GOTO statement. Sometimes it is just more structured to use a GOTO to abort a loop when an error is detected, than to avoid its use. We'll get into that a little farther along. There are several things that should be pointed out regarding the structure of a program. First of all, spaces are ignored by the compiler and may be used freely to separate items for readability. Spaces, of course, may not be used in the middle of identifiers or commands. Blank lines are also ignored by Pascal, and may be used to separate functional groups of program statements. Comments may appear anywhere a space is legal, though it would not usually make sense to use them in the middle of a statement line.

The variables declared at the top of the program before the first procedure are called global variables. References to these variables are valid anywhere in the program or the procedures. Variables declared within a procedure are valid only within that procedure and are called local variables. An exception to the global variable rule is that when a variable in a procedure is declared with the same name as a global variable, it becomes a new and local variable within that procedure (unless it is passed to that procedure as a parameter).

A procedure may be embedded within another procedure. Its variables will be local to it. The variables of the outer procedure will be accessible to it, as will be the global variables. Some microcomputer implementations do not allow such "nesting" of procedures. Any procedure may call another procedure that has been declared before it. This rule eliminates so-called forward references. Actually, that is an oversimplification. A condition may arise in which two procedures have to call each other (in a recursive program). Should this situation arise, Pascal has a means of declaring a procedure partially (giving its name and its parameter list) and then rather than the body of the procedure using FORWARD, which indicates that it will be declared later. This allows forward references by saying "I'm going to declare this procedure later." You can look at this as sort of a sneaky way around forward references. Wirth went to great pains to structure the language in such a way as to make the compiler easier to implement. A function has the same structure as a procedure. Procedures, functions, and programs are called blocks by Wirth.

AN EXAMPLE PROGRAM

Well we've just about arrived at the end of the preliminaries. There are of course still some features of Pascal that haven't been mentioned. However, there comes a time when it is more interesting to start programming, and that time is now. Program Listing 6-1 is a game called REVERSE.

Notice that REVERSE has been written so that the number of numbers in the list is determined by the value of N. N of course must not exceed the array dimension of 20 for the array A. The pieces of the program as presented below will be heavily "overcommented." When the program is presented in one continuous listing later, the comments will be reduced to a more normal level. Where do we start? How about at the beginning.

```
PROGRAM REVERSE (INPUT, OUTPUT);
CONST
N = 9;
```

That takes care of the program title and the number of numbers. Since N won't change during a run of the program, why not make it a constant? Now, what variables do we need. The array to hold the numbers is probably the first that will come to mind. Why not call it List? There are two array indices J and K, and, for the time being, let's not change their names. Then there is R for the player input of how many to reverse. Why not call it HOWMANY? The variable Z holds one of the numbers from the array while two are being swapped. TEMP might be more descriptive than Z for that. Furthermore, we will find that TEMP is only needed locally in one of the procedures, so it will be declared as a local variable later. The player responds to a question about playing another game or not. For the first try, we'll use a character variable RESPONSE. The variable T in the BASIC program counts the number of turns or tries it takes the player to get the numbers in order. TRIES would be suitable. I have a sneaking suspicion that we may want to use a BOOLEAN variable a little later, but we can add that when we come to it. Now we can write the VAR section of the program.

```
VAR
    LIST : ARRAY [1..20] OF INTEGER; (THE LIST OF NUM-
BERS)
    J,K : INTEGER ; (LOOP AND ARRAY INDICES)
```

HOWMANY : INGEGER ; (THE NUMBER TO BE RE-VERSED)

TRIES : INTEGER; (COUNTS PLAYER'S TURNS)

RESPONSE : CHAR; (TO GET PLAYER'S RESPONSE TO QUESTIONS)

That is a good start at all the variables to be used. To take a somewhat casual approach to this problem, how about using the sections of the BASIC program as separated by comments as the major PROCEDURES to be written in Pascal, at least for a first try. There is one problem that has to be taken care of, and we might as well face that one first. Most Pascal implementations don't have a RANDOM function, so we will have to supply it. While we are at it, we might as well let it return a random number between 1 and N. Without going too deeply into the subject, the following will do for a random number generator. We will, later in the program, give the player a chance to "randomize" the "seed" number for it.

FUNCTION RANDOM : INTEGER;

(TO RETURN A NUMBER FROM 1 TO N)

BEGIN

RAND :=RAND / 17; (USE OF PRIME NUMBERS HERE REDUCES CHANCES)

RAND :=RAND * 19; (OF AN EVEN DIVISION AND HELPS RANDOMIZE)

(IN THE MULTIPLICATION TOO)

IF RAND > 16384 THEN RAND := RAND – 16384 (PRE-VENTS OVERFLOW)

RANDOM := TRUNC (RAND) MOD N + 1;

END; (PROCEDURE RANDOM)

Since we are going to have to access the variable RAND from our "main program" later to initialize it, RAND should be a global variable and we will add it to our VAR section.

RAND : REAL;

The MOD function in Pascal returns the remainder for an integer division. RAND MOD N therefore will return a number between 0 and N-1. Adding 1 to this number produces the value between 1 and N that is needed. Successive multiplication of the seed number by 19 and division by 17 produces a series of random numbers with a long repeat period. Now that RANDOM is implemented, it may be used to generate the starting list.

PROCEDURE MAKELIST

(PROCEDURE TO GENERATE A LIST OF NUMBERS FROM 1 TO N WITH NO DUPLICATES, IN RANDOM ORDER]

VAR
    UNIQUE : BOOLEAN; (A LOCAL VARIABLE)
BEGIN
    LIST [1] := RANDOM; (A CALL TO THE FUNCTION RANDOM)
    FOR K := 2 TO N DO
    BEGIN
        REPEAT
            UNIQUE :=TRUE; (INITIALIZE FLAG)
            LIST [K]:= RANDOM; (ASSIGN VALUE TO KTH ELEMENT)
            FOR J :=1 TO K−1 DO (CHECK FOR DUPLICATES AND FLAG)
                IF LIST [K] = LIST [J] THEN UNIQUE := FALSE;
        UNTIL UNIQUE; (END REPEAT LOOP)
    END; (FOR K := 2 TO N DO LOOP)
END; (PROCEDURE MAKELIST)

Do you see how we got rid of the implied GOTO in the BASIC program on line 250? This procedure first assigns a random number to LIST [1]. It then uses a FOR NEXT loop to assign random numbers to the other LIST elements. After each random number is assigned, the newly assigned LIST element is compared to all the earlier elements to check for duplications. If one is found, UNIQUE is set FALSE, and the inner loop repeats, assigning a new value to the current LIST element and making the check again. When all elements in the list so far are different, UNIQUE will be TRUE when the REPEAT is reached, and the inner loop will terminate. The outer loop then will increment K and the next element will be assigned. The process is exactly the same as in the BASIC program, including the looping. The "THEN 230" has been eliminated by using a REPEAT UNTIL loop. Since the variable UNIQUE is only needed within this procedure, it is declared as a local variable.

We can break off another chunk of program to do the reversing of the numbers. How about passing the number to be reversed to the procedure as a parameter? Again, the process is the same as that in the BASIC program.

PROCEDURE REORDER (NUMBER : INTEGER);
(REVERSE THE ORDER OF 'NUMBER' DIGITS FROM THE LEFT END OF
THE LIST)
VAR

TEMP : INTEGER;
(TO SWAP TWO VARIABLES REQUIRES A TEMPORARY LOCATION)
BEGIN (SWAP END ITEMS AND WORK TOWARD CENTER)
    FOR J := 1 TO NUMBER DIV 2 DO (IF ODD, MIDDLE ITEM STAYS PUT)
    BEGIN
        TEMP := LIST [J]; (SAVE IN TEMP)
        LIST [J]: = LIST [NUMBER – J + 1]; (MOVE FIRST ITEM)
        LIST [NUMBER – J + 1] := TEMP; (SWAP COMPLETED)
    END; (FOR J := 1 TO NUMBER LOOP)
END; (PROCEDURE REORDER)

Notice that NUMBER DIV 2 automatically produces an integer result equivalent to the INT(R/2) in line 410 of the BASIC program. Two places in the program GOSUB 610. This is the subroutine that prints the list of numbers. It is rather simple, but since it is to be called from two places in the program, why not include it as a procedure. Actually, REORDER should call it, so it should precede REORDER, and the next to the last line of REORDER should be PRINT_LIST;.

PROCEDURE PRINT_LIST;
(OUTPUT THE LIST OF NUMBERS TO THE TERMINAL)
BEGIN
    FOR J := 1 TO N DO WRITE (LIST [J]:2);
    WRITELN;   (PUT A CR AT THE END OF THE LIST)
    WRITELN   (BLANK LINE AFTER THE LIST)
END; (PROCEDURE PRINT_LIST)

Kind of a simple one, but it combines printing the list and adding a blank line after it. Since the printing of the instructions is just a series of WRITE statements that may or may not be called for, it would make sense to have a PROCEDURE called PRINT_ INSTRUCTIONS.

PROCEDURE PRINT_INSTRUCTIONS;
(OUTPUT THE INSTRUCTIONS FOR THE GAME TO THE TERMINAL)
BEGIN
    WRITELN;
    WRITELN("THIS IS THE GAME OF "REVERSE". TO WIN, ALL YOU HAVE');

```
WRITELN('TO DO IS ARRANGE THE LIST OF NUMBERS
(1 TO,'N:2')');
    WRITELN('IN NUMERICAL ORDER FROM LEFT TO
RIGHT. TO MOVE, YOU');
    WRITELN('TELL ME HOW MANY NUMBERS (COUNT-
ING FROM THE LEFT)TO');
    WRITELN('REVERSE. FOR EXAMPLE IF THE CURRENT
LIST IS:');
    WRITELN;
    WRITELN('2 3 4 5 1 6 7 8 9');
    WRITELN;
    WRITELN ('AND YOU REVERSE 4, THE RESULT WILL
BE');
    WRITELN;
    WRITELN ('5 4 3 2 1 6 7 8 9');
    WRITELN;
    WRITELN ('NOW IF YOU REVERSE 5, YOU WIN.');
    WRITELN;
    WRITELN ('1 2 3 4 5 6 7 8 9');
    WRITELN;
    WRITELN ('NO DOUBT YOU WILL LIKE THIS GAME OF
SKILL, BUT');
    WRITELN ('IF YOU WANT TO QUIT, REVERSE 0
(ZERO)');
    WRITELN;
END;
```

There is certainly nothing new there. It is a direct translation
from the BASIC version. There is not much left to do but a
CHECK_FOR_WIN procedure. An ordinary FOR NEXT loop
would work just as in the BASIC program. However, here is a good
chance to use a WHILE DO loop and exit as soon as a nonwin is
detected. This will speed up the program execution (though
whether a speed increase is necessary or not is academic).

```
PROCEDURE CHECK_FOR_WIN;
(SEE IF THE NUMBERS ARE ALL IN ORDER AND SET THE
VALUE OF WON TO TRUE OR FALSE ACCORDINGLY)
BEGIN
    J := 1; WON := TRUE; (ASSUME WON UNTIL PROVEN
NOT)
    WHILE WON AND (J <= N) DO
        (A COMPOUND CONDITION USING 'AND' RE-
QUIRES THAT)
```

(EXPRESSIONS BE ENCLOSED IN PARENTHESES)
BEGIN
    IF LIST [J] < > J THEN WON := FALSE;
    (NUMBER MUST = INDEX IF IN ORDER)
    J := J + 1 (INCREMENT INDEX)
  END; (WHILE WON := TRUE)
END; (PROCEDURE CHECK_FOR_WIN)

Now it will be necessary to go back to the global VAR declarations and add:

WON : BOOLEAN;

All that remains is the main program that will call these routines. By now, perhaps you have noticed that the original BASIC program has no GOTO as such and is therefore reasonably well structured to begin with. Some Pascal programmers might think the main program that follows is too large. My feeling is that there is not another chunk big enough to break out as a separate procedure. The main program starts things and then stays within an outer loop for each game played and an inner loop for turns within one game. I've put some of the explanations in as comments to associate them with the line in the program. As a minimum though, an END should always have a comment indicating what it is the end of. This is an aid to the programmer too. In a more complex program when there are half a dozen unterminated loops going, several frequently end at the same point in the program, and a little carelessness results in either too few or too many ENDs. A comment after each helps keep things straight for the programmer. Listing 6-2 shows the program complete with the main portion.

BACK TO BASIC

Notice that the program listing has grown from one and a half pages to five. This reflects the "spreading out" of the listing more than added complexity. I've formatted the BASIC program in a more readable form, and it is shown in Listing 6-3. Now it begins to resemble the Pascal program except that the subroutines are at the end. The original program was written to run in a BASIC that does not allow program statements after a THEN but only permits going to another line. I've used statements after THEN to reflect the fact that most BASICs for microcomputers now allow this. This is not intended to be a criticism of the original program, which was written when BASIC was less capable, and memory was as valuable as gold.

Perhaps the point is made that it is also possible to produce a readable structured program in BASIC. It should be apparent,

though, that BASIC lets the programmer get away with less structured programs.

CONCLUSION

There you have the first complete program in Pascal, and
we've translated it from a BASIC program. If you have followed this
from the start, you are now ready to begin to translate some
programs on your own.

Both the Pascal and the BASIC program have been run exactly
as listed here. It is possible that neither will run in your particular
implementations of BASIC and Pascal. I had to change the RND(1)
in the Basic Computer Games listing to RND(0) for my particular
BASIC. The RND function in BASIC is one that is not very stan-
dardized, and you may need to use a different argument or a RAN-
DOMIZE statement in the program to get random numbers. I had a
RANDOM procedure in the Pascal program that ran in one implementation but not in a second. The one given here runs in both.

Listing 6-1. Reverse in BASIC.

```
10 PRINT TAB(22);"REVERSE"
20 PRINT TAB(15);"CREATIVE COMPUTING"
30 PRINT:PRINT:PRINT
100 PRINT "REVERSE -- A GAME OF SKILL"
110 PRINT
130 DIM A(20)
140 REM xxx N = NUMBER OF NUMBERS
150 N=9
160 PRINT "DO YOU WANT THE RULES";
170 INPUT A$
180 IF LEFT$(A$,1)='N' THEN 210
190 GOSUB 710
200 REM xxx MAKE A RANDOM LIST A(1) TO A(N)
210 A(1) = INT((N-1)*RND(0)+2)
220 FOR K=2 TO N
230 A(K)=INT(N*RND(0)+1)
240 FOR J=1 TO K-1
250 IF A(K)=A(J) THEN 230
260 NEXT J: NEXT K
280 REM  PRINT ORIGINAL LIST AND START GAME
290 PRINT:PRINT "HERE WE GO...THE LIST IS:"
310 T=0
320 GOSUB 610
330 PRINT "HOW MANY SHALL I REVERSE";
340 INPUT R
350 IF R=0 THEN 520
360 IF R <=N THEN 390
370 PRINT "OOPS! TOO MANY! I CAN REVERSE";
380 PRINT "AT MOST";N: GOTO 330
390 T=T+1
400 REM REVERSE R NUMBERS AND PRINT NEW LIST
410 FOR K=1 TO INT(R/2)
420 Z=A(K)
430 A(K)=A(R-K+1)
440 A(R-K+1)=Z
450 NEXT K
460 GOSUB 610
```

Listing 6-1. Reverse in BASIC (Continued).

```
470 REM xxx CHECK FOR A WIN
480 FOR K=1 TO N
490 IF A(K)<>K THEN 330
500 NEXT K
510 PRINT "YOU WON IT IN";T;"MOVES!!!";PRINT
520 PRINT
530 PRINT "TRY AGAIN (YES OR NO)";
540 INPUT A$
550 IF LEFT$(A$,1)='Y' THEN 210
560 PRINT: PRINT "O.K.  HOPE YOU HAD FUN!!"
570 GOTO 999
600 REM xxx SUBROUTINE TO PRINT LIST
610 PRINT: FOR K=1 TO N: PRINT A(K);: NEXT K
650 PRINT: PRINT: RETURN
700 REM xxx SUBROUTINE TO PRINT THE RULES
705 PRINT
710 PRINT "THIS IS THE GAME OF 'REVERSE'."
715 PRINT "TO WIN, ALL YOU HAVE TO DO IS"
720 PRINT "ARRANGE A LIST OF NUMBERS (1 TO"
730 PRINT N;") IN NUMERICAL ORDER FROM LEFT"
735 PRINT "TO RIGHT. TO MOVE, YOU TELL ME"
740 PRINT "HOW MANY (COUNTING FROM THE LEFT)"
750 PRINT "TO REVERSE.  FOR EXAMPLE, IF THE"
755 PRINT "CURRENT LIST IS:"
760 PRINT: PRINT "2 3 4 5 1 6 7 8 9"
770 PRINT: PRINT "AND YOU REVERSE 4,"
775 PRINT "THE RESULT WILL BE:"
780 PRINT: PRINT "5 4 3 2 1 6 7 8 9"
790 PRINT: PRINT "NOW REVERSE 5. YOU WIN!"
800 PRINT: PRINT "1 2 3 4 5 6 7 8 9"
810 PRINT "NO DOUBT YOU WILL LIKE THIS GAME."
820 PRINT "IF YOU WANT TO QUIT,"
830 PRINT "REVERSE 0 (ZERO)."
840 PRINT : RETURN
999 END
```

REVERSE is from *BASIC Computer Games,* Microcomputer Edition, Edited by
David H. Ahl, published by Creative Computing Press, Morristown, NJ 07960.
(Used by permission.)

Listing 6-2. Reverse in Pascal .

```pascal
PROGRAM REVERSE (INPUT, OUTPUT);

CONST
   N = 9;

VAR
   LIST : ARRAY [1..20] OF INTEGER; { THE LIST OF NUMBERS }
   J, K : INTEGER;                  { LOOP AND ARRAY INDICES }
   HOWMANY : INTEGER;               { TO BE REVERSED }
   TRIES : INTEGER;                 { COUNT PLAYERS TURNS }
   RESPONSE : CHAR ;
   RAND : REAL ;                    { TO HOLD RANDOM NUMBER }
   WON : BOOLEAN ;

FUNCTION RANDOM : INTEGER;

{ TO RETURN A NUMBER FROM 1 TO N }

BEGIN

   RAND := RAND / 17;
   RAND := RAND * 19;
   IF RAND > 16384 THEN RAND := RAND - 7327;
   RANDOM := TRUNC (RAND) MOD N + 1;

END; { RANDOM }

PROCEDURE MAKELIST;

VAR
   UNIQUE : BOOLEAN; { A LOCAL VARIABLE }

BEGIN
   LIST [1] := RANDOM; { CALL THE FUNCTION }
   FOR K := 2 TO N DO
   BEGIN

      REPEAT
         UNIQUE := TRUE; { INITIALIZE FLAG }
         LIST [K] := RANDOM;
```

Listing 6-2. Reverse in Pascal (Continued).

```
        FOR J := 1 TO K-1 DO
             IF LIST [K] = LIST [J]
                THEN UNIQUE := FALSE;

    UNTIL UNIQUE;  { END REPEAT UNTIL LOOP}
  END;  { FOR K := LOOP }
END; { MAKELIST }



PROCEDURE PRINTLIST;

BEGIN
    FOR J := 1 TO N DO WRITE (LIST [J] : 2);
    WRITELN
END; { PRINTLIST }



PROCEDURE REORDER (NUMBER : INTEGER);

VAR
    TEMP : INTEGER;

BEGIN {SWAP END ITEMS AND WORK TOWARD CENTER}

    FOR J := 1 TO NUMBER DIV 2 DO
    BEGIN
      TEMP := LIST [J];
      LIST [J] := LIST [NUMBER - J + 1];
      LIST [NUMBER - J + 1] := TEMP;
    END; { FOR J }
    PRINTLIST;
END; { REORDER }

PROCEDURE PRINTINSTRUCTIONS ;

BEGIN

    WRITELN;
```

Listing 6-2. Reverse in Pascal (Continued).

```
   WRITE ('THIS IS THE GAME OF "REVERSE ');
   WRITELN ('TO WIN ALL YOU HAVE TO DO IS');
   WRITE ('ARRANGE THE LIST OF NUMBERS ');
   WRITELN ('(1 THROUGH',N:2,') IN');
   WRITE ('NUMERICAL ORDER FROM LEFT TO ');
   WRITELN ('RIGHT.  TO MOVE, YOU TELL ME');
   WRITE ('HOW MANY NUMBERS (COUNTING ');
   WRITELN ('FROM THE LEFT) TO REVERSE.');
   WRITELN ('IF THE CURRENT LIST IS:');
   WRITELN;
   WRITELN (' 2 3 4 5 1 6 7 8 9');
   WRITELN;
   WRITE ('AND YOU REVERSE 4, ');
   WRITELN ('THE RESULT WILL BE');
   WRITELN;
   WRITELN (' 5 4 3 2 1 6 7 8 9');
   WRITELN;
   WRITELN ('NOW REVERSE 5. YOU WIN!');
   WRITELN;
   WRITELN (' 1 2 3 4 5 6 7 8 9');
   WRITELN;
   WRITELN;
   WRITE ('YOU WILL LIKE THIS GAME OF ');
   WRITELN ('SKILL, BUT IF YOU WANT TO');
   WRITELN ('QUIT, REVERSE 0 (ZERO)');
   WRITELN;
END;

PROCEDURE CHECKFORWIN;

     { SETS THE VALUE OF WON TO TRUE OR FALSE }

BEGIN
   J := 1;
   WON := TRUE; {ASSUME WON UNTIL PROVEN NOT}

   WHILE WON AND (J <= N) DO

     {A COMPOUND CONDITION USING 'AND' REQUIRES THAT
      EXPRESSIONS BE ENCLOSED IN PARENTHESES }
```

47

Listing 6-2. Reverse in Pascal (Continued).

```
    BEGIN
        IF LIST [J] <> J THEN WON := FALSE;
        J := J + 1
    END; {WHILE WON }
END; { CHECK }

{ MAIN PROGRAM }

BEGIN

    WRITELN;
    WRITELN ('THIS IS THE GAME OF REVERSE.');
    WRITE ('GIVE ME A NUMBER FROM 1 TO 10000');
    READ (RAND);
    WRITELN;
    WRITE ('DO YOU WANT THE RULES? (Y OR N)');
    READ (RESPONSE);
    WRITELN;
    IF RESPONSE = 'Y' THEN PRINTINSTRUCTIONS;

    { THIS OUTER LOOP REPEATS ONCE PER GAME }

    REPEAT
        WRITELN;
        MAKELIST;
        TRIES := 0;
        WRITELN ('HERE WE GO... THE LIST IS:');
        WRITELN;
        PRINTLIST; { PRINT THE INITIAL ORDER }

      { THE INNER LOOP REPEATS FOR EACH TURN }

      REPEAT
          WRITE (' REVERSE HOW MANY? ');
          READ (HOWMANY);

          IF HOWMANY < 0
            THEN WRITELN ('REALLY NOW, I CAN'T DO THAT!');
          IF HOWMANY > N
            THEN WRITE ('OOPS! TOO MANY! ');
```

48

Listing 6-2. Reverse in Pascal (Continued).

```
            WRITELN ('I CAN REVERSE AT MOST', N : 3);

         IF HOWMANY IN [1..N] THEN
         BEGIN
            WRITELN;
            REORDER (HOWMANY); {INCLUDES PRINTING THE LIST}
            TRIES := TRIES + 1; {COUNT TURN }
            CHECKFORWIN;
         END; { IF HOWMANY IN ...}
      UNTIL WON OR (HOWMANY = 0);

   { BAD ENTRIES WILL SKIP TO HERE AND REPEAT .
     NOW HANDLE THE WIN OR QUIT SITUATIONS }

     IF WON THEN WRITELN
        ('YOU WON IN ',TRIES:3,' TRIES.'),
     WRITELN;
     WRITE ('TRY AGAIN (Y/N) ');
     READ  (RESPONSE);
     WRITELN;
   UNTIL RESPONSE = 'N';
END. { END PROGRAM }
```

Listing 6-3. Reverse in BASIC Formatted.

```
10    REM    GAME OF REVERSE IN BASIC
20    REM
30    REM    VARIABLES USED ARE
40    REM
50    REM    A : ARRAY FOR THE LIST OF NUMBERS
60    REM    N : NUMBER OF NUMBERS IN THE LIST
70    REM    R : NUMBER OF NUMBERS TO REVERSE
80    REM    T : NUMBER OF TURNS TAKEN SO FAR
90    REM    J : LOOP INDEX
100   REM    K : LOOP INDEX
110   REM    A$ : USED FOR USER RESPONSE
120   REM
130      PRINT TAB(32);"REVERSE"
140      PRINT TAB(15);"CREATIVE COMPUTING";
145      PRINT " MORRISTOWN, NEW JERSEY"
150      PRINT:PRINT:PRINT
160      PRINT "REVERSE -- A GAME OF SKILL"
165      PRINT
170   REM
180         DIM A(20)
190   REM       xxx N = NUMBER OF NUMBERS
200         N=9
210   REM
220      PRINT "DO YOU WANT THE RULES";
230      INPUT A$
240      IF LEFT$(A$,1)="Y" THEN GOSUB 780
245   REM    PRINT INSTRUCTIONS
250   REM
260   REM xxx MAKE A RANDOM LIST A(1) TO A(N)
270   REM
280         A(1) = INT((N-1)xRND(0)+2)
290         FOR K=2 TO N
300            A(K)=INT(NxRND(0)+1)
310            FOR J=1 TO K-1
320               IF A(K)=A(J) THEN 300
330            NEXT J
340         NEXT K
350   REM
360   REM x PRINT ORIGINAL LIST AND START GAME
370   REM
```

50

Listing 6.3. Reverse in BASIC Formatted (Continued).

```
375        PRINT
380        PRINT "HERE WE GO... THE LIST IS:"
390        T=0
400        GOSUB 700 : REM PRINT THE LIST
410        PRINT "HOW MANY SHALL I REVERSE";
420        INPUT R
430        IF R=0 THEN 630 :REM QUIT THIS GAME
440         IF R<=N THEN 450
443        PRINT "OOPS TOO MANY!";
445        PRINT "I CAN REVERSE AT MOST";N
447        GOTO 410
450         IF R<0 THEN PRINT"I CAN'T DO THAT"
455         IF R<0 THEN 410
460          T=T+1
470 REM
480 REM REVERSE R NUMBERS AND PRINT NEW LIST
490 REM
500          FOR K=1 TO INT(R/2)
510            Z=A(K)
520            A(K)=A(R-K+1)
530            A(R-K+1)=Z
540          NEXT K
550          GOSUB 700 : REM PRINT THE LIST
560 REM
570 REM          xxx CHECK FOR A WIN
580 REM
590          FOR K=1 TO N
600            IF A(K)<>K THEN 410 :REM NOT YET
610          NEXT K
620          PRINT"YOU WON IT IN";T;"MOVES!!!"
630        PRINT : PRINT
640        PRINT "TRY AGAIN (YES OR NO)";
650        INPUT A$
660        IF LEFT$(A$,1)="Y" THEN 280
665        PRINT
670        PRINT "O.K.  HOPE YOU HAD FUN!!"
680        END
690 REM
700 REM          xxx SUBROUTINE TO PRINT LIST
710 REM
```

Listing 6-3. Reverse in BASIC Formatted (Continued).

```
720      PRINT
730      FOR K=1 TO N
740        PRINT A(K);
750      NEXT K
760      PRINT: PRINT: RETURN
770 REM
780 REM xxx SUBROUTINE TO PRINT THE RULES
790 REM
800    PRINT"THIS IS THE GAME OF 'REVERSE'.";
805    PRINT " TO WIN, ALL YOU HAVE"
810    PRINT "TO DO IS ARRANGE A LIST";
815    PRINT " OF NUMBERS (1 THROUGH";N;")"
820    PRINT "IN NUMERICAL ORDER FROM LEFT";
825    PRINT " TO RIGHT. TO MOVE, YOU"
830    PRINT "TELL ME HOW MANY NUMBERS";
835    PRINT " (COUNTING FROM THE LEFT) TO"
840    PRINT "REVERSE. FOR EXAMPLE, IF":
845    PRINT " THE CURRENT LIST IS:"
850    PRINT: PRINT "2 3 4 5 1 6 7 8 9"
860    PRINT: PRINT "AND YOU REVERSE 4,";
865    PRINT " THE RESULT WILL BE:"
870    PRINT: PRINT "5 4 3 2 1 6 7 8 9"
880    PRINT: PRINT "NOW REVERSE 5, YOU WIN!"
890    PRINT: PRINT "1 2 3 4 5 6 7 8 9"
900    PRINT "NO DOUBT YOU WILL LIKE THIS";
905    PRINT " GAME, BUT"
910    PRINT "IF YOU WANT TO QUIT, REVERSE";
915    PRINT " 0 (ZERO).":PRINT
920    RETURN
```

Chapter 7

Debugging Pascal Programs

Debugging a Pascal program has two phases. The first is to remove all the errors caught by the compiler in your attempts to compile the program. You may at first be annoyed by the compiler being so "picky" about little syntax problems, but later you will wish the compiler could find your more subtle errors as well. I've personally run five Pascal compilers, and they all have the same peculiarity. I assume it is a natural consequence of the way the language is defined. Some errors will cause the compiler to lose its place or get out of sync. Such a problem will cause many meaningless error messages to be generated in succeeding program where no error exists. The proper procedure, therefore, is to fix the first error reported. If it is one of those that causes sync problems, many of the later errors will disappear when it is cured.

Some compilers get so fouled up by an error that they abort rather than continuing. Others try to patch your error and get the compiler back in sync so that they can continue and give you other meaningful information so that multiple errors may be found in a single compile pass. The latter are better from the standpoint of allowing you to correct compiler detected errors.

UNINITIALIZED VARIABLES

The second phase of debugging a Pascal program is that of making the program do what you intended it to do after it has compiled successfully. There are a few pitfalls to watch out for.

There is one area that can be troublesome because someone who has programmed in BASIC may not be aware of it. In BASIC all variables used in the program are automatically cleared to zero before they are used. You may therefore use a variable without putting a value into it first. BASIC programmers may not be aware that BASIC, to my knowledge, is the only programming language in which this is true. In all the others, you may assume that the value of a variable is garbage until you put a value into it for the first time. An exception to this is the language FORTH which forces you to declare an initial value when you define a variable. Putting the initial value into a variable is called initializing it. Failure to initialize a variable means that the program only has reserved memory space for the value of the variable. Whatever was in memory from the previous program remains there. This could result in the contents of a variable being any value of which it is capable. The result can be disaster in several cases in Pascal.

The most obvious area in which an uninitialized variable can cause a problem is the case in which the variable is used as a loop index in a REPEAT—UNTIL or a WHILE DO loop. Suppose N is a loop index as below:

```
WHILE N < 100 DO
BEGIN
    SUM:= SUM + NEWVALUE;
    N := N + 1;
END;
```

If you are fortunate, N will happen to have a value between 0 and 100 and the loop will terminate nicely but with the wrong answer for SUM. In most cases, N will start out with some number far away from the range in question and run the loop for a very long time, perhaps causing an integer overflow somewhere along the way. Of course, the loop should be preceded by a statement setting N := 0; or whatever other initial value you wish.

INCORRECT STATEMENTS

Another sneaky problem with Pascal is a misplaced semicolon. It may be misplaced in such a way that no syntax error is made, but the statement doesn't do what was intended. One place that an extra one is hard to find is illustrated by the following:

```
FOR N := 1 TO 100 DO;
BEGIN
    SUM := SUM + N
END;
```

54

Of course you wouldn't use a BEGIN and END for a single statement, I've just abbreviated to make a point. The semicolon after the DO terminates the loop. In BASIC you have been used to a NEXT N statement to do that. Here, the loop will do nothing 100 times and then execute the compound statement once . . . not quite what was intended. You can get into deep difficulties by adding an extra semicolon if in an IF THEN ELSE structure too. All of the Pascal implementations I have will allow a semicolon after the last statement in a compound statement before END, though Pascal doesn't require one there. However, none will allow a semicolon after the last case in a CASE statement (immediately preceding the END). I don't know why exactly, but this is the case, so beware.

DIVIDE AND CONQUER

Since BASIC is usually implemented as an interpreter, it is generally interactive. Programmers, being lazy like everyone else, sometimes develop debugging techniques that are essentially trial-and-error methods. We're like the TV repair man of the early days of television who could change tubes until the set worked, or take the set back to the shop where someone more knowledgeable could work on it. It is so easy to change a statement in BASIC and run the program again, that this technique usually works. With a compiler, however, the compile step gets in the way. We need to maximize the information gained from each time we recompile and run the program. There are several techniques in programming with a compiled language that result in reduced effort in testing and debugging.

Looking at the program in Chapter 6 in its BASIC and Pascal versions, you've probably noticed that the BASIC version has only 2 subroutines. The other sections that we coded as procedures in Pascal are in-line, and the program doesn't suffer from this, at least functionally. One major reason for greater use of procedures and functions in Pascal is to facilitate debugging. You have of course heard the slogan "divide and conquer." To give you an example, suppose in Chapter 6 you had written the function RANDOM first. Having previously declared the constants and variables, how about a quick program to test RANDOM?

```
(MAIN PROGRAM (TEST RANDOM))
BEGIN
    FOR J := 1 TO 10 DO
    BEGIN
        FOR K := 1 TO 10 DO WRITE (RANDOM:2);
```

        WRITELN
    END;
END.

Now by running what you have of REVERSE, you will get 10 lines of 10 random numbers each, and you can convince yourself that RANDOM works properly before writing MAKELIST. When you are satisfied with RANDOM, you simply delete the "main" program and write the MAKELIST procedure. Now it can be tested with a different main program.

BEGIN
    FOR K := 1 TO 16 DO
    BEGIN
        MAKELIST;
        FOR J := 1 TO 9 DO WRITE (LIST [J]:2);
        WRITELN;
    END;
END.

At this point, running REVERSE will result (if MAKELIST has no bugs) in 16 lines of the numbers 1 to 9 arranged randomly and with no duplicates within a line. You might want to change the limit for K from 16 to 1000 or so and see if the random list ever gets "stuck" and repeats a pattern endlessly (which happened for some of my attempts to write a RANDOM function).

WRITE, WRITE, WRITE

Suppose at this point MAKELIST refuses to function properly. Without the availability of interactive debugging as with BASIC, how do you find out what is wrong? To misquote the previous slogan, "subdivide and conquer." Simply insert some WRITE statements to tell you what is going on. I start all my debug WRITE statements in the first column, i.e., I don't indent them. The reason is that they are easier to see when the time comes to remove them. If one is not obvious, I also comment it with a line of stars. Some thought in the placement of the WRITE statements in a procedure that is not working, can narrow the search down to a few lines of code. Frequently when the variable's values are printed out, the error becomes obvious. The best strategy, of course, is to spread the WRITE statements out within the procedure so that you can see that things are working as planned at one statement, but a few lines farther down, the variables have unplanned values.

PROCEDURE MAKELIST

```
VAR
    UNIQUE : BOOLEAN;
BEGIN
    LIST [1] := RANDOM;
WRITELN ('LIST [1] =',LIST[1]:2);
(****************************)
    FOR K :=2 TO N DO
    BEGIN
        REPEAT
            UNIQUE := TRUE;
            LIST [K] := RANDOM;
WRITELN ('NEW ITEM LIST',K:2,'=',LIST [K]:2);
(***************)
            FOR J := 1 TO K-1 DO
            BEGIN (*** ADDED BECAUSE TEST WRITE
MAKES COMPOUND**)
                IF LIST [K] = LIST [J] THEN UNIQUE:=
                FALSE;
WRITE (LIST [J]:2);
(*****************************************)
            END;
        UNTIL UNIQUE;
    END;
END;
```

Now you will get the first item in the list, the Kth number as it is assigned and all the items in the partial list, repeated as the list is built. With all this information, it should not be very difficult to see just what is going wrong. It is important to include some words that identify the data being printed and not just to print numbers. When the program executes, some of these WRITE statements are in loops, and the printout can be quite confusing. Also, I've been guilty of making an error in my test WRITE statement having forgotten that an array index has been incremented since the statement was executed, resulting in my looking at the next array location where results have not yet been stored. I spent a long evening one time trying to figure out why I couldn't get the right values into an array while they were there all the time. Be careful that you are actually printing out just exactly what you want to look at.

So you see, by breaking your program up into small functional modules and testing each as it is written, using WRITE statements at critical points, debugging is made fast and easy! There is in fact an added bonus in programming this way. Small programs obviously compile faster than large ones. If your disk operating system allows it, you may want to treat each procedure as a separate program for debugging and then append all the text files together and add the main program when all the procedures have been tested separately. As an exercise, after working through the above, continue adding procedures and devise a test program for each new one (except perhaps PRINT_LIST).

FIND IT!

There is a bug in the Pascal program as presented. It will only show up for an unusual combination of player inputs. See if you can think up unusual sequences of play and find the bug after you have the program running. You will find the answer in Appendix C #1.

I've brought this problem up to illustrate a point. This is a simple program as programs go. You might play REVERSE for several months before running across the bug. I doubt that many readers found the symptom by playing the game. Would you rather pick up the Pascal version or the BASIC version of REVERSE a year from now and try to find the bug's cure? My case for clear program documentation rests!

THE "DO SOMETHING UNRELATED" TECHNIQUE

Back to debugging problems. What do you do when you just can't seem to find the problem? From long experience, the best advice I can give you is to quit and go do something else for a while. Frequently a program bug that seems impossible to solve will be easy after a short rest. Frequently when I have such a problem, I will suddenly think of the solution or of other things to try while I am doing something totally unrelated. Your mind goes in circles and you keep looking in the same places, over and over again, when you are tired or fatigued. Keep an open mind. Don't rule out any possibility, even the last procedure that you just finished testing and found to be "correct."

USE THE COMPILER DEBUG FEATURES

Most compiler implementations have built in some debugging aids. These may vary from a minimum of telling you where the program was when the runtime error occurred, to allowing single stepping of the program and examination of variables. Many of the compilers have options that allow line numbers to remain as specially marked comments so that when debugging, the line number may be printed out along with the error information. My P-code compiler generates a listing identical with the source text except that each line is preceded by a number that happens to be the program counter value for the first instruction generated by that line. The runtime error message has the program counter value attached, and it is possible to estimate about how far into the line the error occurred. The only problem with that approach is that as soon as you fix one error, the program counter changes and you must relist the compiler output to get the new P-code values. Another compiler has the line number reporting capability, but you have to enable it by using an option when you compile the program. The point is that you must read the manual that is supplied with your compiler to see if any debug, support is built in.

DON'T OVERLOOK THE OBVIOUS

It is time for an illustration. When I was in college, I earned my spending money by repairing television sets for neighbors and word-of-mouth advertising customers. One evening I went to a home and found the set totally dead. I checked for power at the outlet and found none. Then I asked the customer if they had had any wiring done in the house recently. The response was "yes." I told them that there was no power at that outlet and we proceeded to plug the set in elsewhere. Tubes lit but still no picture. (That reveals my age doesn't it.) I spent a half hour looking at things in the set and finally conceded that I would have to put it on my bench and do some signal tracing.

At home, the next evening, I found a lack of vertical sweep signal. Suddenly the explanation was obvious. Two tubes with their type numbers worn off had been interchanged. Obviously, the people had removed the tubes from the set and taken them to the local store with a tube tester. When they returned them to the set, they switched the two that looked similar but were not. A couple of years of TV servicing had made me familiar with the appearance of the inside of those tubes and I could see that they were swapped. I swapped them back to the correct positions and the set worked. I returned it to the customer and told him that if he had told me that he had tested the tubes I might have looked for swapped ones sooner and saved both of us some time, trouble, and expense. The point is that the owner of the set had overlooked the obvious problem of no power, and then compounded the problem by not giving me enough information so that I could find the obvious problem that he introduced.

When you debug a program, don't overlook the obvious errors such as failure to initialize a variable. Sometimes I have found that I simply failed to call a procedure somewhere in the program flow. A misplaced semicolon can cause mysterious results too. Declaring a local variable (in a procedure), that has a name identical with a global one and then trying to access the global one in the procedure can cause deeply mysterious things to happen in your program, since the local variable will take precedence and block access to the global one. The result is a problem that looks like an uninitialized variable. If you happen to try printing out the value of the variable within the procedure, the cause of the difficulty may suddenly dawn on you. This sort of error is particularly easy to make if you have used BASIC for a long time and are used to all variables being global so that you don't have to worry about any rules of precedence. Some implementations of Pascal won't let you declare a constant, for example NUMBER = 64000;. The TYPE of a constant is decided by the value, and this looks like an INTEGER. However, the number is too large to be represented as an integer, so an error occurs. You must use NUMBER = 6.4E4;, the scientific notation equivalent of 64,000 to represent this number as a constant, to signal the compiler that it is a REAL number and not an INTEGER.

Some of these bugs are introduced by Pascal newcomers simply due to unfamiliarity with the language. You will soon have these sorted out in your mind. Then debugging a Pascal program will become a "fun project."

Chapter 8

Writing a Pascal
Program from Scratch

Now that you have been through the exercise of a program translation from BASIC to Pascal, the next logical step would be to start
from scratch with some goal in mind and see if we can come up with
a working program. I wonder how many of you have ever worked on
a program to find the prime numbers. Prime numbers are those
integers that are not evenly divisible by any other integer than one
and themselves (all integers are evenly divisible by themselves and
one). For example, 7 is a prime number because it has no other
whole divisors than 1 and 7. Two is a prime number, but of course all
other even numbers are divisible by 2 and so are not prime. A
nonprime number is the product of two or more prime numbers
known as its prime factors.

Prime number programs are interesting because they illustrate a point that I would like to make after we've written a few
versions of programs. Suppose that you have a hypothetical "customer" who wants a program that will allow him to input the largest
number to be tested for "primality," and to list neatly to his terminal
all the prime numbers from 1 to that limit. Some of the discussions
of primes include 1 in the list and some do not. Suppose we include
it. It is permissible to "cheat" and start the list with 1, 2, and 3. After
printing out the primes, the program should report the number of
primes found and the limit that was input by the user, in the form:

THERE WERE NNN PRIMES BETWEEN 1 AND NNNN

A FIRST TRY

The brute force method of finding primes would be to test all numbers from 1 to the limit, to see if they are divisible by any number from 1 to the number being tested. Since we already know that all even numbers larger than 2 are not primes, why not just test odd numbers and reduce the work a bit. In order to avoid extra tests, the program should test a number until it finds a factor or runs out of test divisors. As soon as a factor is found, the number being tested is proven to be not a prime. If the program runs out of test divisors without finding a factor, the number must be a prime, and it should be output to the terminal.

What variables will we need? We are dealing with INTEGER numbers only, so no REAL variables will be required. MAX-NUMBER will hold the maximum number to be tested. MAX-NUMBER will be limited to less than 30,000 so that we won't run into trouble with INTEGER arithmetic limited to + / − 32,767 as it is in most microcomputer implementations. A good name for the number being tested would be CANDIDATE (for prime status that is). The test divisor could be TEST_DIVISOR (what else?). The problem specification includes counting the number of primes. COUNT will do nicely for that.

The function MOD will be used for our tests. If A is divisible evenly by B, then A MOD B will be zero. That is, the remainder after the division is zero. We will make use of a BOOLEAN variable set by our test to exit the test loop if a divisor is found. PRIME is a logical name for that variable.

What procedures should we write? One to test each number for primality seems logical. Another could be written to ask the user for the limit. At least one of the variables mentioned above can be local to a procedure, so why not start in the middle and write the procedures first, then decide what variables are to be global.

```
PROCEDURE ASK;
BEGIN
    WRITELN;
    WRITE ('UPPER LIMIT OF PRIMES TO BE FOUND?');
    READ (MAXNUMBER);
    WRITELN;
END;
PROCEDURE TEST (NUMBER:INTEGER);
VAR
    TEST_DIVISOR:INTEGER;
```

```
BEGIN
    PRIME:= TRUE; (ASSUME PRIME UNTIL PROVEN NOT)
    TEST_DIVISOR := 3;
    REPEAT
        IF NUMBER MOD TEST_DIVISOR = 0 THEN
PRIME:= FALSE;
        TEST_DIVISOR := TEST_DIVISOR + 2;
    UNTIL NOT PRIME OR (TEST_DIVISOR > = NUMBER);
END; (TEST - IF NUMBER IS PRIME, PRIME WILL BE TRUE
ON EXIT)
```

I can just hear some of you saying "My gosh, doesn't he know that is a terrible way to find primes?" Of course you are correct. It is also the simplest way, and if you will bear with the discussion for a few pages, we will be looking at a more complicated but vastly more efficient way very soon. It would be nice to be able to output the numbers in a tabular form. How about 10 primes to a line? Here is a PROCEDURE to print the primes in that format:

```
PROCEDURE REPORTPRIME;
BEGIN
    WRITE (CANDIDATE:7); (RIGHT JUSTIFIED IN 7 COL-
UMNS)
    COUNT := COUNT + 1; (COUNT THE PRIMES OUTPUT
SO FAR)
    IF COUNT MOD 10 = 0 THEN WRITELN; (START NEW
LINE)
END;
```

The main program now will consist of three parts. In the first, the program asks for the limit of numbers to be searched and initializes the variables. The second part is the main loop that searches for primes. The last prints the result summary line.

```
BEGIN
    (START THE PROGRAM, INITIALIZE VARIABLES,
START THE PRINTOUT)
    ASK;
    WRITELN;
    WRITE ('1':7,'2':7,'3':7); (FIRST THREE PRIMES)
    COUNT := 3; (INITIALIZE)
    CANDIDATE := 5;
    (MAIN LOOP TO FIND PRIMES)
    WHILE CANDIDATE <= MAXNUMBER DO
    BEGIN
```

```
            TEST (CANDIDATE);
            IF PRIME THEN REPORTPRIME;
            CANDIDATE := CANDIDATE + 2;
            END; (WHILE CANDIDATE)
      (SUMMARIZE RESULTS AND EXIT)
      WRITELN;
      WRITELN ('THERE WERE',COUNT:5' PRIMES FROM 1
TO',
            MAXNUMBER:6);
      WRITELN;
END.
```

Now it is possible to do the VAR declarations.

```
VAR
      PRIME:BOOLEAN;
      CANDIDATE,
      COUNT,
      MAXNUMBER : INTEGER;
```

This runs after putting it in order and adding a title line. See Listing 8-1 for the complete program. For testing this program I have used a P-code compiler that produces efficient code but is not as fast as some others that I have available. For the record, the compiler produced 372 bytes of P code for this program. Compilers have associated with them what is called a "runtime package." This is a group of subroutines for doing things like math functions. In the case of this program, only the integer functions were used. The runtime package for this compiler and program came to about 3500 bytes. The program compiled in about 45 seconds and found the primes to the limit of 1000 in 2 minutes and 3 seconds.

THERE'S A BETTER WAY

How can it be improved? How many test divisors do we have to test to prove that a number is prime? We know that the first (smallest) test divisor is 3. If the number were divisible by 3, the other factor (assuming two) would have to be 1/3 of the number. If a larger number is an even divisor, then the other factor of the division is even smaller than 1/3 of the number. In fact, if the number being tested has two factors, under what conditions will the factors be the largest possible? If both are equal to the square root of the number being tested. Here is the insight. If one factor is larger than the square root of the number, the other has to be smaller. Take for example the number 169 to test for primality. You will find that it is not evenly divisible by 3, 5, 7, 9, or 11. It is divisible by 13, yielding a second factor 13 also. That is, 13 * 13 = 169. It is not necessary to test any divisor larger than the square root of the test number in order to prove a number prime.

Will this help much? The program now has to make almost 500 tests to find that last prime, 997. The odd numbers from 5 to 31 (33 is greater than the square root of 1000) are 15 in number!

Since multiplying a few times is bound to be faster than taking a square root, the new test limit can be implemented in the PROCE-DURE TEST by changing the UNTIL NOT PRIME OR (TESTDIVISOR >= NUMBER); just slightly to UNTIL NOT PRIME OR (TESTDIVISOR * TESTDIVISOR > NUMBER);. Notice that we can't quit the test when the square is equal to the number being tested, or we will get 25, 49, and other perfect squares reported as prime. You are eager to know how much faster this improved program ran, aren't you? Would you believe, under 11 seconds? It is interesting that the time was reduced to the square root of the previous time (almost). That would indicate that we've hit on the part of the program where most of the time is spent. We reduced the number of tests to about the square root of the number in the previously attempted program, and the time was reduced accordingly. The "new" program is all of 8 bytes longer!

BETTER YET!

Is there a possibility of further reductions in what the program has to do? As a matter of fact, considerable improvement may be made. The improvement won't be very significant for a limit of 1000 for the primes, but at 10,000 or 20,000 it will be more significant. It may be shown that we don't have to test divisors that are not primes. To take an example, if the number being tested is divisible by 9, 15, or 21 (all multiples of 3) it will be divisible by 3 also. Furthermore, the factor 3 is smaller than these numbers and would have been found already, so the use of nonprime test divisors is redundant. For the above example of the prime 997, the number of tests were reduced from 497 to 15 with the program change. Of those 15 numbers, 9, 15, 21, 25, and 27 are not primes, leaving 10 tests, and a reduction of 33 percent for the largest prime.

Actual improvement in execution time for the program might not be as large as these numbers predict. Since now it is necessary to save the first primes found and use them to test divisors. An array will be necessary. There are less than 50 primes from 3 to the square root of 30,000, the limit of the program capability, (due to the integer number limit of 32,767 in most microcomputer implementations of Pascal) so an array of dimension 50 will be adequate. The procedure TEST will have to use numbers from the array rather than all odd numbers. The procedure REPORTPRIME, when it prints a prime to the screen, must now also write the first 50 primes to the array. The main program must initialize the first three primes in the array, sort of priming the primes. The changes are listed below:

In the main VAR declarations:

```
PRME : ARRAY [1..50] OF INTEGER;
```

Procedure TEST changes considerably. The new version is:

```
PROCEDURE TEST (NUMBER : INTEGER);
VAR
    N : INTEGER;
BEGIN
    PRIME := TRUE; (ASSUME PRIME UNTIL PROVEN
        NOT)
    N := 2; (INITIALIZE INDEX FOR PRME ARRAY)
    REPEAT
    N := N + 1;
        IF NUMBER MOD PRME [N] = 0 THEN PRIME
            := FALSE;
        UNTIL NOT PRIME OR (PRME [N] * PRME [N] >
NUMBER);
END; (TEST)
```

In the procedure REPORTPRIME, one line is added.

```
COUNT := COUNT + 1; (INCREMENT PRIME COUNT)
IF COUNT < 51 THEN PRME [COUNT] := CANDIDATE;
(THIS LINE ADDED TO PUT EARLY PRIMES IN ARRAY)
```

In the main program, after initializing count, the first three array values are initialized

```
PRME [1] := 1; PRME [2] := 2; PRME [3] := 3;
```

Results in terms of execution time for primes to 1000 are rather disappointing. The program runs in a little over 12 seconds rather than 11. When the limit is increased to 10,000, however, things look more as expected. The previous attempt using all odd numbers as test divisors ran 3 minutes 40 seconds. This program ran 3 minutes and 14 seconds. That is an improvement of about 15 percent. The first improvement was the most dramatic and costs less in terms of program size. The user portion of this last version is 488 bytes, over 100 more than the previous version. We're still a long way away from the most efficient algorithm as reported by Niklaus Wirth, but we've written and improved a program in Pascal from scratch. For the sake of completeness, the final program listing is included as Listing 8-2.

A DIFFERENT APPROACH

There is another method of finding primes. Essentially it consists of initializing an array so that it contains all the odd numbers from 1 to the limit of primes to be found. Then, starting at, but not including 3, zero all the multiples of 3 (which are three array locations apart). Then find the first nonzero prime greater than 3 and zero all its multiples. If this process is repeated until all multiples of primes less than the square root of the maximum number are zeroed, the remaining nonzero entries in the array are primes.

It is then a simple matter to write out all the nonzero array values to the output device. Because of the nature of this method, it is necessary to find all the primes before any are output. There is some overhead in outputting the primes because the program must search the array and skip the zero values. In the Pascal P-code implementation we have been using for all the above tests, the primes are found using this technique in 22 seconds and are output to the terminal in about 7 more. With a native code compiler, results were rather spectacular. Primes to 10,000 were found in 5.5 seconds and output in 8 more. The listing is included here as Listing 8-3. This is a rough translation of an old BASIC version, hence there are no procedures. Since it is a single page program, that is probably acceptable. If you like, for an exercise, break it up into three or four PROCEDURES (GETMAX, CROSOUT, PRINT RESULTS) and a main program. Since each of these will only run once, the division will be for aesthetic reasons and program clarity.

I have a report of the sieve method running in 2.0 seconds in a native code C compiler. If you are wondering what the performance limit is, I've seen a sieve program in 6809 assembler that runs on a 1MHz system in approximately 1/7 second. The person who wrote that program tells me that he has one in assembler that runs in 5 milliseconds (0.005 seconds). The faster of the Pascal compilers is, therefore, in the ballpark of 10 to 20 times slower than a very good assembler program.

The point that I would like to make with the exercises in this chapter is that sometimes a little thought can result in a vast improvement over the first idea that pops into your mind for a program algorithm. One of the cute games in comparing micro-processors is a timing comparison. That is a nice pastime and guaranteed to be published by any of the hobbyist computer magazines. In most cases it is much more fruitful to shorten your algorithm than to try to find a faster microprocessor. You might ask at this point, "How do I make a program run faster?" The answer, though not always very simple, usually involves a few standard principles. First of all, where does the program spend most of its time? In the case of the prime program, the obvious answer was, in the test loop.

Having decided where most of the time is spent, the next question is how to reduce the time there. That may be done either by reducing the number of times through the loop (our approach here) or by reducing the time spent for each loop. One does that by removing all calculations that need not be in the loop to a place before the loop. An example in Listing 8-3 is the pre-calculation of HALFMAX and, of course SEARCHLIM. These are not constants because they depend on the value of MAX entered by the user. However their value does not change within the test loop and it would waste much time to use such a statement as FOR N := 1 TO MAX DIV 2; which would require the division of MAX by 2 each time through the loop. Obviously the statement WHILE INTER-VAL < TRUNC (SQRT(MAX))+1; would require a square root to be calculated each time as well. The most fruitful approach is usually a combination of both approaches.

Some Pascal compilers allow easy interface to procedures written in assembler. Perhaps by writing the TEST procedure in assembler here, you could reduce the execution time a great deal. Another possibility in reducing execution time for programs is to be certain that REAL variables are not used where INTEGER vari-ables will do the job. You may have noticed in the sieve program that the line containing the SQRT is the only place in the program where REAL arithmetic is required. That one statement causes the run-time package to load the floating point math and at least the SQRT function and whatever support routines it needs. It is possible to write an "integer" square root function in three or four lines and eliminate the necessity for the REAL math package. In this present case, we would rather go a little too far with our test than be short, so we may want to add 1 to the integer square root when we calculate SEARCHLIM.

```
FUNCTION SQRT (NUMBER : INTEGER) : INTEGER;
CONST
      INIT = 4; (FIRST GUESS)
```

```
VAR
    RESULT,
    GUESS : INTEGER;
BEGIN
    GUESS := INIT;
    WHILE ABS ((GUESS - RESULT) > 1 DO
    BEGIN
        RESULT := NUMBER DIV GUESS;
        GUESS := (GUESS + RESULT) DIV 2;
    END;
    SQRT := GUESS;
END;
```

That should be a little faster than the REAL SQRT FUNC-
TION since there are less digits involved in the calculation. Since it
is only done once, the speed increase won't be detectable, but less
code will be generated. It was suggested to me that the array
doesn't need to have the odd number values in it, just flags to
indicate whether the number represented by that array position is
or is not a prime. Therefore you can set up an array of BOOLEAN
and initialize all positions to TRUE. At the end of the program, the
number represented by each location is easily calculated to be
$2*N-1$ where N is the array index. See Appendix C, Listing C8-3 for
this version. Code for the original was $CD7 bytes and for the
integer square root version $A0A bytes. A saving of about 700
(decimal) bytes. Because it uses a BOOLEAN array and does not
have to calculate to initialize it, this version finds the primes to
10,000 in 3.5 seconds with the native code compiler. Another
advantage is that the BOOLEAN array is half as large as the
comparable INTEGER array, since BOOLEAN variables are only
one byte, and INTEGER are two. Therefore the big array takes up
only half as much memory. The array could be extended to allow
finding of primes up to the limit of integer number representation in
16-bit form.

Listing 8-1. Prime Numbers, First Try.

```
PROGRAM PRIME (INPUT,OUTPUT);

VAR
   PRIME : BOOLEAN;
   CANDIDATE,
   COUNT,
   MAXNUMBER : INTEGER;

PROCEDURE ASK ;

BEGIN
   WRITELN;
   WRITE ('UPPER LIMIT OF PRIMES? ');
   READ (MAXNUMBER);
   WRITELN;
END;

PROCEDURE TEST (NUMBER : INTEGER);

   { SET PRIME TRUE IF NUMBER IS PRIME }

VAR
   TESTDIVISOR : INTEGER ;

BEGIN
   PRIME := TRUE;       { ASSUME PRIME UNTIL PROVEN NOT }

   TESTDIVISOR := 3;
   REPEAT
     IF NUMBER MOD TESTDIVISOR = 0
        THEN PRIME := FALSE;
     TESTDIVISOR := TESTDIVISOR + 2;
   UNTIL NOT PRIME OR (TESTDIVISOR >= NUMBER);
END; { TEST }

PROCEDURE REPORTPRIME;

BEGIN
   WRITE (CANDIDATE:7);  { RIGHT JUSTIFIED IN 7 COLUMNS
   COUNT := COUNT + 1; { PRIME COUNT }
```

70

Listing 8-1. Prime Numbers, First Try (Continued).

```
   IF COUNT MOD 10 = 0 THEN WRITELN;
END;

            { MAIN PROGRAM HERE }

BEGIN
   ASK;
   WRITELN;
   WRITE ('1':7, '2':7, '3':7);     {FIRST PRIMES}
   COUNT := 3;        {INITIALIZE THE VARIABLE}

   CANDIDATE := 5;
   WHILE CANDIDATE <= MAXNUMBER DO
   BEGIN
      TEST (CANDIDATE);
      IF PRIME
         THEN REPORTPRIME;
      CANDIDATE := CANDIDATE + 2;
   END; {WHILE CANDIDATE }
   WRITELN;
   WRITELN ('THERE WERE ', COUNT : 5,
            ' PRIMES FROM 1 TO ', MAXNUMBER : 6);
   WRITELN;
END.
```

Listing 8-2. Prime Numbers, Improved Version.

```
PROGRAM PRIME2 (INPUT,OUTPUT);

VAR
   PRIME : BOOLEAN;
   CANDIDATE,
   COUNT,
   MAXNUMBER : INTEGER;
   PRME : ARRAY [1..50] OF INTEGER;

PROCEDURE ASK ;

BEGIN
   WRITELN;
   WRITE ('UPPER LIMIT OF PRIMES? ');
   READ (MAXNUMBER);
   WRITELN;
END;

PROCEDURE TEST (NUMBER : INTEGER);

VAR
   N : INTEGER ;

BEGIN
   PRIME := TRUE;    { ASSUME PRIME UNTIL PROVEN NOT }
   N := 2;

   REPEAT
      N := N + 1;
      IF NUMBER MOD PRME [N] = 0
       THEN PRIME := FALSE;
   UNTIL NOT PRIME OR (PRME [N] x PRME [N] > NUMBER);
END; { TEST }



PROCEDURE REPORTPRIME;

BEGIN
   WRITE (CANDIDATE:7);
```

72

Listing 8-2. Prime Numbers, Improved Version (Continued).

```
    COUNT := COUNT + 1; { PRIME COUNT }
    IF COUNT < 51 THEN
          PRME [COUNT] := CANDIDATE; { SAVE THE EARLY PRIMES}

    IF COUNT MOD 10 = 0 THEN WRITELN;
END;

      { MAIN PROGRAM HERE }

BEGIN
   ASK;
   WRITELN;
   WRITE ('1':7, '2':7, '3':7); { FIRST PRIMES }
   COUNT := 3;    { INITIALIZE THE VARIABLE }
   PRME [1] := 1; PRME [2] := 2;
   PRME [3] := 3;    {INITIALIZE}

   CANDIDATE := 5;
   WHILE CANDIDATE <= MAXNUMBER DO
   BEGIN
      TEST (CANDIDATE);
      IF PRIME THEN REPORTPRIME;
      CANDIDATE := CANDIDATE + 2;
   END; {WHILE CANDIDATE }
   WRITELN;
   WRITELN ('THERE WERE ', COUNT : 5,
          ' PRIMES FROM 1 TO ', MAXNUMBER : 6);
   WRITELN;
END,
```

Listing 8-3. Prime Numbers by Sieve Method

```
PROGRAM PRIMESIV (INPUT,OUTPUT);

{ PROGRAM TO FIND PRIME NUMBERS BY THE SIEVE
  OF ERASTOSTHENES METHOD }

VAR
    MAX, { LIMIT OF PRIMES }
    PRIMPTR, { POINTER TO PRIME WHOSE
              MULTIPLES ARE BEING ZEROED }
    J, N, { INDEX VARIABLES }
    INTERVAL, { BETWEEN PRIMES BEING ZEROED }
    COUNT, { OF PRIMES }
    HALFMAX, { HALF OF MAX }
    SEARCHLIM { LIMIT OF MULTIPLES SEARCH }
            : INTEGER;
    PRIME : ARRAY [1..5000] OF INTEGER;

BEGIN
    WRITELN;
    WRITE ('MAXIMUM NUMBER? ');
    READ (MAX);
    WRITELN('FINDING PRIMES TO ',MAX : 6);
    WRITELN;

{ INITIALIZE VARIABLES }
    HALFMAX := MAX DIV 2;
    SEARCHLIM := TRUNC (SQRT(MAX)) + 1;
    INTERVAL := 3;
    PRIMPTR := 2;

{ INITIALIZE ARRAY OF ODD NUMBERS }
    FOR N := 1 TO HALFMAX DO
        PRIME [N] := 2 * N -1;

{ MAIN LOOP }
    WHILE INTERVAL < SEARCHLIM DO
    BEGIN
        J := INTERVAL+ (INTERVAL+1) DIV 2;
        {FINDS FIRST MULTIPLE OF PRIME
            WHOSE MULTIPLES ARE TO
```

Listing 8-3. Prime Numbers by Sieve Method (Continued).

```
            BE CANCELLED }

        WHILE J <= HALFMAX DO
        BEGIN
            PRIME [J] := 0;
            J := J + INTERVAL;
        END; { WHILE J }

        PRIMPTR := PRIMPTR + 1;
        WHILE PRIME [PRIMPTR] =0
            DO  PRIMPTR := PRIMPTR + 1;
            { FINDS NEXT NON-ZERO PRIME }
        INTERVAL := PRIME [PRIMPTR];
    END; { WHILE INTERVAL }

    COUNT := 1;
    WRITE ('      2');
    FOR N := 1 TO HALFMAX DO
    BEGIN
        IF PRIME [N] <> 0 THEN
        BEGIN
            WRITE (PRIME [N] : 7);
            COUNT := COUNT + 1;
            IF COUNT MOD 10 = 0 THEN WRITELN;
        END;
    END; { FOR N }
    WRITELN;
    WRITELN;
    WRITELN ('THERE WERE',COUNT:6,' PRIMES.');
END.
```

Chapter 9

Recursive Programs

Now that you have been through the writing of a program in Pascal from scratch, it is time for a parenthetical insert concerning the subject of recursive programming, which is not easy in BASIC. Because of "the way Pascal works," however, it may be used rather easily to write a recursive procedure or function. A recursive procedure is one that "calls itself." Like a loop, the recursive program must eventually reach a condition for which the call will terminate. A fairly simple example of a recursive program might be one to calculate factorials. Ignoring for the moment, the case of the argument values of 0 or 1, how would we generate such a function? (Recall that 5 factorial (5!) means 5*4*3*2*1.) We could use N! := N*(N-1)! as the basis for a recursive FUNCTION.

```
FUNCTION FACTORIAL (N:REAL):REAL;
VAR
    R : REAL; (RESULT)
BEGIN
    IF N>1 THEN R := N*FACTORIAL (N-1) ELSE R := 1;
    FACTORIAL := R;
END;
```

The FUNCTION calls itself N-2 times, each time being passed the parameter (N-1) from the previous call. It works in Pascal because N is a local variable that "copies" the value passed to it without destroying the parameter in the "calling level." For FAC-TORIAL(7), for example, the FUNCTION calls itself 5 times,

76

generating the successive values at each level for N of 6, 5, 4, 3, and 2.

What happens is that we calculate in steps, the following intermediate answers:

7 * FACTORIAL (6)
7 * 6 * FACTORIAL (5)
7 * 6 * 5 * FACTORIAL (4)
7 * 6 * 5 * 4 * FACTORIAL (3)
7 * 6 * 5 * 4 * 3 * FACTORIAL (2)
7 * 6 * 5 * 4 * 3 * 2 * 1 = 5040

LOCAL VARIABLES REQUIRED

Notice particularly that this FUNCTION would not work if either N and/or R were declared as global variables. The recursive call works because N and R can have a different value in each of the nested calls to FACTORIAL. Notice too, that the calls are not successive, that is to say that FACTORIAL doesn't finish its calculation before it calls itself. Only after the last call when N is not greater than one, do the successive calls get to the return. All the levels of the calls to FACTORIAL are active at one point in the process. If the variables were global, there would not be enough places to store intermediate calculations in the recursive process. This is the reason that recursive programming is not normally done in BASIC. Of course BASIC may be used to set up a structure in which each call saves its intermediate values in a different place. One could set up an array to save the intermediates and increment an index on each recursive call to the function, decrementing the index just before the RETURN. That, essentially, would be doing what Pascal does automatically. We would be creating a stack in BASIC, and the index could be thought of as a stack pointer.

Pascal, whenever a procedure is called, allocates a space on its data stack for the parameters and local variables for that procedure. When the procedure returns, its data area vanishes. One danger in recursive functions is that you must be sure that the number of calls is not so great that the Pascal data stack will overflow.

You may wonder why I have declared the variables in the example above to be REAL. Integer arithmetic, in the implementation of Pascal that I am using, has a limit of 32,767. FACTORIAL(8) is greater than 40,000. By using REAL arithmetic, you can get FACTORIAL to work to the number of digits you have in the REAL arithmetic package, and you can get approximations to the factorials of larger numbers. Notice that at 10! you add another digit. You can't calculate factorials of very large numbers without having special representations of very large integers. Such representations may be programmed with some care.

Of course the function FACTORIAL may be computed non-recursively as follows:

```
FUNCTIONAL FACTORIAL (N : REAL) : REAL;
VAR
    R : REAL;
BEGIN
    R := 1;
    WHILE N > 1 DO
    BEGIN
        R := R * N;
        N := N - 1;
    END;
    FACTORIAL := R;
END;
```

For this simple example the nonrecursive form looks easy and it will work in BASIC too. For some more complicated problems, sometimes a recursive approach can yield a simple solution, one that a chief engineer for whom I once worked would call "elegant." It is rather difficult to program recursively in many high-level languages. It may be done by using an array to save values of variables in successive re-entries to the same routine. This technique would work, for example, in BASIC. However, Pascal is designed so that implementation of a recursive algorithm is very easy. A few chapters later in this book, we will use a recursive approach to a sorting algorithm called Quicksort.

Listing 9-1. Recursive Factorial Program.

```
PROGRAM FACTEST (INPUT,OUTPUT);

        { RECURSIVE SOLUTION TO FACTORIAL FUNCTION }

VAR
   NUMBER : REAL ;

FUNCTION FACTORIAL (N : REAL) : REAL ;

VAR
   R : REAL ; { RESULT }

BEGIN
   IF N > 1
     THEN R := N * FACTORIAL (N-1)
     ELSE R := 1;
   FACTORIAL := R;
END;

BEGIN
   REPEAT
     WRITELN;
     WRITE ('INPUT NUMBER FOR FACTORIAL ');
     READ (NUMBER);
     WRITELN;
     WRITELN (FACTORIAL (NUMBER) : 8:0);
   UNTIL FALSE;
END.
```

Listing 9-2. Nonrecursive Factorial Program.

```
PROGRAM FACTEST (INPUT,OUTPUT);

      { NON RECURSIVE FACTORIAL PROGRAM }

VAR
   NUMBER : REAL ;

FUNCTION FACTORIAL (N : REAL) : REAL ;

VAR
   R : REAL ; { RESULT }

BEGIN
   R := 1;
   WHILE N > 1 DO
   BEGIN
      R := R * N;
      N := N - 1;
   END;
   FACTORIAL := R;
END;

BEGIN
   REPEAT
      WRITELN;
      WRITE ('INPUT NUMBER FOR FACTORIAL ');
      READ (NUMBER);
      WRITELN;
      WRITELN (FACTORIAL (NUMBER) : 8 : 0);
   UNTIL FALSE;
END.
```

Chapter 10

Basic
RIP

String Functions in Pascal

Earlier, it was pointed out that Pascal has minimal string functions available. It might therefore be fun and informative to try to write some string functions that duplicate those of most BASIC interpreters. First it will be necessary to examine the limited string functions that Pascal does have. It is possible to declare a single dimensioned array of CHAR which can be considered a string. A singly dimensioned array is sometimes called a vector. The TYPE declaration in Listing 10-1 will indicate how a type STRING may be defined. You will note the use of a constant to set the string length. Several of the string functions will use this length, and the use of a constant makes it easy to adapt this set of functions for many uses without having to edit extensively.

Pascal will allow you to write a string to an output file or the terminal with a WRITE statement as below:

```
TYPE
     STRING = ARRAY [1..32] OF CHAR;
VAR
     A : STRING;
BEGIN
     WRITE (A);
END;
```

That is, you don't need to use a loop to write each character, increment the index, etc. Standard Pascal will output characters until it reaches the end of the string. Standard Pascal will not allow

81

you to READ (A) as a means of inputting a string. You must use a loop and index through the array one character at a time. With these limitations in mind, let's start looking at the string functions. Those here are presented in order, as is necessary with Pascal. That is, the first ones are called by later ones. The matter of being able to build on previously declared functions and procedures is important. You will find that if you can write a set of procedures in this way, the result will be considerably less code generated by the compiler.

Since the string input function is one that will be used many times in a program, it needs to be done neatly and well. There should be a means to honor a backspace if the user wants to correct an error. The procedure RSTRNG for readstring should fulfill this function nicely. See Listing 10-1. This function reads the string a character at a time. If the input character is a backspace, it destroys the last character entered in the array. It accepts characters until a CR is detected. The CR sets the EOLN condition. After that, the remaining array elements are filled with nulls.

BASIC STRING FUNCTIONS

Since Pascal doesn't allow a '$' in an identifier, the function names are the same as those used in BASIC, less the '$'. The first function is LEN, which returns the length of the string. LEN searches for the first null character to find the end of the string. It returns the position of the first null minus 1 as the length of the string. You will remember that a function may be passed parameters as required and returns one "value" as a result. You will find that by using functions rather than procedures, we can make the function calls identical to those used in BASIC. That is, if ASTR is a string variable containing a string, we use K := LEN (ASTR); and the length of ASTR will be found in the variable K, which must be declared as an INTEGER. Note that we have declared local variables for each function, and that all necessary parameters are passed to the function without using GLOBAL variables. This greatly increases the usefulness of these functions, since they can be "prepended" to a program with a guarantee that they won't interfere with the main program's variables even if the same names are used for global variables.

The next function to be done is MID. The syntax of the call is BSTR := MID (ASTR,3,4); where ASTR is a string variable containing a string, 3 is the position of the first character to be "pulled out" of the string, and 4 is the number of characters. The above statement, assuming that ASTR contains 'abcdefgh' would result in

BSTR containing 'cdef'. The returned string should be filled with nulls after the string contents, and the function takes care of this too. The comments in the listing are rather self explanatory for this simple function.

LEFT is the next function to be implemented. BSTR := LEFT (ASTR,3) in the case of the above string would return 'abc'. This function receives only two parameters. It simply adds a third and calls MID (ASTR,1,3). That is, it simply makes the midstring function start at the first character of the string. RIGHT is a little more complex. Suppose that ASTR were 8 characters as in the above example and we want RIGHT (ASTR,5). We want to subtract the 5 from LEN (ASTR), yielding 8 - 5 = 3. The last 5 characters of this string of length 8 are, however, characters 4 through 8. We therefore must add 1 to the result of the subtraction to get the position of the first character. Then, of course, we simply use MID again, the result being MID(ASTR,4,5), which will give us the correct result, 'defgh'.

MORE FUNCTIONS

A very useful string function is one that will search for a smaller string within a larger one. I am aware of two implementations of BASIC that have this function. One calls it INSTR for instring, and the other calls it SUBSTR for substring. I will use INSTR here. This function returns not a string but the position of the first character of the smaller string in the larger one. N := INSTR (ASTR,'ef'); should return the value 5 for N. The smaller string (which we will call the substring) doesn't need to be a string "literal" as in the example above. If BSTR had the contents 'def' we could use N := INSTR (ASTR, BSTR); and get the value 4 for N. (This again assumes that we have the previously stated value for ASTR.) If the smaller string is not found within the larger, the function returns the value 0. Of course, you may use more imaginative names for the string variables than I have done for this discussion.

BASIC allows the concatenation of strings (either the contents of string variables or literal strings in quotes) simply by using the + operator, C$ = A$+B$ or C$ = A$ + "TESTING" are valid expressions in BASIC. Pascal reserves the + operator for numerical operations only. We can simulate this function in Pascal with the function called CAT. It is very hard in Pascal to pass a variable number of parameters to a procedure or function. We will therefore limit CAT to concatenating two strings. However, CAT may be nested to concatenate any number of strings whose total length doesn't exceed STRLEN. The listing contains an example of concatenating three strings with a nested CAT function call. This results in CAT being called recursively, which is no problem since we are passing the strings to local variables. If these functions were to be implemented using global variables, however, we would find that this recursive call would result in catastrophe.

I should note here that it is possible to print out a string without its 'trailing nulls' by using the program fragment below:

```
BEGIN
    FOR N := 1 TO LEN (ASTR) DO WRITE (ASTR [N]);
    WRITELN;
END;
```

In fact, you may want to implement that one statement as a PROCEDURE for printing the contents of string variables. It could be called PSTRING or some such and would be passed only the name of the string variable, as PSTRNG (ASTR);. Related to these functions, are the pre-declared functions CHR and ORD, CHR is identical to CHR$ in BASIC, and ORD, when used on variables of type CHAR, is the same as ASC in BASIC. ORD has other uses on noncharacter variables as well, as explained earlier.

EXTENDED FUNCTIONS

In the first draft of this chapter, I had decided that VAL and STR could not be implemented in a practical way in Pascal. My co-worker Shawn Morrisy pointed out to me a straightforward (though rather cumbersome) way to convert a string to a numerical value. Since in Pascal we must specify the TYPE of the data returned by a function, two functions called VALI and VALR have been written for INTEGER and REAL conversions respectively.

VALI removes the leading spaces from the string and tests to see if the next character is a minus sign. If so, a NEGATIVE flag is set and the array index is incremented to point at what must be the high order digit of the number. N is the result being calculated. The conversion algorithm is to multiply N by 10 and add the next digit of the number, converted from its ASCII representation by using the ORD function and removing the offset or bias. Trailing spaces or any nonnumerical character will terminate the conversion. If the negative flag is set, the number is negated, and the function is assigned the value of N.

VALR sets up a string containing a decimal point (period) and does an INSTR function search for the decimal point in the string representation of the REAL number. Since the number to the left of the decimal point is an integer, it used VALI to convert that portion of the string. If VALI returns a negative number, the negative flag is set, and the number is treated as positive for the remainder of the conversion. Next, the remainder of the string is scanned, each converted digit being divided by a constant K and added to the previous result. K is initialized to 0.1 and divided by ten each time through the loop. When the string representation of the number runs out, the negative flag is tested, and if true, the result is complemented and assigned to VALR.

STRI is a function that follows from the above. It converts an integer number to a string. Conversion proceeds from low to high order. The number is successively divided by 10 and the remainder becomes the next digit. The ASCII bias is added and the digit put into the string. As in the other functions, a negative flag is set if the input number is negative. The absolute value is taken, and the number is treated as positive. At the end, a minus sign is inserted in the string if negative is true, and a space is inserted if it is false. The resulting number is adjusted to remove the leading zeros, and the result is assigned to STRI.

The descriptions of these last three functions have been somewhat more brief than some of the previous ones. By now, you should be getting used to Pascal and should be able to analyze some of the detail for yourself. These last three functions more than double the byte count for the STRING FUNCTIONS. Their value is, at best, marginal. The function STRI is at least not very useful. STRR could be written too, but one would have to decide whether to represent numbers in scientific notation or not. The only reason I can think of for having such a function would be to assist in formatting the output of numbers from Pascal. Since Pascal already has good ways of specifying the format, the STR functions are not needed in general.

I trust that these examples will give you some further insight into writing a program in Pascal as well as provide some useful tools in the area of string manipulations. As you will find out in later chapters, the inclusion of all of these functions in a program would probably be overkill. You will see that it is possible to write a reasonably efficient mailing-list program set using only a few of the functions developed here. Perhaps an advantage of Pascal is that the string functions need not be part of the program or runtime package if they are not used.

In keeping with the philosophy of testing functions and procedures as they are developed, Listing 10-1 also includes a main program that "exercises" the functions and allows you to enter various strings and be satisfied that they work properly. You should recognize that these functions are not intended to work as a "stand-alone" program, but as part of another program. Of course under these circumstances, the "main program" given here would be deleted, and the functions would be included as part of your proram. Most microcomputer operating systems will allow concatenation or appending of disk files, and this set of functions could have your main program appended to them. Then the new file could be edited to insert the program name, constant, type, and variable declarations before the functions. If you have an editor that allows loading of files into the edit buffer while you are editing a program listing, you may load the string functions directly at the proper place in a larger program.

Listing 10-1. String Functions in Pascal.

```pascal
PROGRAM STRINGS (INPUT,OUTPUT);

CONST
    STRLEN = 32;        { LENGTH OF STRING VARIABLES}
    NULL = CHR(0);
    BACKSP = CHR(8);

TYPE
    STRING = ARRAY[1..STRLEN] OF CHAR;

VAR A,B,C : STRING ;
    N : INTEGER ;
    CH : CHAR ;
    RESULT : REAL;



PROCEDURE RSTRNG (VAR X : STRING) ;

{ READ A STRING FROM TERMINAL. }

VAR
    N : INTEGER ; { LOOP INDEX }
    CH : CHAR ;

BEGIN
    FOR N := 1 TO STRLEN DO X [N] := NULL;
                { FILL WITH NULLS FIRST }
    N := 1 ;
    REPEAT
        READ (CH) ;
        IF (CH = BACKSP) AND (N > 1)
            THEN BEGIN
                    N := N - 1;
                    X [N] := NULL;
                END
            ELSE IF NOT EOLN THEN X [N] := CH ;
                    {EOLN WOULD ADD A SPACE OTHERWISE}

        IF CH <> BACKSP THEN N := N + 1 ;
```

Listing 10-1. String Functions in Pascal (Continued).

```
    UNTIL EOLN OR (N > STRLEN);
END;




FUNCTION LEN (X : STRING) : INTEGER;

{ RETURNS LENGTH OF STRING }

VAR N : INTEGER;
    CH : CHAR;

BEGIN
   N := 0; { INITIALIZE LOOP INDEX }
   REPEAT
      N := N + 1 ;
   UNTIL (X [N] = NULL) OR ( N = STRLEN);

   IF N = STRLEN THEN LEN := STRLEN ELSE LEN := N-1;
END;




FUNCTION MID (X : STRING; FIRST, NUMBER: INTEGER): STRING ;

{ RETURNS A STRING CONTAINING 'NUMBER'
      CHARACTERS STARTING AT 'FIRST' }

VAR N,M : INTEGER;
    Y : STRING ;

BEGIN
   FOR N := 1 TO STRLEN
     DO Y [N] := NULL;    { FILL WITH NULLS }

   FOR N := 1 TO NUMBER DO
     IF FIRST + N - 1 <= STRLEN
       THEN Y [N] := X [FIRST + N - 1] ;
       { TRANSFER NUMBER CHARACTERS FROM
         MIDDLE OF X TO NEW STRING Y }
```

Listing 10-1. String Functions in Pascal (Continued).

```
   MID := Y ;
END;




FUNCTION LEFT (X : STRING; NUMBER : INTEGER) : STRING ;

{ RETURNS A STRING CONTAINING THE LEFTMOST
   'NUMBER' CHARACTERS OF STRING. LEFT IS
   SAME AS MID, STARTING AT FIRST CHARACTER }

BEGIN
   LEFT := MID (X,1,NUMBER);
END;




FUNCTION RIGHT (X : STRING; NUMBER : INTEGER) : STRING ;

{ RETURNS THE RIGHTMOST 'NUMBER' CHARACTERS OF STRING }

BEGIN
   IF LEN (X) > NUMBER THEN
   RIGHT := MID (X, LEN (X) - NUMBER + 1, NUMBER)
   ELSE RIGHT := X ;
END;




FUNCTION INSTR (X,Y : STRING) : INTEGER ;

{ RETURNS THE STRING POSITION (INDEX) OF
   THE FIRST CHARACTER OF STRING Y
   IF IT IS FOUND WITHIN STRING X,
   ELSE RETURNS ZERO }

VAR
```

Listing 10-1. String Functions in Pascal (Continued).

```
    K,N : INTEGER ;
    LENGTH : INTEGER ;

BEGIN
    K := 0; N := 1;
    LENGTH := LEN (Y) ;

    REPEAT
      IF MID (X, N, LENGTH) = Y THEN K := N ;
      N := N + 1;
    UNTIL (K <> 0) OR ( N = STRLEN - LENGTH );
    INSTR := K ;
END;



FUNCTION CAT (X,Y : STRING) : STRING ;

{ CONCATENATE TWO STRINGS.  TOTAL LENGTH
  MUST NOT EXCEED STRLEN. SPACES ARE KEPT
  DURING CONCATENATION PROCESS }


VAR
    N,K : INTEGER ; { INDEX FOR LOOP }

BEGIN
    K := LEN (X);
    FOR N := 1 TO LEN (Y) DO X [N+K] := Y [N];
    CAT := X;
END;



FUNCTION VALI (NUMBER : STRING) : INTEGER;

VAR
    I : INTEGER;          { INDEX FOR LOOP }
    N : INTEGER;          { FOR CONVERTED NUMBER }
    NEGATIVE : BOOLEAN ;
```

Listing 10-1. String Functions in Pascal (Continued).

```pascal
BEGIN
   N := 0;  I := 1;
   NEGATIVE := FALSE;  { INITIALIZE VARIABLES}
   WHILE NUMBER [I] = CHR(32)
     DO I := I + 1;  { REMOVE LEADING SPACES }

   IF NUMBER [I] = '-' THEN
   BEGIN
      NEGATIVE := TRUE;
      I := I + 1
   END;
   WHILE NUMBER [I] IN ['0'..'9'] DO
   BEGIN
      N := N x 10 ;
      N := N + ORD (NUMBER [I]) - 48;  { REMOVE ASCII BIAS }
      I := I + 1
   END;
   IF I <> LEN (NUMBER) + 1
     THEN WRITELN ('INPUT FORMAT ERROR');
   IF NEGATIVE THEN N := - N;
   VALI := N;
END;



FUNCTION VALR (NUMBER : STRING) : REAL;

VAR
   A,I,N : INTEGER;
   PARTIAL,B : STRING;
   RESULT : REAL;
   K : REAL;
   NEGATIVE : BOOLEAN;

BEGIN
   B [1] := '.';
   FOR N := 2 TO STRLEN
     DO B [N] := NULL;          { SET UP FOR INSTR }
   A := INSTR (NUMBER,B);       { DECIMAL POINT }
   IF A = 0
```

91

Listing 10-1. String Functions in Pascal (Continued).

```
      THEN WRITELN ('INPUT FORMAT ERROR');
   PARTIAL := LEFT (NUMBER,A - 1);
   N := VALI (PARTIAL);
   IF N < 0
      THEN NEGATIVE := TRUE
      ELSE NEGATIVE := FALSE;
   RESULT := ABS(N);
                  { ASSIGN INTEGER VALUE TO REAL VARIABLE }
   K := 0.1; I := A+1;
   WHILE NUMBER [I] IN ['0'..'9'] DO
   BEGIN
      RESULT := RESULT + (ORD (NUMBER [I]) - 48) X K;
      I := I + 1;
      K := K/10;
   END;
   IF NEGATIVE THEN RESULT := - RESULT;
   VALR := RESULT;
END;

FUNCTION STRI (NUMBER : INTEGER) : STRING;

VAR
   RESULT : STRING;
   N : INTEGER;
   NEGATIVE : BOOLEAN;

BEGIN
   FOR N := 1 TO STRLEN DO RESULT [N] := NULL;
   IF NUMBER = 0 THEN RESULT [2] := '0';

   IF NUMBER < 0
      THEN NEGATIVE := TRUE
      ELSE NEGATIVE := FALSE;

   NUMBER := ABS (NUMBER) ;
   FOR N := 6 DOWNTO 2 DO
   BEGIN
      RESULT [N] := CHR (NUMBER MOD 10 + 48);
                     { ADD ASCII BIAS }
      NUMBER := NUMBER DIV 10;
```

Listing 10-1. String Functions in Pascal (Continued).

```
    END;

    IF NEGATIVE
      THEN RESULT [1] := '-'
      ELSE RESULT [1] := CHR(32);

    WHILE (RESULT [2] = '0')
      AND (RESULT [3] <> NULL)
      DO FOR N := 2 TO 6
          DO RESULT [N] := RESULT [N+1];
      STRI := RESULT;
  END;



{ MAIN PROGRAM TO TEST STRING FUNCTIONS }

BEGIN
    REPEAT
      WRITELN ('INPUT A STRING LESS THAN',
                      STRLEN : 3,' CHARACTERS LONG');
      RSTRNG (A) ;
      WRITELN ;
      WRITELN (LEN (A) : 4);

      WRITE ('MID (A,3,4) =');
      B := MID (A,3,4);
      WRITELN (B) ;

      WRITE ('LEFT (A,5) =');
      B := LEFT (A,5);
      WRITELN (B) ;

      WRITE ('RIGHT (A,5) =') ;
      B := RIGHT (A,5);
      WRITELN (B) ;

      WRITE ('INSTRING FUNCTION: ');
      WRITELN ('INPUT SUBSTRING FOR SEARCH ');
      RSTRNG (B) ;
```

Listing 10-1. String Functions in Pascal (Continued).

```
      WRITELN ;
      N := INSTR (A,B);
      WRITELN ('INSTR =',N:3);
      WRITELN ;

      WRITELN ('CONCATENATED ', CAT (A, B));
      WRITELN ('NESTED CAT ', CAT (A, CAT (B, B)));

   { NOTE THAT THE ABOVE CAUSES A RECURSIVE
     CALL TO CAT AND THAT A LITERAL STRING
     MUST BE STRLEN CHARACTERS LONG.
     TRAILING BLANKS WILL BE
     THROWN AWAY WHEN CONCATENATED }

   WRITE ('INPUT INTEGER STRING FOR VALI ');
   RSTRNG (A);
   WRITELN;
   N := VALI(A);
   WRITELN (N :5);

   WRITE ('INPUT REAL STRING FOR VALR ');
   RSTRNG (A);
   WRITELN;
   RESULT := VALR(A);
   WRITELN (RESULT:12:6);

   WRITE ('INPUT INTEGER FOR STRI ');
   READ (N);
   WRITELN;
   A := STRI(N);
   WRITELN(A);

   UNTIL FALSE OR (CH = CHR(27)) ;
END.
```

Chapter 11

Sorting

There have been whole books written on the subject of sorting, so we won't be able to go into it very deeply in a few pages. This should be considered a brief introduction to the subject.

Sorting programs in general improve with regard to efficiency at the cost of increased complexity of the program. A measure of the efficiency of a sort program is the number of "swaps" required to sort a list of items in random order. To get a list of items from a random order to a sorted order, generally items are swapped in pairs according to some predetermined algorithm until the sort is completed. Swaps are made or not made based on the comparison of two items in the list, and so, the number of comparisons made sorting the list is another measure of the efficiency of the sorting method. The third measure, a somewhat simpler "bottom line" measurement, is the time required to sort the list.

In order for us to be able to compare the sorting algorithms and programs as we develop them, I am going to use a data file of 100 random integers with values from 1 to 100. Since the numbers were generated with a random number generator, some will be included several times, and others will be missing. When we're done, we will show a table of the sorting times and number of swaps and comparisons for our list for each method. See Listing 11-1 for my RANGEN program that generates a file of random numbers.

BUBBLE SORT

The first method we will look at is what is commonly called the "bubble" sort, though the way it is usually programmed, it would more accurately be called the "sinker" sort. Suppose you want to sort a list of numbers in order from lowest to highest (reverse order sorts are easily done by reversing the comparison of the items). The bubble sort starts at the top of the list comparing adjacent items. If the larger is before the smaller, the two are swapped. The effect of a pass from top to bottom, comparing and swapping, is to sweep the largest item to the bottom of the list and a number of large items down until a larger item is found. On the next pass through the list, we need not look at the bottom item since it has been found to be the largest. On succeeding passes, the comparisons stop one item shorter. Since it frequently happens that the items reach their final order before all the passes are completed, a Boolean DONE flag is set TRUE at the start of each pass. If items are swapped, the swap routine sets DONE FALSE. If at the end of any pass, DONE is TRUE, that means that no swaps were made and the sort must be complete.

There are a few enhancements to the bubble sort. One is to make passes alternately from top to bottom and bottom to top, which results in the smallest number being swept to the top after the largest is swept to the bottom. The output list then grows from each end toward the middle. This sounds like it might be a significant improvement, but it reduces the compares and swaps only marginally for an average set of randomly ordered items. All the programs given in this chapter will be run for a list of 100 items and then later for a list of 1000 items. The programs are written so that they may be used for both runs by changing a constant called NUMBER at the beginning of the program. The variables SWAPS and COMPARES or MOVES will hold the count of these operations for each sort. Since for 1000 items, some of the counts will overflow the limit of integer arithmetic for the Pascal implementations available, they have been declared as REAL variables in the programs. The times for the 100 item sorts are all with these variables declared as INTEGER. See Listing 11-2 for the bubble sort.

INSERTION SORT

It is possible to sort in another way. You can start with a "full" random ordered list and move items sequentially to an initially empty list, inserting the item in its proper place each time. This, of course, involves moving many items in the output list as new items are inserted in their proper place. With some clever programming, the input and output lists can occupy the same memory space, since items are removed from one and added to the other. This is called an "insertion sort." A sample of such a sort program is shown in Listing 11-3.

When I first wrote this chapter, I had never tried an insertion sort, and I had assumed it would be less efficient than the bubble sort. Surprise! It is considerably more efficient, though a little more complex. Its execution time for my random list was about 60 percent of the time for the bubble sort, and I had to rearrange the order of the programs in this discussion since I wanted to go from the least to the most efficient. It now occurs to me that if we were to implement what is known as a binary search in the procedure FINDPLACE, we would considerably reduce the compares, and this sort might become as efficient as the Shell Metzner sort to be discussed next.

INSERTION SORT WITH BINARY SEARCH

A binary search is the fastest way to find a place to insert an item in an already ordered list, exactly the problem for FINDPLACE. We first do our compare on the "middle" item of the list. If CURITEM is smaller, we go to the ¼ point, and if it is larger, we try the ¾ point. The interval for successive tries continues to be divided in half. For our list of 100 items, in 7 tries, we are guaranteed to have found the first item in the list greater than our CURITEM. That means that toward the end of the sort, an item can be inserted with 7 compares rather than up to 90 or more. If you have ever played a game called "guess my number," you may have discovered that you can find it in a minimum number of tries by using a binary search. If the number is between 1 and 100, and the computer tells you whether your number is too large or too small, you can use the binary search. Guess 50 for the first try. If your number is too small, guess 50 + 50/2 or 75. If it is too large, guess 50 - 50/2 or 25. Repeat the process of splitting the interval, and you will find the answer in a minimum number of tries.

Listing 11-4 shows the binary search version of the FINDPLACE procedure. There are a few more "if's" to keep everything straight. Since we are not looking for a definite value, but for the place where CURITEM is less than the INSPTR item but greater than the INSPTR - 1 item, things get more complicated. Two conditions must be handled. If CURITEM is less than LIST [1], we can't see if it is greater than the value in LIST [0], since that array position does not exist. CURITEM less than the first item in the list is therefore a special case, and we must move all items in the output list down. We have the other special case that we had in the first sequential search version, where the INSPTR reaches the INITEM pointer, which means that the CURITEM has to be inserted at the bottom of the list. Other than these two cases, the binary search procedure finds an item greater than CURITEM and checks to see whether the preceding item in the list is less than CURITEM. If this condition is fulfilled, FINDPLACE is done. This improved version of the insertion sort ran 30 percent faster than the original version and in 42 percent of the time required for the bubble sort.

I must point out that the improvement in going to a binary search for the insertion will become more apparent as the list grows. For example, for a list of 1000 items, only 10 compares are required near the end of the sort, to find the place for the item, as compared to nearly 1000 for the sequential sort method. Unfortunately, comparisons take considerably less time than moves or swaps, and the binary search for the insertion point does nothing to reduce the number of moves, which increase drastically with the size of the list of items to be sorted.

SHELL-METZNER SORT

The next sort, and next in complexity, is the Shell-Metzner, named after its originators (or inventors). Listing 11-5 shows this sort. These men decided to try comparing and swapping items that are farther apart at first, and then reduce the comparison interval gradually until adjacent items are compared. The compare interval may start at half of the list length, but it has been shown that prime numbers used for intervals produce better results. The program will find the highest power of 2 that is less than the list length and subtract 1 from this for the first interval. For our list of 100 items, the search interval will be 63. We then divide this by 2 when a pass has been made with no swaps. Remember that we are using integer arithmetic and 63/2=31, which happens to be the next lower power of 2 minus 1 also. Not all (2^N)-1 numbers are prime, but they are sufficiently unrelated so that the efficiency of the sort is good, and they are extremely easy to calculate.

The results with the initial interval set at 63, are given in Table 11-1. There were 721 compares and 296 swaps. Runtime was 4.5 seconds. I tried using 64 as the initial interval, so that successive intervals would be 32, 16, 8, 4, 2, and 1. These values of course are the successively smaller powers of two. They are too related. The results using the same data file were 989 compares, 468 swaps, and a run time of 7 seconds! Having gotten interested, I decided to try an initial value of 50. Since this at least produces a less regular series: 50, 25, 12, 6, 3, and 1. Results were somewhat better. There were 782 compares, 330 swaps, and runtime was approximately 5 seconds. Lastly, I tried 47, since this yields a series of all prime numbers, 47, 23, 11, 5, 2, and 1. The results on the "standard" random numbers were 768 compares and 307 swaps. Results with four different data files, however, averaged slightly better than with the initial interval of 63. There were on the average 22.5 more compares and 7.5 less swaps. The average run time seemed to be closer to 4 seconds than with the initial interval of 63.

Shell-Metzner uses another means to get items moved a long distance if that is required. When two items are swapped, the item pointers are "backed up" by a whole interval (if backing up does not put the pointer above the top of the list), and another comparison is made. For example suppose we are comparing item 50 with item 81, the sort interval being 31. We swap these items, and then compare the new item 50 with item 19. If we swap these, we see that the next compare would be item 19 with item -12, so we stop and resume comparing item 51 with item 82. When a pass results in no swaps, we again reduce the interval by dividing by 2 and proceed until the interval is 1 and no swaps are made in a pass. This sort is much faster than the bubble sort. The results would indicate that Shell and Metzner were correct in their initial assumption that moving items larger distances first would reduce the work that had to be done.

QUICKSORT

I hesitate a bit to include this next and last sorting technique called Quicksort, because of its complexity. It requires a stack to keep track of pending operations, a fact that suggests a recursive implementation. Wirth, in his book *Algorithms + Data Structures = Programs,* (Prentice Hall, 1976), discusses various sorting methods and includes the algorithm for the Quicksort procedure. Listing 11-6 is a program to test that algorithm with our standard list of 100 numbers. I've added the statements that keep track of swaps, compares, and recursion depth. As a matter of interest, recursion got to a level of 12 for the standard list. You probably will notice that as we go to more complex algorithms, it gets more difficult to count the compares. Wirth's discussion of the algorithm and his analysis of its performance are both well done, and the book is an excellent one for anyone interested in further pursuing the subject of sorting.

For the sake of completeness, I will attempt to describe the action of this algorithm. I have run Quicksort on a list of 25 items and inserted print statements to print the information before and after each swap. Figure 11-1 is a printout that consists of three lines of information, repeated after each swap. The first of these lines indicates the comparison value on which swaps are based. The second is the list as it stands at that point in the sort, and the third is the portion of the list being considered by the procedure SORT at that point in the program execution. The third line shows that portion of the list after a swap has taken place, so you can see what values were swapped.

The algorithm first divides the list in two and uses the VALUE of the middle item as a comparison value. It searches from the left of the list for an item greater than or equal to that comparison value, and from the right for an item less than that value. When it finds such a combination, it swaps those two items. This process is repeated until the two search pointers bump each other or cross over. You will note by looking at Fig. 11-1, that the algorithm results in the swapping of equal values, which is of course unnecessary. It turns out that it costs more time to check for this condition and eliminate the swap, than it takes to do these extra swaps. In the case of the list of 25 items, 30 swaps are made but only 24 are required. While looking at the results, I did find that the pointers I and J frequently end up pointing at the same item, and the original algorithm performed a swap in this case also. A simple test eliminates this condition and results in the saving of several "swaps." The improvement in time made by this change is not detectable in the sort for 100 items, but it does save one second and about 10 percent of the swaps in the test below for 1000 items.

When the pointers bump, early in the sort, the left portion of the remaining list is sorted (IF LEFT < J THEN SORT (LEFT, J)). That is, if the left item pointer is not bumping the left end of the list, sort from the left end to the left item pointer. The next line of the program takes over when the left item pointer gets to the beginning of the list after successive sorts of smaller and smaller left parts of lists. This then sorts the right portion of the lists, continuing to subdivide the list into smaller and smaller parts. When the left pointer (J) is at the left end of the list and the right pointer (I) is at the right (which happens only after the sublist is reduced to two items and they are in order), no further sorting is possible on that list, and SORT ends and returns one level of recursion.

The complication is that SORT calls itself. When it does this, it suspends working on the current sort and sorts the sublist. However, LEFT, RIGHT, I, and J for the current sort are not lost because they are local variables that are not destroyed by the recursive call to SORT. The parameters passed to SORT become new local variables for that new call of SORT. When the smallest subsort is done, and SORT returns, it finishes the sort at the next level, using the variables still there on the stack. It is all less complicated than it sounds. See Chapter 9 for a quick review of recursive programs. I've marked the items swapped in Fig. 11-1 so that you can see the progress. It is interesting to trace the progress of, for example, the 2 that is the third item from the right of the list, and note that it is moved only three times before it reaches its final location as the second item in the list.

It is also of interest that although the first comparison item happened to be 24, which is almost the maximum value in the list, after four swaps, the top quarter of the list is nearly in order. After ten swaps, the top half of the list is in fairly good order.

SORTING RESULTS COMPARED

My standard random list is given in Fig. 11-2. The results of the sort programs are given in Table 11-1. As a test, I have run the programs with other random lists with very similar results.

Times are approximate. As mentioned above, the insertion sorts don't swap two items in the array being sorted. They read an item from the array, find where it should go in the output list, move everything in the list below that point down, and insert the item. A move reads a value from the array and writes it back to the array. A swap does two reads from the array, two writes to the array, and a read and a write to a simple variable. Accessing a variable in an array requires the software to calculate the memory address of the array element and, therefore, accessing variables in an array is slower than accessing a simple variable. We will use the rough estimate that a swap will take about 2.5 times as long as a move. Compares in the Bubble and Shell-Metzner sorts are between two array elements. Those in the insertion sorts and Quicksort, are between the contents of a simple variable and an array element, so we could conclude that these would be faster. Of course, the more complex sorts have some added overhead. The Shell-Metzner sort has several pointers that must be assigned values on the basis of

```
                    WHOLE LIST SHOWN BEFORE SWAP
              PORTION BEING CONSIDERED SHOWN AFTER SWAP


COMPARE WITH ITEM  13  WHOSE VALUE IS  24

  1 10  5 16 22  4 18 20 17 19 10 24 24 22  9 24 12 16 25 24  3  6  2  5 25
  1 10  5 16 22  4 18 20 17 19 10  5 24 22  9 24 12 16 25 24  3  6  2 24 25
                                  x                                x


  1 10  5 16 22  4 18 20 17 19 10  5 24 22  9 24 12 16 25 24  3  6  2 24 25
  1 10  5 16 22  4 18 20 17 19 10  5  2 22  9 24 12 16 25 24  3  6 24 24 25
                                     x                          x


  1 10  5 16 22  4 18 20 17 19 10  5  2 22  9 24 12 16 25 24  3  6 24 24 25
  1 10  5 16 22  4 18 20 17 19 10  5  2 22  9  6 12 16 25 24  3 24 24 24 25
                                             x                 x


  1 10  5 16 22  4 18 20 17 19 10  5  2 22  9  6 12 16 25 24  3 24 24 24 25
  1 10  5 16 22  4 18 20 17 19 10  5  2 22  9  6 12 16  3 24 25 24 24 24 25
                                                      x        x

COMPARE WITH ITEM  10  WHOSE VALUE IS  19

  1 10  5 16 22  4 18 20 17 19 10  5  2 22  9  6 12 16  3 24 25 24 24 24 25
  1 10  5 16  3  4 18 20 17 19 10  5  2 22  9  6 12 16 22
              x                                     x


  1 10  5 16  3  4 18 20 17 19 10  5  2 22  9  6 12 16 22 24 25 24 24 24 25
  1 10  5 16  3  4 18 16 17 19 10  5  2 22  9  6 12 20 22
                    x                                x


  1 10  5 16  3  4 18 16 17 19 10  5  2 22  9  6 12 20 22 24 25 24 24 24 25
  1 10  5 16  3  4 18 16 17 12 10  5  2 22  9  6 19 20 22
                       x                          x


  1 10  5 16  3  4 18 16 17 12 10  5  2 22  9  6 19 20 22 24 25 24 24 24 25
  1 10  5 16  3  4 18 16 17 12 10  5  2  6  9 22 19 20 22
                                      x     x
COMPARE WITH ITEM   8  WHOSE VALUE IS  16
  1 10  5 16  3  4 18 16 17 12 10  5  2  6  9 22 19 20 22 24 25 24 24 24 25
  1 10  5  9  3  4 18 16 17 12 10  5  2  6 16
           x                             x


  1 10  5  9  3  4 18 16 17 12 10  5  2  6 16 22 19 20 22 24 25 24 24 24 25
  1 10  5  9  3  4  6 16 17 12 10  5  2 18 16
                    x                    x


  1 10  5  9  3  4  6 16 17 12 10  5  2 18 16 22 19 20 22 24 25 24 24 24 25
  1 10  5  9  3  4  6  2 17 12 10  5 16 18 16
                       x           x


  1 10  5  9  3  4  6  2 17 12 10  5 16 18 16 22 19 20 22 24 25 24 24 24 25
```

Fig. 11-1. Quicksort run on 25 random numbers.

102

```
                 1 10  5  9  3  4  6  2  5 12 10 17 16 18 16
      COMPARE WITH ITEM   6 WHOSE VALUE IS   4
                 1 10  5  9  3  4  6  2  5 12 10 17 16 18 16 22 19 20 22 24 25 24 24 24 25
                 1  2  5  9  3  4  6 10  5 12 10
                    X                 X


                 1  2  5  9  3  4  6 10  5 12 10 17 16 18 16 22 19 20 22 24 25 24 24 24 25
                 1  2  4  9  3  5  6 10  5 12 10
                       X        X


                 1  2  4  9  3  5  6 10  5 12 10 17 16 18 16 22 19 20 22 24 25 24 24 24 25
                 1  2  4  3  9  5  6 10  5 12 10

      COMPARE WITH ITEM   3 WHOSE VALUE IS   4
                 1  2  4  3  9  5  6 10  5 12 10 17 16 18 16 22 19 20 22 24 25 24 24 24 25
                       3  4
                       X  X


      COMPARE WITH ITEM   8 WHOSE VALUE IS  10
                 1  2  3  4  9  5  6 10  5 12 10 17 16 18 16 22 19 20 22 24 25 24 24 24 25
                          9  5  6 10  5 12 10
                                X        X                  (SWAP OF EQUAL VALUES)

      COMPARE WITH ITEM   7 WHOSE VALUE IS   6
                 1  2  3  4  9  5  6 10  5 12 10 17 16 18 16 22 19 20 22 24 25 24 24 24 25
                          5  5  6 10  9
                          X        X

      COMPARE WITH ITEM   5 WHOSE VALUE IS   5
                 1  2  3  4  5  5  6 10  9 12 10 17 16 18 16 22 19 20 22 24 25 24 24 24 25
                          5  5
                          X  X                              (SWAP OF EQUAL VALUES)

      COMPARE WITH ITEM   8 WHOSE VALUE IS  10
                 1  2  3  4  5  5  6 10  9 12 10 17 16 18 16 22 19 20 22 24 25 24 24 24 25
                                   9 10

      COMPARE WITH ITEM  10 WHOSE VALUE IS  12
                 1  2  3  4  5  5  6  9 10 12 10 17 16 18 16 22 19 20 22 24 25 24 24 24 25
                                     10 12
                                      X  X

      COMPARE WITH ITEM  13 WHOSE VALUE IS  16
                 1  2  3  4  5  5  6  9 10 10 12 17 16 18 16 22 19 20 22 24 25 24 24 24 25
                                           16 16 18 17
                                           X        X
      COMPARE WITH ITEM  14 WHOSE VALUE IS  18
                 1  2  3  4  5  5  6  9 10 10 12 16 16 18 17 22 19 20 22 24 25 24 24 24 25
                                                 17 18
                                                 X  X

      COMPARE WITH ITEM  17 WHOSE VALUE IS  19
                 1  2  3  4  5  5  6  9 10 10 12 16 16 17 18 22 19 20 22 24 25 24 24 24 25
```

```
                              19 22 20 22
                               X  X


COMPARE WITH ITEM  18  WHOSE VALUE IS  20
  1  2  3  4  5  5  6  9 10 10 12 16 16 17 18 19 22 20 22 24 25 24 24 24 25
                                              20 22 22


COMPARE WITH ITEM  18  WHOSE VALUE IS  22
  1  2  3  4  5  5  6  9 10 10 12 16 16 17 18 19 20 22 22 24 25 24 24 24 25
                                                 22 22
                                                  X  X    (EQUAL VALUES)


COMPARE WITH ITEM  23  WHOSE VALUE IS  24
  1  2  3  4  5  5  6  9 10 10 12 16 16 17 18 19 20 22 22 24 25 24 24 24 25
                                                       24 24 24 25 25
                                                        X        X


  1  2  3  4  5  5  6  9 10 10 12 16 16 17 18 19 20 22 22 24 24 24 24 25 25
                                                       24 24 24 25 25
                                                              X  X


COMPARE WITH ITEM  21  WHOSE VALUE IS  24
  1  2  3  4  5  5  6  9 10 10 12 16 16 17 18 19 20 22 22 24 24 24 25 25
                                                       24 24
                                                        X  X


COMPARE WITH ITEM  24  WHOSE VALUE IS  25
  1  2  3  4  5  5  6  9 10 10 12 16 16 17 18 19 20 22 22 24 24 24 24 25 25
                                                             24 25 25
                                                              X  X
```

Fig. 11-1. Quicksort run on 25 random numbers (continued from page 103).

several logical conditions. The Quicksort requires a stack for pending operations. Pascal is ideal for this algorithm since pending operations are automatically saved when SORT is called recursively by the program.

SORTING LARGER LISTS

Theoretically, for a list of 1000 items, Quicksort would make an average of 2800 swaps. For the same list, Shell-Metzner sort

77	21	71	26	88	57	35	21	18
25	46	81	31	100	88	98	33	96
89	17	84	94	52	64	36	76	90
89	82	80	95	41	34	91	4	87
97	50	62	51	12	61	56	16	32
18	31	88	4	99	66	20	23	90
15	10	35	4	34	43	27	1	25
16	67	93	51	56	28	57	58	88
63	100	17	10	93	28	31	95	36
11	36	28	81	8	67	75	49	80
84	17	96	36	58	56	44	85	95
67								

Fig. 11-2. Random numbers used in sort testing.

would need almost 4500, and the Insertion and Bubble sorts would use about 250,000 moves or swaps respectively. The spread in performance between Bubble sort and Quicksort should increase from the approximate 10 to 1 shown for 100 items, to 60 to 1 for 1000 items. On this basis, with the Pascal implementation I have used to run these tests, the Bubble sort would take 40 minutes, and the Quicksort would take about 40 seconds!

Now, we will sort a list of 1000 items with each method and see how close the actual runs come to the theoretical results. For the SHELL sort I will use an initial interval of 511. Remember that we have added some overhead in counting swaps and compares, and that the less efficient programs, having more of these, will probably do even worse than the theoretical predictions would indicate. In the case of the Bubble and both Insertion sorts, the number of swaps and compares become so large that they overflow the maximum integer (32767) of the implementations of Pascal that I have. Therefore it is necessary to change the types of those variables to REAL. This adds additional overhead because it takes longer to add 1 to a

Table 11-1. Comparison of Sort Program Results for 100 Items.

Type of Sort	Compares	Swaps or Moves	Time for 100 Items
Bubble	4797	2521 swaps	23 sec
Insertion	2528	2617 moves	14
Insertion Binary	688	2644 moves	10
Shell-Metzner	721	296 swaps	4.5
Quicksort	929	197 swaps	2.5

REAL variable than an INTEGER. The results are given in Table 11-2.

It is interesting to note the ratio of the time taken for 1000 items to the time taken for 100 items for each of these:

Sort	Time 1000 items /100 items
Bubble	154
Insertion	147
Insertion Bin.	105
Shell Metzner	22
Quicksort	19

THE WINNER

Quicksort is the clear winner as a sorting algorithm. As a matter of interest, recursion reached a level of 22 for the list of 1000 numbers that I used for these tests. Also, out of curiosity, I prepared a "stripped down" version without the counting of swaps and compares, and it executed the sort of 1000 items in 38 seconds. The best sort took only 19 times as long for 1000 items as it did for 100. The worst took 154 times as long. Our theoretical values of 40 seconds and 40 minutes for the best and worst sort were not too far away from the actual times of 47 seconds and 59 minutes. Some other numbers bear mentioning. The Bubble sort made N*N/2 compares and N*N/4 swaps approximately. (N is the number of items.) The insertion sorts also made N*N/4 swaps, but the straight insertion made N*N/4 comparisons too. The Binary Insertion program made only 11,496, which is roughly 11 comparisons per item in the list. For 1000 items, N times Log(base 2) of N is very nearly 10,000. The comparisons approach what the theoreticians call an N*log (N) process. The Shell sort is a little worse with regard to comparisons, but the number of swaps is reduced to a number close to 2/3 the N*log (N) value. Lastly, Quicksort approaches N*log (N) comparisons and 1-4 N*log (N) swaps!

CONCLUSIONS

It should be quite plain from this discussion that the type of sort algorithm used is not critical for sorting a small number of items (less than 100 or so), but it is crucial for sorting large numbers of items. I have run the Bubble and Quicksort programs for 100 items in another Pascal that produces native code, and the results were approximately 6 times faster for both.

Table 11-2. Comparison of Sort Program Results for 1000 Items.

Type of Sort	Compares	Swaps or Moves	Time for 1000 Items
Bubble	499479	242428 swaps	3538 sec.
Insertion	25870	243421 moves	2060 sec.
Insertion Bin.	11496	243623 moves	1045 sec.
Shell Metzner	14160	6711 swaps	100 sec.
Quicksort	13444	2639 swaps	47 sec.

There is some order of input list for each of these, that is a worst case. The worst case for the Shell-Metzner and Quicksort are the same as the worst case for the bubble sort in terms of swaps and compares. Since they have more overhead, they would actually run slower in the worst case condition. The old rule "There's no such thing as a free lunch" works here too. On the average, however, over many tries with different "random" input data, the Shell-Metzner and Quicksort are vastly faster than the bubble sort.

We have only discussed the subject of sorting an array of items here. What happens if the list is too big to fit in memory? There are simple ways to sort the contents of sequential data files by successive reads and writes of the data. Since our main purpose here is to learn Pascal and not sorting methods (and since I am now rather out of sorts), this is a good place to stop. You will find a good discussion of these methods in Wirth's book mentioned above.

Pascal is a natural for a slightly different approach to the test programs presented here. It is not difficult to write a general (main) program to include all the housekeeping such as getting the file of random numbers into an array, keeping track of the swaps and compares, and printing the results. Having that, it is reasonable to write each of the different sort methods as a procedure that will be compatible with the same main program. Testing various sort methods, then involves only the writing of the sort procedure to be used with the same main program. At this point you should be familiar enough with Pascal to try your own hand at doing this with the sort programs here. Give it a try, and then see Appendix C for my solution to this problem. You need not implement the feature of finding the recursion depth for the Quicksort program.

Listing 11-1. Random Number Generator.

```pascal
PROGRAM RANGEN (INPUT, OUTPUT, DATA);

CONST
  N = 100;

VAR
  RAND : REAL ; { TO HOLD RANDOM NUMBER }
  K : INTEGER;
  DATA: FILE OF CHAR;{USE FILE OF CHAR FOR EASE OF READING}


FUNCTION RANDOM : INTEGER;

{ TO RETURN A NUMBER FROM 1 TO N }

BEGIN

  RAND := RAND / 17;
  RAND := RAND * 19;
  IF RAND > 16384 THEN RAND := RAND - 7327;
  RANDOM := TRUNC (RAND) MOD N + 1;

END; { RANDOM }

BEGIN
  WRITE ('INPUT A NUMBER FROM 1 TO 10000');
  READ (RAND);
  REWRITE (DATA);
  FOR K := 1 TO N DO WRITE (DATA, RANDOM);
END.
```

Listing 11-2. Bubble Sort.

```
PROGRAM BUBBLE (INPUT,OUTPUT,DATA);

CONST
   NUMBER = 100;

VAR
   LIST : ARRAY [1..NUMBER] OF INTEGER;
   DATA : FILE OF CHAR;

   LASTITEM,    { POINTER TO THE LAST ITEM TO BE COMPARED }
   N : INTEGER; { ARRAY INDEX }

   SWAPS,       { COUNT OF SWAPS }
   COMPARES : INTEGER; { COUNT OF COMPARES }

   DONE : BOOLEAN;

PROCEDURE SWAP (FIRST : INTEGER);

VAR
   TEMP : INTEGER;
        { TO HOLD ONE VALUE FOR SWAP }

BEGIN
   TEMP := LIST [FIRST];
   LIST [FIRST] := LIST [FIRST + 1];
   LIST [FIRST + 1] := TEMP;
   SWAPS := SWAPS + 1;
   DONE := FALSE;
END;

BEGIN
   RESET (DATA);

   FOR N := 1 TO NUMBER
    DO READ (DATA,LIST [N]);    { GET THE LIST TO SORT }
   LASTITEM := NUMBER - 1;
   SWAPS := 0;  COMPARES := 0;

    WRITELN ('SORTING');          { FOR TIMING }
```

Listing 11-2. Bubble Sort (Continued).

```
REPEAT
  DONE := TRUE;

  FOR N := 1 TO LASTITEM DO
  BEGIN
    IF LIST [N] > LIST [N+1]
      THEN SWAP (N);
    COMPARES := COMPARES + 1; { COUNT }
  END;

  LASTITEM := LASTITEM - 1;  { REDUCE INPUT LIST BY 1 }
  WRITELN (LASTITEM : 7);
UNTIL DONE;

FOR N := 1 TO NUMBER DO
BEGIN
  WRITE (LIST [N] : 7);
  IF N MOD 10 = 0 THEN WRITELN;
END;

WRITELN;
WRITELN ('COMPARES ',COMPARES : 6);
WRITELN ('SWAPS ',SWAPS : 6);
END.
```

Listing 11-3. Insertion Sort.

```
PROGRAM INSERT (INPUT, OUTPUT, DATA);

CONST
   NUMBER = 100;

VAR
   CURITEM,      { CURENT ITEM FOR COMPARISON }
   LASTOUT,      { POINTER TO END OF OUTPUT LIST }
   INITEM,       { POINTER TO ITEM IN INPUT LIST }
   MOVES,        { COUNT OF MOVES FOR COMPARISON }
   N : INTEGER;  { ARRAY INDEX }

   INSPTR,       { POINTER TO PLACE FOR INSERTION
                   OF CURRENT ITEM IN OUTPUT LIST}
   COMPARES : INTEGER;
        { COUNT OF COMPARES FOR EVALUATION }

   LIST : ARRAY [1..NUMBER] OF INTEGER;
   DATA : FILE OF CHAR;

{ NOTE, THE OUTPUT LIST STARTS AT THE TOP
  OF THE ARRAY AND GROWS TO REPLACE
  ITEMS REMOVED FROM THE INPUT LIST }

PROCEDURE FINDPLACE ;

{ FIND PLACE FOR INSERTION OF CURRENT ITEM }

BEGIN
   INSPTR := 0;

   REPEAT
      INSPTR := INSPTR + 1;
      COMPARES := COMPARES + 1;
   UNTIL (CURITEM < LIST [INSPTR])
      OR (INSPTR = INITEM);

END; { EXIT WITH INSPTR POINTING AT PLACE
       TO INSERT CURITEM AFTER MOVING ALL
       OTHER ITEMS IN OUTPUT LIST DOWN }
```

111

Listing 11-3. Insertion Sort (Continued).

```
PROCEDURE INSERT;

BEGIN
   IF INSPTR <> INITEM THEN
   BEGIN
      FOR N := LASTOUT DOWNTO INSPTR DO
      BEGIN
         LIST [N+1] := LIST [N];
            { MOVE THE ITEMS TO MAKE ROOM }
         MOVES := MOVES + 1;
      END;
      LIST [INSPTR] := CURITEM;
       { INSERT THE CURRENT ITEM IN ITS PLACE }

      MOVES := MOVES + 1; { MOVED CURRENT ITEM TOO }
   END; { ELSE ITEM IN PROPER PLACE ALREADY }
END;


BEGIN
   RESET (DATA);
   FOR N := 1 TO NUMBER
      DO READ (DATA,LIST [N]); {GET LIST}

   LASTOUT := 1; { INITIALIZE VARIABLES }
   INITEM := 2; COMPARES := 0; MOVES := 0;

   WRITELN ('SORTING'); { FOR TIMING }

   REPEAT
      CURITEM := LIST [INITEM];
      FINDPLACE;
      INSERT;
      LASTOUT := LASTOUT + 1;
      INITEM := LASTOUT + 1;
   UNTIL LASTOUT = NUMBER;

   FOR N := 1 TO NUMBER DO
```

112

Listing 11-3. Insertion Sort (Continued).

```
    BEGIN
        WRITE (LIST [N] : 7);
        IF N MOD 10 = 0 THEN WRITELN;
    END;
    WRITELN;
    WRITELN ('COMPARES ',COMPARES : 6);
    WRITELN ('MOVES ',MOVES : 6);
END.
```

Listing 11-4. Insertion Sort with Binary Search

```
PROGRAM INSERT (INPUT, OUTPUT, DATA);

CONST
   NUMBER = 100;

VAR
   CURITEM,        { CURENT ITEM FOR COMPARISON }
   LASTOUT,        { POINTER TO LAST ITEM IN OUTPUT LIST }
   INITEM,         { POINTER TO CURRENT ITEM IN INPUT LIST }
   INSPTR,         { POINTER TO PLACE FOR INSERTION
                     OF CURRENT ITEM IN OUTPUT LIST}
   N : INTEGER;    { ARRAY INDEX }

   COMPARES,       { COUNT COMPARES FOR EVALUATION }
   MOVES : INTEGER; { COUNT OF MOVES }

   LIST : ARRAY [1..NUMBER] OF INTEGER;
   DATA : FILE OF CHAR;

{ NOTE, THE OUTPUT LIST STARTS AT THE TOP OF
  THE ARRAY AND GROWS TO REPLACE
  ITEMS REMOVED FROM THE INPUT LIST }

PROCEDURE FINDPLACE ;

{ FIND PLACE FOR INSERTION }

VAR
   INTVAL : INTEGER;        { SEARCH INTERVAL }
   FOUND : BOOLEAN ;        { FLAG FOR DONE }

BEGIN
   FOUND := FALSE;
   IF LASTOUT > 2
    THEN INTVAL := LASTOUT DIV 2
    ELSE INTVAL := 1;
   INSPTR := INTVAL;
   REPEAT
      IF INTVAL > 1
        THEN INTVAL := INTVAL DIV 2;
```

114

Listing 11-4. Insertion Sort with Binary Search (Continued).

```
      IF CURITEM > LIST [INSPTR]
        THEN INSPTR := INSPTR + INTVAL
        ELSE BEGIN  { TEST SPECIAL CASES OF INSERT AT
                          TOP OR BOTTOM OF LIST }
         IF (INSPTR = INITEM) OR (INSPTR = 1)
           THEN FOUND := TRUE
           ELSE BEGIN
            IF CURITEM >= LIST [INSPTR - 1]
              THEN FOUND := TRUE
              ELSE INSPTR := INSPTR - INTVAL;
            COMPARES := COMPARES + 1;
           END;
        END;
      COMPARES := COMPARES + 1;
   UNTIL FOUND;
END; { EXIT WITH INSPTR POINTING AT PLACE TO
       INSERT CURITEM AFTER MOVING ALL OTHER
       ITEMS IN OUTPUT LIST DOWN }

PROCEDURE INSERT;

BEGIN
   IF INSPTR <> INITEM THEN
   BEGIN
      FOR N := LASTOUT DOWNTO INSPTR DO
      BEGIN
        LIST [N+1] := LIST [N];
             { MOVE THE ITEMS TO MAKE ROOM }
        MOVES := MOVES + 1;
      END;
      LIST [INSPTR] := CURITEM;
             { INSERT THE CURRENT ITEM IN ITS PLACE }
      MOVES := MOVES + 1;
             { MOVED CURRENT ITEM TOO }
   END;        { ELSE ITEM IN PROPER PLACE ALREADY }
END;


BEGIN
   RESET (DATA);
```

Listing 11-4. Insertion Sort with Binary Search (Continued).

```
FOR N := 1 TO NUMBER
  DO READ (DATA,LIST [N]); {GET LIST }

LASTOUT := 1;   { INITIALIZE VARIABLES }
INITEM := 2;
COMPARES := 0;   MOVES := 0;

WRITELN ('SORTING'); { FOR TIMING }

REPEAT
   CURITEM := LIST [INITEM];
   FINDPLACE;
   INSERT;
   LASTOUT := LASTOUT + 1;
   INITEM := LASTOUT + 1;
UNTIL LASTOUT = NUMBER;

FOR N := 1 TO NUMBER DO
BEGIN
   WRITE (LIST [N] : 7);
   IF N MOD 10 = 0 THEN WRITELN;
END;
WRITELN;
WRITELN ('COMPARES ',COMPARES : 6);
WRITELN ('MOVES ',MOVES : 6);
END.
```

Listing 11-5. Shell-Metzner Sort.

```
ROGRAM SHELL (INPUT,OUTPUT,DATA);

CONST
   NUMBER = 100; { NUMBER OF ITEMS FOR SORT }
   FIRSTINT = 47; {STARTING SORT INTERVAL }

VAR
   INTERVAL,     { THE INTERVAL BETWEEN ITEMS
                   TO BE COMPARED }
   INDEX,        { POINTER, HOLDS PLACE WHEN
                   SWAP POINTERS BACK UP }
   ITEM1,        { POINTER FOR FIRST ITEM
                   FOR COMPARISON }
   COMPARES,     { COUNT OF COMPARES }
   SWAPS : INTEGER; { COUNT OF SWAPS }

   LIST : ARRAY [1..NUMBER] OF INTEGER;
                          { ARRAY OF ITEMS TO BE SORTED }
   DATA : FILE OF CHAR; { THE RANDOM LIST }

   SWAPPED : BOOLEAN; { FLAG FOR SWAPPED DATA}

PROCEDURE SWAP;

VAR
   TEMP : INTEGER; { NEEDED FOR SWAP }
BEGIN
   TEMP := LIST [ITEM1];
   LIST [ITEM1] := LIST [ITEM1 + INTERVAL];
   LIST [ITEM1 + INTERVAL] := TEMP;
   SWAPPED := TRUE;
   SWAPS := SWAPS + 1;
END;


BEGIN

   RESET (DATA);     { GET UNSORTED LIST }
   FOR INDEX := 1 TO NUMBER
     DO READ (DATA, LIST [INDEX]);
```

Listing 11-5. Shell-Metzner Sort (Continued).

```
{ INITIALIZE VARIABLES }
INTERVAL := FIRSTINT ;
INDEX := 1;
ITEM1 := 1;
SWAPS := 0;
COMPARES := 0;

WRITELN ('SORTING'); { FOR TIMING }

REPEAT
   SWAPPED := FALSE;
   COMPARES := COMPARES + 1;
   IF LIST [ITEM1] > LIST [ITEM1 + INTERVAL]
     THEN BEGIN
             SWAP;
             ITEM1 := ITEM1 - INTERVAL;
          END;
   IF (NOT SWAPPED) OR (ITEM1 < 1)
     THEN BEGIN
             INDEX := INDEX + 1;
             IF INDEX > (NUMBER - INTERVAL)
               THEN BEGIN
                       INTERVAL := INTERVAL DIV 2;
                       INDEX := 1;
                    END;
             ITEM1 := INDEX;
          END;
UNTIL INTERVAL = 0;

FOR INDEX := 1 TO NUMBER DO
BEGIN
   WRITE (LIST [INDEX] : 7);
   IF INDEX MOD 10 = 0 THEN WRITELN;
END;
WRITELN;
WRITELN ('COMPARES ',COMPARES : 6);
WRITELN ('SWAPS ',SWAPS : 6);
END.
```

Listing 11-6. Quicksort.

```pascal
PROGRAM QUICK (INPUT,OUTPUT,DATA);

VAR
   LIST : ARRAY [1..100] OF INTEGER;

   COUNT,
   SWAPS,
   LEVEL, { CURRENT LEVEL OF RECURSION }
   MAXIMUM, { MAXIMUM LEVEL OF RECURSION }
   COMPARES : INTEGER;

   DATA : FILE OF CHAR;

PROCEDURE SWAP (ITEM1, ITEM2 : INTEGER);

VAR
   TEMP : INTEGER:

BEGIN
   TEMP := LIST [ITEM1];
   LIST [ITEM1] := LIST [ITEM2];
   LIST [ITEM2] := TEMP;
   SWAPS := SWAPS + 1;
END;


PROCEDURE SORT (LEFT, RIGHT : INTEGER);

VAR
   I,
   J,
   X : INTEGER;

BEGIN
   I := LEFT;    J := RIGHT;
   X := LIST [(LEFT + RIGHT) DIV 2];
   LEVEL := LEVEL + 1;
   IF LEVEL > MAXIMUM THEN MAXIMUM := LEVEL;
   REPEAT
```

119

Listing 11-6. Quicksort (Continued).

```
      WHILE LIST [I] < X DO
      BEGIN
         I := I + 1; COMPARES := COMPARES;1;
      END;
      COMPARES := COMPARES + 1;
{ ONE FOR THE COMPARE THAT ENDED THE WHILE }

      WHILE X < LIST [J] DO
      BEGIN
         J := J - 1; COMPARES := COMPARES+1;
      END;
      COMPARES := COMPARES + 1;

      IF I <= J THEN
      BEGIN
         SWAP (I,J);
         I := I + 1;
         J := J - 1;
      END;
   UNTIL I > J;

   IF LEFT < J THEN SORT (LEFT,J);
   IF Y < RIGHT THEN SORT (I,RIGHT);
   LEVEL := LEVEL - 1;
      { DUCREMENT RECURSION LEVEL ON EXIT }
END;

  { PROGROM TO TEST QUICKSORT ALGORITHM }
BEGIN
   RESET (DATA);
   SWAPS := 0;
   COMPARES := 0;
   LEVEL := 0;
   MAXIMUM := 0;

   FOR COUNT := 1 TO 100 DO
      READ (DATA, LIST [COUNT]);

   WRITELN ('SORTING '); { FOR TIMING }
```

120

Listing 11-6. Quicksort (Continued).

```
   SORT (1,100);

   FOR COUNT := 1 TO 100 DO
   BEGIN
      WRITE (LIST [COUNT] : 7);
      IF COUNT MOD 10 = 0 THEN WRITELN;
   END;

   WRITELN;
   WRITELN ('COMPARES ',COMPARES : 6);
   WRITELN ('SWAPS ',SWAPS : 6);
   WRITELN ('RECURSION LEVEL ',MAXIMUM : 6);
END. {QUICK}
```

Chapter 12

Records

Pascal has the data type RECORD. A record is a group of related items that make up one logical unit of information. For example in a program for handling a list of names and addresses, a record might be comprised of name, address, city, state, zip code, and telephone number. It would be feasible to put all those parts of the record in one long STRING but that doesn't lend itself to accessing the various parts of the record very well. Suppose, for example, that you want to sort your name and address records by last name for some purposes and by zip code for others. Furthermore, when you print mailing labels, you don't want the phone number to appear, but you do want the phone number when you print your personal phone directory, using the information from the records.

It should be plain that the data could be manipulated more easily if there were a way to access the components of the record more easily. Pascal allows such a structure by allowing the user to divide the record into various "fields." Suppose we have set up a record variable that contains the fields LAST, FIRST, MIDDLE, ADDRESS, CITY, STATE, ZIP, and PHONE. Let's call the record NAMAD for NAMe and ADdress. Now, you can access the CITY part of the record by using NAMAD.CITY. That is, the field is specified in the same way as most disk operating systems specify a file extension. Having access to the various parts of the records allows you to manipulate data in a much more efficient manner. Suppose you want to sort your file of name and address records so that they may be listed in order of last name. It would be nice, too, to have people with the same last name listed in order of first name. Suppose you have the following list of names:

    Smith   John
    Anderson   Ronald
    Anderson   Richard
Sorted by first name, the order would be:
    Smith   John
    Anderson   Richard
    Anderson   Ronald
Now sorting by last name using a sort that won't rearrange the order of the Andersons:
    Anderson   Richard
    Anderson   Ronald
    Smith   John

RECORDS DIVIDED INTO FIELDS

We could complicate matters more by adding another level of sort by middle initial, which would have to be first. Then John B. Smith would end up ahead of John M. Smith. To hold these three parts of the name for the sort in BASIC would require three arrays. We could use F$ for first name, L$ for last name, and I$ for initial. The three parts—first, last, and middle initial—taken together may be represented in Pascal as a RECORD. Each of the three components is a FIELD of that RECORD.

```
TYPE
    NAMES = RECORD
            FIRST : ARRAY [1..12] OF CHAR:
            LAST : ARRAY [1..14] OF CHAR;
            INITIAL : CHAR
            END;
VAR
    NAME : NAMES;
    LIST ARRAY [1..100] OF NAMES;
```

Yes, you can have an array of records. Now you have a data structure that can be used for storing and sorting names. The various parts or fields of the record are accessed easily.
NAME.FIRST := 'RONALD   ';

Pascal also has another way of designating labels for fields of a specific record. Unfortunately the only implementation of Pascal that I have available with RECORDS doesn't have this feature implemented, so it will not be used in the example programs here. It is included for the sake of completeness. If you are to work with one record or array of records you may use:

```
WITH NAME DO
    FIRST := 'WILLIAM    ';
    LAST := 'CARMICHAEL    ';
    INITIAL := 'G'
END;

FOR INDEX := 1 TO 10 DO
    WITH LIST [INDEX] DO
        WRITELN ('FIRST NAME');
        READ (FIRST);
        WRITELN ('LAST NAME');
        READ (LAST);
        WRITELN ('INITIAL');
        READ (INITIAL);
        WRITELN
    END;
END;
```

You may access the parts of the array by LIST [9]. FIRST :='RUDOLPH   ';. Rather than declaring LIST as an array, it can just as well be declared as a file of the type NAMES. LIST : FILE OF NAMES;. Then after opening the file and assuming that it existed previously, one could read the records in the file sequentially by: READ (LIST, NAME);. That is, the contents of one record of type NAMES in the file would be read into the variable NAME of type NAMES. You may then manipulate the values in the variable NAME and write it back to the same or another file. You may not read NAME.FIRST. You must read the whole record and assign it to a variable of the same type.

Do you begin to see the value of this structure? In our example here, all the fields have been characters. We could easily extend the idea here to a RECORD that holds a name and address, including zip code. The .ZIP part of the record can be of type INTEGER. However, you will soon find a problem if you do that. Integer numbers are limited to a maximum of 32,767 in many microprocessor implementations of Pascal, and you won't be able to put in an address west of somewhere in Pennsylvania! In addition, you will find that Canadian and many other foreign zip codes are mixed letters and numbers. It is therefore better to use a string for the zip too.

```
TYPE
    NAMAD = RECORD
        LASTNAME : ARRAY [1..12] OF CHAR;
        FIRSTNAME : ARRAY [1..12] OF CHAR;
        INITIAL : CHAR;
        STREETAD : ARRAY [1..30] OF CHAR;
        CITY   : ARRAY [1..15] OF CHAR;
        STATE  : ARRAY [1..2] OF CHAR;
        ZIP    : ARRAY [1..7] OF CHAR;
    END;
```

Here, I must warn that we are getting into features of Pascal that are not supported in all the implementations. For example, I have one that supports only FILE of CHAR. It doesn't support RECORD types at all. Another implementation supports RECORD types and files of all types, but the WITH statement is not implemented. We are going to build up a name and address program, in case you hadn't guessed, and I am going to use the implementation that allows everything but the WITH statement.

First, let's do something very simple. How about a brief program to see if we can get data input from the terminal and written to a data file. Next, the inverse should be done and we will get data from the file and display it on the terminal. Listing 12-1 and 12-2 do just that. I've used a Pascal implementation that associates the data disk file name with the parameter DATA by means of its inclusion on the command line that causes the program to be run. My programs are called RECTEST (to write names to a record file) and RECREAD (to read records from a file and list them). I simply type RUN,RECTEST,DATA,DAT.1, and the file is opened for write by the REWRITE (DATA) instruction in the program. The same procedure is used to associate the file name with DATA in the RECREAD program.

This implementation of Pascal has a peculiarity. I can't declare the parts of a record as ARRAY [1..N] OF CHAR;. I must declare a variable type STRING = ARRAY [1..15] OF CHAR;. Then I can declare LAST and FIRST as type STRING as I have done in the listings. The declaration used as examples in the text are according to the Pascal standard, and these limitations are peculiar to the particular implementation. They, along with the lack of WITH, will simply add a few lines to the program.

Oh, yes, I nearly forgot another detail. This implementation not only has implemented WRITE (NAME.LAST) to write the contents of the array to the terminal, it also has an extension whereby it allows READ (NAME. LAAST);. You simply type in the name and terminate input with a carriage return. The Pascal fills the string with blanks. In addition, it honors a backspace as the string is being input. Of course, if you input a number of characters equal to the array size, the input terminates and the string is truncated or cut off at the array size. We may want to add our trailing blank removal procedure developed in Chapter 11 on STRINGS so that we can print the output in better format. For now, though, we have accomplished the writing of RECORDS of data to a file and reading them back.

There is nothing else very startling about the program listings. You may think the way to terminate the data input loop is rather clumsy. I agree. How about modifying the RECTEST program to accept a null input (only a CR) for the last name as the condition for termination. It would still be well to write a string of Z's to the file as the last name. We will use this later when we get to sorting a file. Also, it would be nice to format the screen nicely so the user can see the prompts clearly. If your terminal has a screen clear and home cursor function, implement it so that the screen is cleared at the start of the prompt for each new record. If your terminal doesn't allow this, you could output a couple of blank lines to separate the records, or possibly enough blank lines to cause the previous record to scroll off the screen. While you are modifying, add the procedure RSTRNG or a modification of it that will allow you to use these programs with Standard Pascal without the special extension mentioned above. Try the modification and check your answer with Listing C12-1 in Appendix C. Now modify the RECREAD program to work properly with the data file generated by using RSTRNG in RECTEST. RSTRNG fills the string with nulls rather than blanks, so there is no space output after the first name. It will run together with the initial unless you add a space there. You might like to format the output to print one name to a line so that it looks like it would if you were to write it as part of an address on a label or envelope (i.e., John Q. Jones). You will find my solution Listing C12-2 in Appendix C.

In the next chapter we will continue to develop a mailing-list system and include the means for putting phone numbers in the record too. We will write a program to allow printing of labels and one to allow printing of a name address and phone number list. We will write a program to sort the records in the file as well.

Listing 12-1. Write Record Variables.

```pascal
PROGRAM RECTEST (INPUT, OUTPUT, DATA);

{ WRITE TO A FILE OF RECORDS }

TYPE
   STRING = ARRAY [1..15] OF CHAR;
   NAMES = RECORD
                LAST : STRING;
                FIRST : STRING;
                INITIAL : CHAR
           END;

VAR
   NAME : NAMES;
   DATA : FILE OF NAMES;

BEGIN
   REWRITE (DATA);
   REPEAT
      WRITE ('INPUT FIRST NAME ');
      READ (NAME.FIRST);
      WRITELN;
      WRITE ('INPUT MIDDLE INITIAL ');
      READ (NAME.INITIAL);
      WRITELN;
      WRITE ('INPUT LAST NAME ');
      READ (NAME.LAST);
      WRITELN;
      WRITE (DATA, NAME);
   UNTIL NAME.LAST = 'ZZZZZZZZZZZZZZZ'
END.
```

Listing 12-2. Read Record Variables.

```
PROGRAM RECREAD (INPUT, OUTPUT, DATA);

{ READ RECORDS FROM A FILE AND DISPLAY DATA }

TYPE
   STRING = ARRAY [1..15] OF CHAR;
   NAMES = RECORD
              LAST : STRING;
              FIRST : STRING;
              INITIAL : CHAR
           END;

VAR
   NAME : NAMES;
   DATA : FILE OF NAMES;


BEGIN
   RESET (DATA);
   WRITE (CHR(26)); { CLEAR SCREEN }
   READ (DATA, NAME);
   WHILE NAME.LAST <> 'ZZZZZZZZZZZZZZZ'
   DO BEGIN
      WRITELN ( NAME.FIRST,' ',
                NAME.INITIAL,'. ',
                NAME.LAST);
      READ (DATA, NAME)
   END;
END.
```

Chapter 13

A Mailing List Program

This chapter will be a sort of "talk through" of the writing of a set of programs that will support a data file of names, addresses, and telephone numbers. These programs have not yet been written. I have chosen to do this chapter in this manner because it might provide you with some insight into how a set of programs come into being. Most of the more formal books on programming strongly stress a "problem definition" or "program specification" that is supposed to be supplied by the "customer." Perhaps in the area of data processing at least some of the customers know precisely what they want the software to do. In the area of machine control applications in which I work, I have never seen a customer supplied specification. Usually, the total input from the customer is "Build me a machine to do this." Frequently, hindsight adds quite a few requirements to the specification after the program is done. It is of course easier to see what is needed after looking at something working. As you will probably see at the end of this chapter, the application of some hindsight will reveal several possibilities for improvements. For the time being, let's take a stab at the task of putting together a set of mailing-list programs.

THE DATA STRUCTURE

The first and most important part of writing a group of programs to support a data file is to determine the structure of the file. All the other parts of the system will depend on that structure, and changes found necessary at a later time will require changes in all the support programs.

How many programs will we be generating? We will need a program to create a data file, one to edit it, one to sort it, and probably at least two to print the data out. One will print mailing labels, and the other will print a list that could be used as a personal address and phone book. That is five for a start.

Let's define our basic RECORD first:

```
TYPE
    STRING32 = ARRAY [1..32] OF CHAR;
    STRING15 = ARRAY [1..15] OF CHAR;
    STRING12 = ARRAY [1..12] OF CHAR;
    STRING 7 = ARRAY [1..7] OF CHAR;
    STRING 2 = ARRAY [1..2] OF CHAR;
    STRING 1 = ARRAY [1..1] OF CHAR;

    NAME = RECORD
        FIRST  : STRING12;
        INITIAL  :STRING1;
        LAST   : STRING15;
        STREET  :STRING32;
        ADDITIONAL : STRING32;
        CITY  : STRING15;
        STATE  : STRING2;
        ZIP  : STRING7;
        PHONE  : STRING12
    END;
```

Should we decide that some of these are too small, we may expand them in the type declarations in each program without too much trouble. We know how to create a file, input data, and write it to the file. We just did that in the last chapter. Let's do it again using this more complicated RECORD structure, maintaining or expanding all the features of RECTEST. We will call our program CREATE because we will use it to create our data file. Listing 13.1 is the program. You may wonder about the string length 1 used for the middle initial. If you use a CHAR type, Pascal only looks for one character and immediately accepts it without a CR. (Some Pascal implementations treat a character input just like a string, but not this one). By using a string, the initial input waits for a CR just like all the others and operation is uniform. Such things are important to a good operator interface, particularly when the program is to be used by a nonprogrammer.

We come quickly to our first disappointment in Pascal. It would be very nice if we could use RSTRING to read in strings of various lengths, and pass it the string name and length as parameters. We cannot. PROCEDURE RSTRNG (VAR X : STRING32); defines the string length as 32. Any attempts to pass RSTRNG the length first and then define X as VAR X : ARRAY [1..length] OF CHAR; results in an error message saying that a variable may not be used here. You might think that defining X as an array of the largest size to be used (32) would allow you to read into smaller arrays by passing the length and only reading, for example 15 characters for the last name. Pascal objects if you declare X as type STRING32 and try to pass it NAME.FIRST, which is defined as STRING12. It sees and complains about a TYPE conflict. Seemingly the only way out of this "overprotective" nature of Pascal is always to read the input from the terminal into a string of type STRING32. Then it is necessary to read the first N characters of that string into the variable of STRINGN type. You will see that I have done just that for all the variables except those that happened to be STRING32 in the first place.

Other than that little dilemma, there is nothing remarkable about the CREATE program. It is simply an extension of our first experiment to write names to a file. Now we must do something with our data file if it is to be useful. Perhaps it would be easy and show some tangible progress in the set of programs to do a label program next. PLABEL will print the contents of all the records in the file in mailing label format. (See Listing 13-2.)

PRINTING LABELS

The label printing program does no more than read the file and print its contents (omitting the phone number, of course) in a formatted manner. Notice that there is provision for an additional address line for apartment number or other additional information. If this string is null, a blank line is not printed at that point in the label, but it is added later after the city, state, and zip line. Mailing labels are normally 1 inch "long" and they require 6 lines. Once the printer is properly adjusted, the labels will stay in sync with the address information.

The listing has an additional parameter in the program parameter list, that of PRINTER. This implementation of Pascal uses the parameter, a declaration of PRINTER : FILE OF CHAR; and the specification of a device number in the command line to run the program, to link the printer to the program. Any WRITE or

WRITELN statement then specifying the file PRINTER will be written to the printer or, if the link is not made in the command line, will default to the terminal. Your Pascal probably will link to the printer in a very similar manner. You will have to read the manual to be certain.

PRINT A DIRECTORY FROM THE SAME DATA

Since the PLABEL program was rather easy, let's tackle the PDIR program next. It will print an address and phone number listing. Since the total number of positions in all the fields of our name, address, and phone number record is 128, it is not possible to fit all on one line of a reasonably sized printout. Full 132-column 14-inch-wide paper is not too handy for such purposes. Let's format the printout in two lines. The first will contain the name and street address. The second will contain additional address, city, state, zip, and phone number. A third blank line will separate entries. The second line will be indented from the first by 5 spaces. There will be 20 items to a page, after which we will issue a formfeed to the printer. For our first try, let's not tab the data into columns, but rather let's let it be in free form with spaces between adjacent items. (See Listing 13-3.)

NOW TO CHANGE THE DATA FILE

Now, what we have so far seems to work, and studying the programs will give you a good feel for how to use RECORDS and also some further insight into how strings may be treated in Pascal. The three programs won't do us much good, however, without the real workhorse program. We need one to allow us to edit information in a record to handle a change of address, for example. It must also allow us to delete a record or add a new one. Rather than try to do these very similar functions in three different programs, let's try to combine them into one called CHANGE. To do any of those operations, we need a way to find records in order to operate on them. Assuming we have sequential files only, we will have to read the original file and write a new file, copying all the records that are not to be changed as well as handling edits, additions, and deletions. Let's assume that we won't necessarily be working with sorted files. If we add a SORT program later, that won't change our CHANGE program. First, we should decide on a procedure to find a record.

For a personal name and address file, we would normally find records by people's names. CHANGE should allow us to enter more than one name (perhaps 10 or 20) and then search for all of those entered as it reads the input file. When it finds a record that we need, it should ask if it has the correct record, and then let us change it. At the end of the list, the program should report any records that it couldn't find using the information we input. We must know if we didn't change one of the records. We will first need a procedure to get the list of names to search for. We will add a TYPE definition for a RECORD called SEARCH that will consist of the three parts of the name. (See Listing 13-4 for the program.)

I decided while writing CHANGE that it would be simple to let CHANGE ask for each field in turn as a record is being changed. When the information in a particular field is to remain the same as before, a CR is accepted as a signal to leave that field alone. Thus only the changed information needs to be typed in when you change a record. It became evident that it would be possible to take advantage of a seeming inconvenience to do this. The program tests the input string INSTR to see if the first character is a null. If it is, the data is left unaltered in that field. If we had input the user response directly into the record held in the variable NAME, that would not have been possible. It is a great operator convenience to be able to leave chosen parts of the record as is with a single keystroke.

The program first asks for a list of names to match with records that need to be changed or deleted. Then it reads the input file, a record at a time, and compares the name in each record with the list of those to be changed. If it does not find a match, it writes that record unchanged to the output file. If a match is found, the information from that record is presented and it may be changed. When the change is complete, it is written to the output file and another input record is read and compared to the list until the end of file is reached. If a record is to be deleted, it is simply not written to the output file. It turns out that it would be simpler to include the ADD a record function in the CREATE program. All that program has to do in addition to what it already does, is to ask if the file is new or not. If not, it will first read the old file to the output file and then add names in the same manner as it already adds names to a new file. Listing 13-5. shows the modified CREATE program, which I have renamed CREADD.

This brings up a point. If you hadn't guessed, I am writing these programs concurrently with the text. I have left the text and the original CREATE program here to show how you might change your mind while in the middle of a set of programs. At this point the only function we have not yet implemented is a program to sort our file by name.

SORTING THE DATA RECORDS

In keeping with a simple approach, let's first write a program using the Shell-Metzner sorting method. We will assume that there is enough memory in the computer for us to read the whole data file into memory and sort it all at once. If you have 48K or so of memory, you will probably have 40K free for the data array. You can sort 8 records per 1K of memory, so that with 40K you could sort 320 records. I am going to use 200 for an array dimension in this program. We will use a trick to speed up the sort. Since the sorted list will be written back to a file, we don't need to move the records around in memory. We will generate another array, initially filled with the numbers from 1 to 200 in order. We will do the sort operation but swap only the numbers in our pointer array. When the sort is finished, we will write the records to the output file in the order specified by the shuffled pointers, and the output will be in order. This "trick" saves execution time because we only swap pointers (integer numbers). It should run as fast as our Shell-Metzner sort a few chapters back, except for some additional overhead in accessing the subparts of the records for sorting and a string comparison procedure we will have to write.

Initially, we will allow sorting only by one field, so that all the people named Smith will be grouped together but not necessarily in order of first names. Later, after the program is working, we will add secondary field sorts. We will allow sorting by name or zip code in the initial version. You will recognize PROCEDURE SORT as the Shell-Metzner sort. I've automated the choice of the initial interval. Starting at 255, it is divided by two until it is less than the number of items to be sorted. Of course we found previously that the (2 to the nth power)—1 series of intervals is not quite as efficient as some all-prime series, but they are easier to calculate in this automatic mode.

Looking at the listing, you will see a variable BIGARRAY : ARRAY [1..200] OF NAMES;. That one bears some thinking about. Expressing it a little less formally, it boils down to BIGARRAY : ARRAY [1..200] OF (GROUP OF CHARACTER ARRAYS OF VARIOUS LENGTHS);. It is an array of RECORDS, each of which contains 9 arrays of characters! If this isn't complex enough, we are accessing the RECORD with an index that is an element of an array TAGS : ARRAY [1..200] of INTEGER;. Remember, we said that we were going to swap only the "tags" that correspond with the record numbers and not the records themselves. When the sort is done, the contents of TAG [7] is the number of the record that is to be seventh in the sorted output list. The contents of TAG [1] is the number of the record that is to be first in the output list. Perhaps showing an example of how to specify a particular character in a particular field of a specific record would help to clarify the accessing of a field in an array of records.

BIGARRAY [record number].fieldname [character_position]

This specifies the "character_positionth" character in the field "fieldname" of the "record numberth" record stored in BIGARRAY. The records are put into BIGARRAY in the order in which they are read from the input file. If we swap the contents of two locations in the TAGS array and then use the contents of TAGS to specify the order of the output records, the effect is the same as if we had swapped the contents of those two records and then output BIGARRAY in order from top to bottom.

IMPROVEMENTS

In the process of getting the sorts to work I found that I had to change CREAD to put 'ZZZZZZZ' into the .ZIP portion of the last record as well as filling the last name field with Z's. It has become rather apparent that we don't really need the dummy last record with the Z's for sorting. How about modifying the programs to remove that feature and rely on EOF (INDATA) to find the end of the input file. It will simplify the programs somewhat.

While you are modifying, notice that I've not provided for the case of no middle initial. The PLABEL and PDIR programs will print a period and space even if the initial is a null. Modify these programs to skip the period and only print a single space between first and last names if there is no middle initial. We have also not provided for a "prefix" such as Mr., Mrs., Ms., Dr., or Mr. & Mrs. For a personal mailing list it would be nice to have those. You might even want to add Dr. & Mrs. I suggest another field called order of the prefixes above; MR,RS,MS,DR,MM, and DM. This abbreviation has two advantages. It gets very tiresome typing in Mr. & Mrs. over and over again, and the memory usage is considerably reduced with the coding. It is also rather easy to remember. The choices could be included in the prompt for that field. The PDIR and PLABEL programs could use a CASE statement to print the proper prefix based on the code.

There are some other things that could be done to improve

these programs. Operator interface is very important in this sort of program set. As the CREADD and CHANGE programs stand, there is no way to go back to a previous field and make a correction once the operator has hit a CR. Modify the programs so that when all data for a record has been input, the program asks "OK TO WRITE RECORD TO DISK?". If the response is anything but 'Y', the program should return to the start of that record and input the information again.

Another possible modification to reduce the operator's work would be for CHANGE. If a field is to be left as is, have the program accept a CR for the first character as a signal to go on to the next field and leave the current one unchanged. As sometimes happens, this change necessitated a change in the RSTRNG procedure so that I could backspace to the first position of the input buffer and put a NULL there if return were hit at that point. As you work on these, pay particular attention to clear prompts and clean format of the information presented on the CRT. An extra WRITELN here and there is much better than one too few.

My solutions to the above are included in Appendix C under the same listing numbers with a prefixed C. That is, PLABEL is found as Listing C 13-2 in Appendix C. You will find that you will quickly learn a great deal about Pascal programming if you tackle these modifications one at a time after you have the programs running as presented in this chapter. I hope that these programs will be useful, and that as you work through them you will see just how they work. If you come up with any interesting extensions and modifications, please write me, c/o TAB Books Inc. I will be most interested in what you can add to them.

As an advanced project, you might want to look at sorting by first name and then by last. This will get the first names in order within a group of people with the same last name. I'll leave that as an exercise for you.

I've used my enhanced programs to input my personal name and address book of 70 entries. In the process, I found it necessary to make some of the improvements suggested above. I was pleased to find that the program SORTNAME was able to read a file of 70 records initially sorted in order of zip code, sort them in last name order, and write them to the output file in just over 40 seconds.

If you need for a mailing-list program for a business, you might want to add one more field to the end, or use the phone number field for a different purpose, that of categorizing your list. You can divide the names and addresses into various categories and then modify the PLABEL program to print labels only for the names that fall into selected categories. If you are an insurance agent, for example, you might want to send a special holiday greetings calendar to all your customers at the beginning of the year but, only your best customers. If you have need for this, you may modify the programs for that feature too.

You may have seen (or own) some database management software. You'll find that the heart of most of these program systems is a way of specifying the fields of a record to be used to hold the data items for your application. You will notice that Pascal allows you to specify your record directly as you write the program. Though the program CHANGE has grown to over four pages of listing (as computer printout on 8½-by-11-inch paper), it is not overly complex. We've built it up in small blocks of procedures. Though the main program is over a page long, it consists of repeated blocks of the same lines for input of each field of the record. Once you understand the function of one of these blocks, you understand them all. The main program then is reduced to half a page or so of statements that start and terminate four loops.

Just one more point needs making. You will make liberal use of an editor that allows reading parts of existing text files into the file that you are editing. This approach eliminates the necessity of typing in such things as the TYPE declarations for each program several times. You might notice that the section used to input the information for each field in the CHANGE program is very similar to that of the CREADD program. I used the editor to get those lines from CREADD and then modified them slightly for CHANGE. The largest P-code file for these is CHANGE, and it runs just over 3K with my compiler. The runtime package is another 3.5K or so. I have ample room to expand the maximum number of records that can be sorted in one pass.

If you need data files larger than 200 records, you might write a SORT program that will sort 200 items and save them to an intermediate file, read and sort 200 more and merge these with the data read from the intermediate file, writing the resulting 400 records in order to an output file, etc. This procedure may be repeated as required to sort any number of items, and indeed is faster than sorting a very large number of items all in one sort. To merge two sorted lists, you simply compare the two top items on the lists and write the lesser to the output file, repeating until one file is empty, and then write the rest of the items in the remaining file to the output file.

Listing 13-1. Create a Data File.

```pascal
PROGRAM CREATE (INPUT, OUTPUT, DATA);

LABEL
   10;

CONST
   CLRSCRN = CHR(26); { CHARACTER CONSTANT }
   NULL = CHR(0);

TYPE
   STRING32 = ARRAY [1..32] OF CHAR;
   STRING15 = ARRAY [1..15] OF CHAR;
   STRING12 = ARRAY [1..12] OF CHAR;
   STRING7  = ARRAY [1..7] OF CHAR;
   STRING2  = ARRAY [1..2] OF CHAR;
   STRING1  = ARRAY [1..1] OF CHAR;
     { ARRAY OF 1 USED FOR UNIFORM
       OPERATION WITH REGARD TO CR }

   NAMES = RECORD
              FIRST      : STRING12;
              INITIAL    : STRING1;
              LAST       : STRING15;
              STREET     : STRING32;
              ADDITIONAL : STRING32;
              CITY       : STRING15;
              STATE      : STRING2;
              ZIP        : STRING7;
              PHONE      : STRING12
           END;


VAR
   CH : CHAR;
   NAME : NAMES;
   DATA : FILE OF NAMES;
   INSTR : STRING32;
   N : INTEGER ; { LOOP INDEX }
```

Listing 13-1. Create a Data File (Continued).

```
PROCEDURE RSTRNG (VAR X : STRING32);


BEGIN
   FOR N := 1 TO 32 DO X [N] := CHR (0);
                    { FILL WITH NULLS }
   N := 1;
   REPEAT
      READ (CH);
      IF (N>1) AND (CH = CHR(8))
         THEN N := N - 2
         ELSE IF NOT EOLN THEN X [N] := CH;
      N := N + 1;
   UNTIL EOLN OR (N > 32);
END;

BEGIN
   REWRITE (DATA);
   WRITE (CLRSCRN);
   WRITE ('INPUT DATA AS PROMPTED. ');
   WRITELN ('TO QUIT, ENTER RETURN');
   WRITE (' ONLY FOR LAST NAME. ');
   WRITELN (' (HIT RETURN TO CONTINUE.)');
   READ (CH);

   REPEAT
      WRITE (CLRSCRN);
      WRITE
       ('INPUT FIRST NAME              ');
      RSTRNG (INSTR);
      FOR N := 1 TO 12
        DO NAME.FIRST [N] := INSTR [N];
      WRITELN;

      WRITE
       ('INPUT MIDDLE INITIAL          ');
      RSTRNG (INSTR);
      NAME.INITIAL [1] := INSTR [1];
```

139

Listing 13-1. Create a Data File (Continued).

```
WRITELN;

WRITE
  ('INPUT LAST NAME                ');
RSTRNG (INSTR);
FOR N := 1 TO 15
  DO NAME.LAST [N] := INSTR [N];
WRITELN;
IF NAME.LAST [1] = NULL THEN GOTO 10;

WRITE
  ('INPUT STREET ADDRESS           ');
RSTRNG (NAME.STREET);
WRITELN;

WRITE
  ('ADDITIONAL ADDRESS (CR IF NONE)');
RSTRNG (NAME.ADDITIONAL);
WRITELN;

WRITE
  ('CITY                           ');
RSTRNG (INSTR);
FOR N := 1 TO 15
  DO NAME.CITY [N] := INSTR [N];
WRITELN;

WRITE ('STATE                        ');
RSTRNG (INSTR);
FOR N := 1 TO 2
  DO NAME.STATE [N] := INSTR [N];
WRITELN;

WRITE ('ZIP                          ');
RSTRNG (INSTR);
FOR N := 1 TO 7
  DO NAME.ZIP [N] := INSTR [N];
WRITELN;

WRITE ('PHONE (AAA PPP-NNNN)          ');
```

140

Listing 13-1. Create a Data File (Continued).

```
        RSTRNG (INSTR);
        FOR N := 1 TO 12
          DO NAME.PHONE [N] := INSTR [N];
        WRITELN;

   10:  IF NAME.LAST [1] = NULL
            THEN NAME.LAST := 'ZZZZZZZZZZZZZZZZ';
        WRITE (DATA, NAME);
      UNTIL NAME.LAST = 'ZZZZZZZZZZZZZZZZ'
END.
```

Listing 13-2. Print Labels.

```
PROGRAM PLABEL (INPUT, OUTPUT, DATA, PRINTER);

CONST
   NULL = CHR(0);

TYPE
   STRING32 = ARRAY [1..32] OF CHAR;
   STRING15 = ARRAY [1..15] OF CHAR;
   STRING12 = ARRAY [1..12] OF CHAR;
   STRING7  = ARRAY [1..7] OF CHAR;
   STRING2  = ARRAY [1..2] OF CHAR;
   STRING1  = ARRAY [1..1] OF CHAR;

   NAMES = RECORD
             FIRST      : STRING12;
             INITIAL    : STRING1;
             LAST       : STRING15;
             STREET     : STRING32;
             ADDITIONAL : STRING32;
             CITY       : STRING15;
             STATE      : STRING2;
             ZIP        : STRING7;
             PHONE      : STRING12
           END;


VAR
   NAME : NAMES;
   DATA : FILE OF NAMES;
   N : INTEGER ; { LOOP INDEX }
   PRINTER : FILE OF CHAR;

BEGIN
   RESET (DATA);
   READ (DATA,NAME);
   WHILE NAME.LAST [15] <> 'Z' DO
   BEGIN
      WRITELN (PRINTER,NAME.FIRST,' ',NAME.INITIAL,'. ',
                       NAME.LAST);
      WRITELN (PRINTER, NAME.STREET);
```

142

Listing 13-2. Print Lables (Continued).

```
      IF NAME.ADDITIONAL [1] <> NULL
         THEN WRITELN (PRINTER, NAME.ADDITIONAL);

      WRITELN (PRINTER,NAME.CITY,', ',
                       NAME.STATE,' ',NAME.ZIP);
      WRITELN (PRINTER);
      WRITELN (PRINTER);

      IF NAME.ADDITIONAL [1] = NULL
         THEN WRITELN (PRINTER);
           { 6 LINES TO A ONE INCH LABEL }
      READ (DATA,NAME);
   END;
END.
```

Listing 13-3. Print a Directory.

```
PROGRAM PDIR (INPUT, OUTPUT, DATA, PRINTER);

CONST
   NULL = CHR(0);
   FORMFEED = CHR(12);

TYPE
   STRING32 = ARRAY [1..32] OF CHAR;
   STRING15 = ARRAY [1..15] OF CHAR;
   STRING12 = ARRAY [1..12] OF CHAR;
   STRING7  = ARRAY [1..7] OF CHAR;
   STRING2  = ARRAY [1..2] OF CHAR;
   STRING1  = ARRAY [1..1] OF CHAR;

   NAMES = RECORD
             FIRST      : STRING12;
             INITIAL    : STRING1;
             LAST       : STRING15;
             STREET     : STRING32;
             ADDITIONAL : STRING32;
             CITY       : STRING15;
             STATE      : STRING2;
             ZIP        : STRING7;
             PHONE      : STRING12
           END;


VAR
   NAME : NAMES;
   DATA : FILE OF NAMES;
   N : INTEGER ; { LOOP INDEX }
   PRINTER : FILE OF CHAR;
   ITEMCOUNT : INTEGER; { FOR PAGE FORMAT }

PROCEDURE THREELINES;

BEGIN
   WRITELN (PRINTER);
   WRITELN (PRINTER);
   WRITELN (PRINTER);
```

144

Listing 13-3. Print a Directory (Continued).

```
END;


BEGIN
   RESET (DATA);
   READ (DATA,NAME);
   ITEMCOUNT := 1;
   WRITE (PRINTER, FORMFEED);
   THREELINES;
   WHILE NAME.LAST [15] <> 'Z' DO
   BEGIN
      WRITELN (PRINTER,NAME.FIRST,' ', NAME.INITIAL,'. ',
                         NAME.LAST,'   ', NAME.STREET);

      WRITELN (PRINTER, NAME.ADDITIONAL,'   ',NAME.CITY,
                   ', ',NAME.STATE,' ', NAME.ZIP,'   ',
                         NAME.PHONE);

      WRITELN (PRINTER);

      ITEMCOUNT := ITEMCOUNT + 1;
      IF ITEMCOUNT = 20 THEN
      BEGIN
         WRITE (PRINTER, FORMFEED);
         THREELINES;
         ITEMCOUNT := 1;
      END;
      READ (DATA,NAME);
   END;
END.
```

145

Listing 13-4. Edit a Data File.

```
PROGRAM CHANGE (INPUT, OUTPUT, INDATA, OUTDATA

LABEL
   10;

CONST
   CLRSCRN = CHR(26); { CHARACTER CONSTANT }
   NULL = CHR(0);

TYPE
   STRING32 = ARRAY [1..32] OF CHAR;
   STRING15 = ARRAY [1..15] OF CHAR;
   STRING12 = ARRAY [1..12] OF CHAR;
   STRING7  = ARRAY [1..7] OF CHAR;
   STRING2  = ARRAY [1..2] OF CHAR;
   STRING1  = ARRAY [1..1] OF CHAR;


   NAMES = RECORD
             FIRST      : STRING12;
             INITIAL    : STRING1;
             LAST       : STRING15;
             STREET     : STRING32;
             ADDITIONAL : STRING32;
             CITY       : STRING15;
             STATE      : STRING2;
             ZIP        : STRING7;
             PHONE      : STRING12
         END;


   SEARCH = RECORD
             FIRST      : STRING12;
             INITIAL    : STRING1;
             LAST       : STRING15
         END;

VAR
   CH        : CHAR;
   NAME      : NAMES;
   INDATA,
   OUTDATA   : FILE OF NAMES;
```

146

Listing 13-4. Edit a Data File (Continued).

```
    INSTR        : STRING32;
    K,N          : INTEGER ; { LOOP INDEX }
    SEARCHLIST   : ARRAY [1..20] OF SEARCH;
                   {LIST OF RECORDS}


PROCEDURE RSTRNG (VAR X : STRING32);

BEGIN
    FOR N := 1 TO 32
      DO X [N] := CHR (0); { FILL WITH NULLS }
    N := 1;
    REPEAT
      READ (CH);
      IF (N>1) AND (CH = CHR(8))
         THEN N := N - 2
         ELSE IF NOT EOLN THEN X [N] := CH;
      N := N + 1;
    UNTIL EOLN OR (N > 32);
END;



PROCEDURE GETLIST;

BEGIN

    { INITIALIZE ALL ENRIES TO FOUND }
    FOR N := 1 TO 20
      DO SEARCHLIST [N].LAST [1] := NULL;
    K := 1;
    REPEAT
      WRITE (CLRSCRN);
      WRITE (NULL);
       { TERMINAL REQUIRES TIME FOR CLEAR }
      WRITELN
           ('IDENTIFY RECORD TO BE CHANGED');

      WRITE ('FIRST NAME              ');
      RSTRNG (INSTR);
```

147

Listing 13-4. Edit a Data File (Continued).

```
     FOR N := 1 TO 12
      DO SEARCHLIST [K].FIRST [N]:=INSTR [N];
     WRITELN;

     WRITE ('INITIAL                    ');
     RSTRNG (INSTR);
     SEARCHLIST [K].INITIAL [1] :=INSTR [1];
     WRITELN;

     WRITE ('LAST NAME                  ');
     RSTRNG (INSTR);
     FOR N := 1 TO 15
      DO SEARCHLIST [K].LAST [N]:=INSTR [N];
     WRITELN;

     K := K + 1;
  UNTIL (K = 21) OR (SEARCHLIST [K-1].LAST [1] = NULL);
END;

PROCEDURE FINDRECORD;

VAR
   FOUND : BOOLEAN;

BEGIN
   READ (INDATA, NAME);
   FOUND := FALSE;

   WHILE (NOT EOF (INDATA)) AND (NOT FOUND)
   DO BEGIN
     N := 1;
     REPEAT
        FOUND := TRUE;

        IF NAME.LAST <> SEARCHLIST [N].LAST
          THEN FOUND := FALSE;

        IF NAME.FIRST<> SEARCHLIST [N].FIRST
          THEN FOUND := FALSE;
```

Listing 13-4. Edit a Data File (Continued).

```
            IF NAME.INITIAL <> SEARCHLIST [N].INITIAL
              THEN FOUND := FALSE;

            N := N + 1;
        UNTIL FOUND OR (N = K);

        IF FOUND
          THEN SEARCHLIST [N-1].LAST [1] : NULL;
                    { MARK AS FOUND }
        IF NOT FOUND
          THEN BEGIN
                 WRITE (OUTDATA, NAME); {NOT CHANGED}
                 READ (INDATA,NAME);    {GET ANOTHER}
               END; { IF NOT FOUND }
    END; {WHILE NOT EOF }
END; { FINDRECORD }



BEGIN
  RESET (INDATA);
  REWRITE (OUTDATA);
  GETLIST;

  REPEAT
    FINDRECORD;
    IF NOT EOF (INDATA)
      THEN BEGIN
        WRITE (CLRSCRN);
        WRITELN ('IS THIS A RECORD TO BE CORRECTED? ');
        WRITELN (NAME.FIRST,' ', NAME.INITIAL,'. ',
                 NAME.LAST);
        WRITELN (NAME.STREET);
        WRITELN (NAME.ADDITIONAL);
        WRITELN (NAME.CITY,', ', NAME.STATE,' ',
                 NAME.ZIP);
        WRITELN (NAME.PHONE);
        READ (CH);
        WRITELN;
```

149

Listing 13-4. Edit a Data File (Continued).

```
IF CH ='Y' THEN
  BEGIN
    WRITE ('DELETE (D) OR CHANGE (C) ');
    READ (CH);
    WRITELN;
    IF CH = 'C' THEN
    BEGIN
     WRITE ('TYPE RETURN TO RETAIN');
     WRITELN ('SAME INFORMATION IN FIELD');
     WRITE ('INPUT FIRST NAME             ');
     RSTRNG (INSTR);
     IF INSTR [1] <> NULL
       THEN FOR N := 1 TO 12
         DO NAME.FIRST [N] := INSTR [N];
     WRITELN;

     WRITE ('INPUT MIDDLE INITIAL         ');
     RSTRNG (INSTR);
     IF INSTR [1] <> NULL
       THEN NAME.INITIAL [1]:=INSTR [1];
     WRITELN;

     WRITE ('INPUT LAST NAME              ');
     RSTRNG (INSTR);
     IF INSTR [1] <> NULL
       THEN FOR N := 1 TO 15
         DO NAME.LAST [N] := INSTR [N];
     WRITELN;
     IF NAME.LAST [1] = NULL
       THEN GOTO 10;

     WRITE ('INPUT STREET ADDRESS         ');
     RSTRNG (INSTR);
     IF INSTR [1] <> NULL
         THEN NAME.STREET := INSTR;
     WRITELN;

     WRITE ('ADDITIONAL ADDRESS (CR IF NONE)');
     RSTRNG (INSTR);
     IF INSTR [1] <> NULL
```

Listing 13-4. Edit a Data File (Continued).

```
            THEN NAME.ADDITIONAL := INSTR;
        WRITELN;

        WRITE ('CITY                        ');
        RSTRNG (INSTR);
        IF INSTR [1] <> NULL
          THEN FOR N := 1 TO 15
            DO NAME.CITY [N] := INSTR [N];
        WRITELN;

        WRITE ('STATE                       ');
        RSTRNG (INSTR);
        IF INSTR [1] <> NULL
          THEN FOR N := 1 TO 2
            DO NAME.STATE [N] := INSTR [N];
        WRITELN;

        WRITE ('ZIP                         ');
        RSTRNG (INSTR);
        IF INSTR [1] <> NULL
          THEN FOR N := 1 TO 7
            DO NAME.ZIP [N] := INSTR [N];
        WRITELN;

        WRITE ('PHONE (AAA PPP-NNNN)         ');
        RSTRNG (INSTR);
        IF INSTR [1] <> NULL
          THEN FOR N := 1 TO 12
            DO NAME.PHONE [N] := INSTR [N];
        WRITELN;

        WRITE (OUTDATA, NAME);
      END; { IF CH = 'C' }
    10: { DUMMY LINE }
    END; {IF CH = 'Y' }
  END; { IF NOT ENDFILE }
UNTIL EOF (INDATA);

FOR N := 1 TO 20 DO
BEGIN
```

Listing 13-4. Edit a Data File (Continued).

```
       IF SEARCHLIST [N].LAST [1] <> NULL
          THEN WRITELN (SEARCHLIST [N].FIRST,
             ' ',SEARCHLIST [N].INITIAL,'. ',
                SEARCHLIST [N].LAST,
                ' NOT FOUND xxxxxxx');
     END;
END.
```

Listing 13-5. Create or Add to a File.

```
PROGRAM CREADD (INPUT, OUTPUT, DATA, INDATA);

LABEL
   10;

CONST
   CLRSCRN = CHR(26); { CHARACTER CONSTANT }
   NULL = CHR(0);

TYPE
   STRING32 = ARRAY [1..32] OF CHAR;
   STRING15 = ARRAY [1..15] OF CHAR;
   STRING12 = ARRAY [1..12] OF CHAR;
   STRING7  = ARRAY [1..7] OF CHAR;
   STRING2  = ARRAY [1..2] OF CHAR;
   STRING1  = ARRAY [1..1] OF CHAR;

   NAMES = RECORD
              FIRST      : STRING12;
              INITIAL    : STRING1;
              LAST       : STRING15;
              STREET     : STRING32;
              ADDITIONAL : STRING32;
              CITY       : STRING15;
              STATE      : STRING2;
              ZIP        : STRING7;
              PHONE      : STRING12
           END;


VAR
   CH : CHAR;
   NAME : NAMES;
   INDATA,
   DATA : FILE OF NAMES;
   INSTR : STRING32;
   N : INTEGER ; { LOOP INDEX }


PROCEDURE RSTRNG (VAR X : STRING32);
```

153

Listing 13-5. Create or Add to a File (Continued).

```
BEGIN
   FOR N := 1 TO 32 DO X [N] := CHR (0);
                  { FILL WITH NULLS }
   N := 1;
   REPEAT
      READ (CH);
      IF (N>1) AND (CH = CHR(8))
         THEN N := N - 2
         ELSE IF NOT EOLN THEN X [N] := CH;
      N := N + 1;
   UNTIL EOLN OR (N > 32);
END;
BEGIN
   REWRITE (DATA);
   WRITE (CLRSCRN);
   WRITE ('CREATE A NEW FILE (C) OR ADD TO');
   WRITELN (' AN OLD ONE (A) ');
   READ (CH);
   IF CH = 'A'
      THEN BEGIN
               RESET (INDATA);
               READ (INDATA,NAME);
               WHILE NAME.LAST <> 'ZZZZZZZZZZZZZZZ' DO
               BEGIN
                  WRITE (DATA,NAME);
                  READ (INDATA,NAME);
               END; { WHILE NAME.LAST }
            END; {IF CH = 'A' }

   WRITE ('INPUT DATA AS PROMPTED.');
   WRITELN ('  TO QUIT, ENTER RETURN');
   WRITE (' ONLY FOR LAST NAME.');
   WRITELN ('  (HIT RETURN TO CONTINUE.)');
   READ (CH);
REPEAT
   WRITE (CLRSCRN);
   WRITE ('INPUT FIRST NAME           ');
   RSTRNG (INSTR);
   FOR N := 1 TO 12
      DO NAME.FIRST [N] := INSTR [N];
   WRITELN;
```

154

Listing 13-5. Create or Add to a File (Continued).

```
WRITE ('INPUT MIDDLE INITIAL              ');
RSTRNG (INSTR);
NAME.INITIAL [1] := INSTR [1];
WRITELN;

WRITE ('INPUT LAST NAME                   ');
RSTRNG (INSTR);
FOR N := 1 TO 15
   DO NAME.LAST [N] := INSTR [N];
WRITELN;
IF NAME.LAST [1] = NULL
   THEN GOTO 10;

WRITE ('INPUT STREET ADDRESS              ');
RSTRNG (NAME.STREET);
WRITELN;

WRITE ('ADDITIONAL ADDRESS (CR IF NONE)');
RSTRNG (NAME.ADDITIONAL);
WRITELN;

WRITE ('CITY                              ');
RSTRNG (INSTR);
FOR N := 1 TO 15
   DO NAME.CITY [N] := INSTR [N];
WRITELN;

WRITE ('STATE                             ');
RSTRNG (INSTR);
FOR N := 1 TO 2
   DO NAME.STATE [N] := INSTR [N];
WRITELN;

WRITE ('ZIP                               ');
RSTRNG (INSTR);
FOR N := 1 TO 7
   DO NAME.ZIP [N] := INSTR [N];
WRITELN;
```

Listing 13-5. Create or Add to a File (Continued).

```
      WRITE ('PHONE (AAA PPP-NNNN)           ');
      RSTRNG (INSTR);
      FOR N := 1 TO 12 DO NAME.PHONE [N] := INSTR [N];
      WRITELN;

 10:  IF NAME.LAST [1] = NULL
         THEN BEGIN
            NAME.LAST := 'ZZZZZZZZZZZZZZZZ';
            NAME.ZIP  := 'ZZZZZZZ';
         END;
      WRITE (DATA, NAME);
   UNTIL NAME.LAST = 'ZZZZZZZZZZZZZZZZ'
END.
```

Listing 13-6. Sort a Data File.

```
PROGRAM SORTNAME (INPUT, OUTPUT, INDATA, OUTDATA);

CONST
   CLRSCRN = CHR(26); { CHARACTER CONSTANT }
   NULL = CHR(0);

TYPE
   STRING32 = ARRAY [1..32] OF CHAR;
   STRING15 = ARRAY [1..15] OF CHAR;
   STRING12 = ARRAY [1..12] OF CHAR;
   STRING7  = ARRAY [1..7] OF CHAR;
   STRING2  = ARRAY [1..2] OF CHAR;
   STRING1  = ARRAY [1..1] OF CHAR;

   NAMES = RECORD
           FIRST      : STRING12;
           INITIAL    : STRING1;
           LAST       : STRING15;
           STREET     : STRING32;
           ADDITIONAL : STRING32;
           CITY       : STRING15;
           STATE      : STRING2;
           ZIP        : STRING7;
           PHONE      : STRING12
       END;

VAR
   CH          : CHAR;
   NAME        : NAMES;
   INDATA,
   OUTDATA     : FILE OF NAMES;
   INSTR       : STRING32;
   N, NUMITEMS : INTEGER ; { LOOP INDEX }
   TAGS        : ARRAY [1..200] OF INTEGER;
   BIGARRAY    : ARRAY [1..200] OF NAMES;
   ZIP         : BOOLEAN ; { SORT MODE LAST NAME IF NOT ZIP }


PROCEDURE SORT (FIRST, LAST:INTEGER);
```

157

Listing 13-6. Sort a Data File (Continued).

```
CONST
   FIRSTINT = 255;

VAR
   INTERVAL, { THE INTERVAL BETWEEN ITEMS TO BE COMPARED }
   INDEX,    { POINTER, HOLDS PLACE WHEN SWAP
                   POINTERS BACK UP }
   ITEM1 : INTEGER;{ POINTER FOR FIRST ITEM FOR COMPARISON }


   TOSWAP,              { FLAG TO SWAP ITEMS }
   SWAPPED : BOOLEAN; { FLAG FOR SWAPPED }

PROCEDURE SWAP;

VAR
   TEMP : INTEGER; { FOR SAVING ONE VALUE DURING SWAP }
BEGIN
   TEMP := TAGS [ITEM1];
   TAGS [ITEM1] := TAGS [ITEM1 + INTERVAL];
   TAGS [ITEM1+INTERVAL] := TEMP;
   SWAPPED := TRUE;
END;

PROCEDURE COMPAREZIP;

VAR
   FIRST,SECOND : CHAR;

BEGIN
   TOSWAP := FALSE;
   N := 1;
   REPEAT
      FIRST:= BIGARRAY [TAGS [ITEM1] ].ZIP [N];
      SECOND := BIGARRAY [TAGS [ITEM1 + INTERVAL]].ZIP [N];
      IF FIRST > SECOND THEN TOSWAP := TRUE;
      N := N + 1;
   UNTIL (FIRST <> SECOND) OR (N = 8);
END;
```

Listing 13-6. Sort a Data File (Continued).

```
PROCEDURE COMPARENAME;

VAR
    FIRST,SECOND : CHAR;

BEGIN
    TOSWAP := FALSE;
    N := 1;
    REPEAT
        FIRST := BIGARRAY [TAGS [ITEM1] ].LAST [N];
        SECOND := BIGARRAY [TAGS [ITEM1+INTERVAL] ].LAST [N:
        IF FIRST > SECOND THEN TOSWAP := TRUE;
        N := N + 1;
    UNTIL (FIRST <> SECOND) OR (N = 16);
END;




BEGIN

    { INITIALIZE VARIABLES }
    INTERVAL := FIRSTINT ;
    REPEAT
        INTERVAL := INTERVAL DIV 2;
    UNTIL INTERVAL < LAST;
    INDEX := FIRST;
    ITEM1 := FIRST;

    WRITELN;
    WRITELN ('SORTING BY SHELL METZNER SORT');
    WRITELN;

    REPEAT
        SWAPPED := FALSE;

        IF ZIP
            THEN COMPAREZIP
            ELSE COMPARENAME;
```

Listing 13-6. Sort a Data File (Continued).

```
PAGE        IF TOSWAP THEN
            BEGIN
               SWAP;
               ITEM1 := ITEM1 - INTERVAL;
            END;
            IF (NOT SWAPPED) OR (ITEM1 < 1) THEN
            BEGIN
               INDEX := INDEX + 1;
               IF INDEX > (LAST - INTERVAL) THEN
               BEGIN
                  INTERVAL := INTERVAL DIV 2;
                  INDEX := 1;
               END;
               ITEM1 := INDEX;
            END;
         UNTIL INTERVAL = 0;
      END; { SHELL SORT }

   BEGIN
      RESET (INDATA);
      REWRITE (OUTDATA);

      FOR N := 1 TO 200
         DO TAGS [N] := N;  {INITIALIZE POINTER ARRAY }

      REPEAT
         WRITE ('SORT BY LAST NAME (N) OR ZIP CODE (Z)?');
         READ (CH);
         WRITELN
      UNTIL CH IN ['N','Z'];

      IF CH = 'N' THEN ZIP := FALSE;
      IF CH = 'Z' THEN ZIP := TRUE;

      READ (INDATA, NAME);
      N := 1;
      WHILE NOT EOF (INDATA) DO
      BEGIN
         BIGARRAY [N] := NAME;
         READ (INDATA, NAME);
```

Listing 13-6. Sort a Data File (Continued).

```
    N := N + 1;
  END;
  NUMITEMS := N-1;
  SORT (1,NUMITEMS);
  FOR N := 1 TO NUMITEMS DO
  BEGIN
    WRITE (OUTDATA, BIGARRAY [TAGS [N]]);
  END;
END.
```

Chapter 14

Formatting a Program Listing

No two people will agree on just what constitutes good programming practice with regard to the format of the listing. This book has used (mostly) one style of formatting in which the most important consideration is what is called the "lexical level" of statements. There are some other styles that are more readable than those presented here, and there are some "ground rules" for good readability that have not been followed to the letter in the listings presented here. This chapter will present examples of some alternative formats for listings. There are, however, some more or less universal rules.

One of these is to use some white space. Think for a moment how hard it would be to read this text if it were not paragraphed. The same holds true for a program listing. If a group of statements are related and there is a definite "new thought" in the next statement, put a blank line there.

TABULARIZE IT

Another way to improve readability is to tabularize. Look at Listing 13-1. Notice in particular the type definitions on the first page. Mentally remove the extra spaces in the RECORD definition that are used to align all the colons. In fact, look at the VAR definitions just below. Columnarizing would help improve the readability of these also.

END OF WHAT?

Another rule is to comment an END to indicate which loop or compound statement it ends. I have trouble with that one, though I have done it rather consistently in some of the programs here and not in many of the others. I hasten to add that it is possible to overcomment a program so that the program statements get lost in the comments. Very few programmers are guilty of that, however.

USE MULTIPLE LINES

Putting the key words at the start of a line will improve the readability of complex compound statements as in a long IF THEN ELSE statement. Perhaps an example of bad and good structure will help.

IF (A=B AND (C=D) THEN E:=F ELSE E := G;
IF (A=B AND (C=D)
    THEN E := F
    ELSE E := G; (THE STRUCTURE IS MUCH MORE APPARENT HERE)

The added clarity is apparent even in the example above with very short variable names. If the structure contains compound statements and long names, the improvement is more dramatic. Let me use an example from the mailing list programs of a complicated write statement and how it might be made easier to read.

WRITELN (PRINTER,NAME.FIRST,",NAME.LAST,",
    NAME.STREET);
WRITELN (PRINTER, NAME.FIRST, ",
    NAME.LAST, ",
    NAME.STREET);

We who are old hands at BASIC programming find it hard to realize that carriage returns have no significance in a Pascal program. Only the semicolon ends a statement.

INDENTATION

The following examples are taken from Listing 13.3 I prefer the first form. A good friend, who is a good programmer, prefers the latter.

IF ITEMCOUNT = 20 THEN
BEGIN
    WRITE (PRINTER, FORMFEED);
    THREELINES;
    ITEMCOUNT := 1;
END; (IF ITEMCOUNT)

IF ITEMCOUNT = 20

```
THEN BEGIN
        WRITE (PRINTER, FORMFEED);
        THREELINES;
        ITEMCOUNT := 1;
    END;
```

NEXT STATEMENT STARTS WITH THIS INDENTA-
TION.

The first form has the advantage of the indentation corresponding to the lexical level. The BEGIN and END bracket the compound
statements and are indented identically. The next statement will
start at the same indentation as the END. In the second form, the
key word THEN is at the start of a line. The whole compound
statement is indented under the IF statement, and the scope or
length of the statement is more apparent. Probably only because I
have gotten used to the first form, the second doesn't seem quite as
natural to me. You may take your choice. The second form is
consistent with the example above of the IF THEN ELSE structure.

USE BLANK LINES TO SEPARATE BLOCKS

In reading someone else's Pascal program, you frequently have
to find a FUNCTION or a PROCEDURE above the main program. If
the PROCEDURES are separated by several blank lines, they are
much easier to find. It is also very good practice to put a line or two
comment at the start of each procedure to describe what it does
unless it is very simple and its function is quite apparent. I prefer
that the comment follow the PROCEDURE name line, though it
could precede the entire procedure just as well.

USE THE RIGHT VARIABLE NAMES

A very important means of communicating function in your
program listing is the thoughtful choice of meaningful identifiers.
That includes names of functions and procedures as well as names of
variables. I firmly believe that long variable names can be overdone
and result in a listing that is difficult to read. Having had some
college math courses, using N or K for an array index is less
cluttered to my way of thinking and just as clear as using INDEX or
ITEM or STEP. A good friend disagrees with me on this point.
STRING_ARRAY [N] in my opinion is not significantly less meaningful than STRING_ARRAY [INDEX].

SECOND_SEGMENT_NUMBER   :=   FIRST_SEG-
MENT_NUMBER + 1;

164

```
    IF SECOND_SEGMENT_NUMBER > NUMBER_OF_
SEGMENTS
        THEN SECOND_SEGMENT_NUMBER := 1;
    SEG2_NUM := SEG1_NUM + 1;
    IF SEG2_NUM > NUM_SEGS
        THEN SEG2_NUM := 1;
```

You decide which is clearer. Of course, you must be familiar with the program application to know precisely what the variables stand for, but I contend that anyone familiar enough with the application to understand the first, would understand the second as well, and not have as much trouble reading it. I have to mention the fact that the first form takes longer to type in and is also more prone to hidden typographical errors than the second. Again, I've received and noted strong disagreement from another programmer.

There is another area where you might like to adopt a personal standard (or company standard). The Pascal standard doesn't permit lowercase letters in identifiers. Most current implementations do. Some don't distinguish case, though allowing upper and lower, and the rest recognize them as different. If you have one of the latter, you might like to adopt a standard for identification in which, for example, VARIABLE_NAME is a variable global to the whole program. Variable_name is global to one large procedure, and variable_name is local to a subprocedure of a larger one. With proper programming practice one would tend to have very few global variables referenced in procedures, and this standard helps to identify these places and call them to the programmer's attention. Since modifying a global variable tends to be a dangerous practice, it should be called to the attention of the programmer or program reviewer.

This chapter is just an introduction to the subject of program format or prettyprinting as it is sometimes called. You will probably develop your own style that is in some way unique as you progress as a Pascal programmer.

Chapter 15

Basic
RIP

Pointers

This chapter is not about hot tips on Pascal programming. Pascal has a type of variable called a POINTER. If you have done much assembler programming, you are probably familiar with the concept of pointers. Refer to Listing 13-6 SORTNAME. TAGS [3] is the location containing a pointer that identifies the third item to be output after BIGARRAY is sorted. BIGARRAY [TAGS[3]] is the location of that third item. If the seventeenth item in BIGARRAY is to be output third, TAGS [3] will contain the value 17. That is, the contents of BIGARRAY [17] will be the third value to be output. It is necessary to be careful not to confuse the four different quantities. There is a location where the pointer is stored, the value of the pointer, the location pointed at, and the contents of that location. In our example, TAGS [3] is the location of the pointer; 17 is its value. BIGARRAY [17] is the location pointed at, and the contents of BIGARRAY [17] is the data being pointed at.

The pointers used in the SORTNAME program are not "official" Pascal POINTER variables. They may be called pointers because they were used for that function.

PASCAL POINTER VARIABLES

POINTER variables in Pascal may point only at RECORDS. Pointers and their associated record types are declared thus:

TYPE
      STRING15 = ARRAY [1..15] OF CHAR;

```
          LINK = ^PERSON; (LINK = POINTER TO RECORD
TYPE PERSON)
          PERSON = RECORD
          NAME : STRING15;
          NEXT : LINK; (WILL POINT AT NEXT RECORD)
     END;
```

The type LINK is defined as a pointer to records of type PERSON. This is the only place in Pascal where a reference to a not yet declared type is allowed. In the implementation of Pascal that I am using to run these programs (the only one available for my system with pointers implemented), the record type must be defined immediately after the pointer type. Having defined the types, we may declare some variables:

```
VAR
     FIRST,
     CURRENT : LINK;
```

MAKING SPACE FOR DATA

At this point we have two pointers declared but not initialized. We've not allocated any memory for a record of type PERSON yet. The statement NEW (FIRST); will assign a value to FIRST (i.e., the location FIRST will now contain a pointer that points at an uninitialized record of the type PERSON). The statement NEW (CURRENT) will allocate space for a second record pointed at by CURRENT.

Of course if we needed a pointer for each record, each with its own name, there would be little use for pointers. Note that the second part of the record definition is a pointer. What we are going to do is to create a linked list, in which each record includes a pointer at the next record in the list. We need two or three pointers other than those associated with the records in order to access the list and move through it searching for data. Of course we must not lose the beginning of the list. The variable FIRST will always be left pointing at the first record.

ASSIGNING DATA TO A RECORD

The statement FIRST^.NAME := 'TESTING   '; will assign the value TESTING with blanks to fill the array, to the .NAME field of the first record. Now, FIRST^.NEXT := CURRENT; causes the pointer field (.NEXT) of the first record to point at the second record. FIRST^.NEXT might be read "the .NEXT field of

the record pointed at by FIRST". Now, CURRENT^.NAME :=
'SECOND RECORD '; would assign that string value to the second
record .NAME field.

A LINKED LIST

If you have been following this, you will recognize that we now
have a problem. CURRENT now points at the second record. We
can't now set CURRENT^.NEXT to point at the third record because we haven't created the third record yet. If we use NEW
(CURRENT) to create the third record, we've lost the pointer to the
second record. A solution to this problem is to use a third pointer
variable, which we might call PREVIOUS. Now we can use PRE-
VIOUS := CURRENT; followed by NEW (CURRENT);. Now we
have PREVIOUS pointing at the second record and CURRENT at
the third. We can link the second record to the third by PREVI-
OUS^.NEXT := CURRENT. A value for CURRENT^.NAME may
be assigned, and it should be clear that a repeat loop may be used to
set PREVIOUS := CURRENT and NEW (CURRENT) again to
create and link records until we run out of memory. The following
code segment could generate a linked list of 10 records;

```
NEW (FIRST);
NEW (CURRENT);
FIRST^.NEXT := CURRENT;
FIRST^.NAME :=' ';
FOR N := 3 TO 10 DO
BEGIN
    CURRENT^.NAME :='     ';
    PREVIOUS := CURRENT;
    NEW (CURRENT);
    PREVIOUS^.NEXT := CURRENT;
END;
CURRENT^.NEXT := NIL;
```

ENDING THE LIST

NIL is a special value for the pointer that indicates "no pointer." It may be detected and used to signal the end of the list.
Normally, in taking full advantage of a linked list, we wouldn't
initialize all the name fields with blanks and then go through it again
and insert data, but the above clearly shows how the pointers may
be set up. There are about four pages of the Jensen Wirth Pascal
Report devoted to pointer variables. In that document, Wirth gives

an example of creating a linked list from the bottom up. Each record points at the previous one rather than the next one. The code is simpler, but the list is traversed backwards. That is, you put data in from the bottom up, but reading it out in order of the links gets it back from the top down, so that the first item entered is the last read out. This might be a good way to simulate a push down stack, but it doesn't seem very useful in handling data from files. (See Listing 15-2).

SEARCHING A LINKED LIST

Suppose we have a linked list, and we wish to search for a particular name in the .NAME field of the records in the list. The following fragment could do just that:

```
VAR
     NAMSTR : STRING15;
     FOUND : BOOLEAN;
     PREV,
     CURRENT;
     SEARCH,
     FIRST : LINK;
BEGIN
(MUST HAVE A LINKED LIST IN MEMORY WITH FIRST
RECORD POINTED AT BY FIRST.)
NAMSTR :='JONES      '; (COULD BE READ IN FROM A
DATA FILE OR TERMINAL)
CURRENT := FIRST;
FOUND := FALSE;
REPEAT
     IF CURRENT^.NAME = NAMSTR
          THEN FOUND := TRUE
          ELSE CURRENT := CURRENT^.NEXT;
     UNTIL FOUND OR (CURRENT^.NEXT = NIL);
     IF NOT FOUND THEN WRITELN ('NAME NOT
FOUND');
     END;
```

INSERTION SORT INTO A LINKED LIST

We will now put all the pieces together and write a program that will read any reasonable number (up to memory overflow) of last names input from the terminal and insert them into a linked list in alphabetical order. Notice that we can't use the binary search method we used for one of the insertion sort programs, since we must access the records in sequence. The main advantage of the linked list over the array to hold the data, of course, is that we don't have to relocate all the data below the insertion point. We just have to break the link and insert the new item. It turns out that when the place to insert a new item is found, the insertion is to be done between the item pointed at by PREV and the item pointed at by SEARCH (see Listing 15-1). CURRENT points at the item to be inserted.

I've used a technique here that could have been used in the insertion sort program done previously. Two records have been set up. One contains a name smaller than any that will be entered, and one contains a larger name. Since we are assured that all the new records will be inserted after the first record and before the last, we eliminate the two special cases of insertion at the head or end of the list. Perhaps a better choice for the first record would be 15 blanks (ASCII decimal 32) rather than 15 A's (ASCII decimal 65). 15 nulls (ASCII 0) would be even better if the names had the possibility of containing punctuation. Two lines of code take care of switching the pointers so that the PREV record points at the new item, and the new item points at the next record when a record is inserted.

PREV^.NEXT := CURRENT;
CURRENT^.NEXT := SEARCH;

The value of the input string NAMESTR is assigned to CURRENT^.NAME, and a flag FOUND is set true. The search is terminated as soon as the item is inserted. Execution of this program is quite fast. For a list of 100 names or so, the prompt for the next name is delayed less than a second when inserting an item near the bottom of the list. Since the operator entry is the slow part of the chain, it seems reasonable to have the sort done as names are entered. A space in the first array position is used as a signal to terminate the entry process, and an output file is written. In most Pascal implementations, if a destination file is not specified in the command line, the output file defaults to the terminal and you may want to verify that the program is correct before actually writing a file.

DYNAMIC VARIABLE ALLOCATION

There are two other procedures used only in connection with pointer variables. They are MARK and RELEASE. If a procedure is to be used as in the program listed here, and then the memory space

170

used is no longer needed, you use the statement MARK; before allocating memory with NEW. At the end of the procedure you use RELEASE; and all the memory is "deallocated." You may do this several times within one procedure, using memory more than once within that procedure. That cannot be done using regular variables, all of which are allocated by the VAR declarations at the start of the block and remain so until the execution of that block is terminated.

Listing 15-2 is my interpretation of the Wirth example that builds the list from the bottom. One less pointer is used because FIRST is continuously redefined to point at the last record to be entered. The use of MARK and RELEASE is shown in this program though their use here is unnecessary since the released memory is not reallocated in the program.

CONCLUSION

You may agree with me that pointer variables are a rather specialized feature of Pascal since their use is limited to linked list applications. You may stretch your understanding of this feature of Pascal by working through the examples here. For an extra challenge, how about rewriting the CREADD program for the mailing list to sort entries as they are input. Call it CREALINK or something similar. You can add a prompt to ask whether sorting is required to be by name or zip. Notice that you don't have to include the LINK field in the record to be put in the disk file. You simply define the record without the link as it is now and read the records from the disk into a variable. Then you assign the fields of that record to the fields of the linked list record and assign the link pointer value as you read in records from the file for adding to a list, or from the terminal for creating a list. When the records are written back to the disk you can assign the linked list record fields to the record variable without the link field and then write the record back to the file. To change the order of the record from Name order to Zip order, you would use CREADD to ADD to a file, except that you wouldn't add any records. This would make SORTNAME unnecessary. The solution to this problem is this time left to you.

Listing 15-1. Insertion Using a Linked List.

```
PROGRAM POINTEST (INPUT, OUTPUT, OUTDATA);

{ PROGRAM TO READ A LIST OF NAMES FROM
  TERMINAL AND INSERT INTO A LINKED
  LIST IN ALPHABETICAL ORDER, THEN WRITE
  IN ORDER TO A FILE }

TYPE
   STRING15 = ARRAY [1..15] OF CHAR;

   LINK = ^PERSON;

   PERSON = RECORD
               NAME : STRING15;
               NEXT : LINK
            END;

VAR
   FIRST,
   CURRENT,
   PREV,
   SEARCH : LINK;

   I       : INTEGER;
   NAMESTR : STRING15;
   OUTDATA : FILE OF CHAR;
   FOUND   : BOOLEAN;

BEGIN
   REWRITE (OUTDATA); { OPEN FILE FOR OUTPUT}
   NEW (FIRST); { CREATE FIRST ITEM IN LIST }
   NEW (CURRENT);{ CREATE SECOND "   " " }

   FIRST^.NAME := 'AAAAAAAAAAAAAAA';
   FIRST^.NEXT := CURRENT;
   CURRENT^.NAME := 'ZZZZZZZZZZZZZZZ';
   CURRENT^.NEXT := NIL;
     {SPECIAL "NO POINTER" VALUE TO END LIST}
```

Listing 15-1. Insertion Using a Linked List (Continued).

```
WRITELN ('INPUT A LIST OF NAMES, SPACE/CR TO EXIT');
WRITELN;
REPEAT
   WRITE ('NAME: ');
   READ (NAMESTR);
   WRITELN;
   IF NAMESTR [1] <> ' '
     THEN
     BEGIN
        SEARCH := FIRST;
          { INITIALIZE SEARCH POINTER }
        NEW (CURRENT); {CREATE NEW RECORD}
        FOUND := FALSE;
        REPEAT
           IF SEARCH^.NAME > NAMESTR
              THEN BEGIN { FOUND PLACE TO PUT NEW ENTRY }

                       PREV^.NEXT := CURRENT;
                       CURRENT^.NEXT := SEARCH;
                       CURRENT^.NAME := NAMESTR;
                       FOUND := TRUE;
                    END
              ELSE BEGIN
                       PREV := SEARCH;
                       SEARCH := SEARCH^.NEXT;
                    END;
        UNTIL FOUND;
   END; { IF NAMESTR [1] }
UNTIL NAMESTR [1] = ' ';

{ NOW WRITE TO FILE }

CURRENT := FIRST^.NEXT; { SKIP 'AAA..A' }
WRITELN;
WHILE CURRENT^.NEXT <> NIL DO
BEGIN
   WRITELN (OUTDATA, CURRENT^.NAME);
   CURRENT := CURRENT^.NEXT;
END; {WHILE CURRENT^.NEXT }
END. { POINTEST }
```

Listing 15-2. Linked List Test.

```
PROGRAM TEST (INPUT, OUTPUT);

TYPE
   NAMES = ARRAY [1..25] OF CHAR;

   LINK = ^PERSON;

   PERSON = RECORD
                  NAME : NAMES;
                  NEXT : LINK
              END;

VAR
   FIRST,P : LINK;
   I : INTEGER;
   NAMESTR : NAMES;

BEGIN
   MARK;
   FIRST := NIL;
   REPEAT
      READ (NAMESTR);
      WRITELN;
      NEW (P);
      P^.NEXT := FIRST;
      P^.NAME := NAMESTR;
      FIRST := P;
   UNTIL NAMESTR [1] = ' ';

   P := FIRST;
   REPEAT
      WRITELN (P^.NAME);
      P := P^.NEXT;
   UNTIL P = NIL;
   RELEASE;
END.
```

Chapter 16

Set Variables

There is yet another useful data type that we haven't yet discussed, the SET type. The SET is usually closely associated with a SCALAR variable. A SET is declared as below:

    TYPE
        PRIMARY = (RED, GREEN, BLUE); (A SCALAR
    TYPE)
        GROUP = SET OF PRIMARY; (A SET TYPE)
    VAR
        COLOR : PRIMARY; (A SCALAR VARIABLE)
        COLORS : GROUP; (A SET VARIABLE)

Since COLOR is a scalar or enumerated variable, it may have the value RED, GREEN, or BLUE. That is, there are three possible values for COLOR. The SET variable COLORS, may include none, any, or all of the three possible values for COLOR. That is, COLORS may have the values:

1. [   ] (EMPTY)
2. RED
3.   GREEN
4. RED   GREEN
5.   BLUE
6. RED   BLUE
7.   GREEN BLUE
8. RED   GREEN   BLUE

For an N element SET, therefore, there are 2 to the Nth power possible values.

SETS MAY BE ASSIGNED VALUES

The following assigns the values RED and BLUE to the set of COLORS.

COLORS : = [RED,BLUE];

SET OPERATORS

A set may be ANDed by using *. The AND function of two sets is called its intersection. Suppose we have three set variables SET1, SET2, and SET3 defined as type GROUP.

SET1 := [RED];
SET2 := [GREEN];
SET3 := SET1 + SET2;

SET3 now contains RED and GREEN. The + is the OR function for the sets. (In the theory of symbolic logic, this is called the union of two sets.) The result is that SET3 contains any value contained in either SET1 or SET2. The OR function resembles addition, so the use of + is logical. The IN structure that we have used for testing a variable's range really belongs with the SET variables.

IF NUMBER IN [0..9] THEN DIGIT := TRUE;
IF RED IN SET1 THEN . . .
IF COLOR (A SCALAR VARIABLE) IN [RED,GREEN] THEN . . .

Sets may also be subtracted with the expected results.

SET1 := [RED,GREEN];
SET2 := [RED];
SET3 := SET1 - SET2;

SET3 now contains only GREEN. Division, however, has no meaning with regard to SETS. Most microprocessor implementations of Pascal limit a SET to a number of elements less than 255. Usually, the number of elements in a set is limited to the same number as the maximum number of values for a SCALAR variable. The implementation I have, has a limit of 64 elements for a set, and 128 values for a Scalar variable.

CONCLUSION

Though SET types have limited use, they can be used very effectively to model some "real world" problems. Listing 16-1 is an example of their use. This demonstration program is one of a set supplied by Lucidata Ltd. with their Pascal compiler for 6800 and 6809. The listing here is a slight modification of their program to conform to the listing width restriction in this book and to change some of the code that demonstrated a couple of extensions to Pascal provided in the Lucidata version. See Appendix D for a list of the Pascal compilers that have been used to test the programs in this book. I realize that most probably many more readers will be running systems that are based on other processors, and for that reason I've not dwelt on the details of the implementations I have used.

The demonstration program shows how to define a SET variable and then how to manipulate sets. It pretty much uses the features outlined above and should be easy to follow.

Listing 16-1. Set Variable Demonstration.

```
PROGRAM SETS (INPUT, OUTPUT);

{ PROGRAM TO DEMONSTRATE SET OPERATIONS }

TYPE
   PEOPLE = ( ANN,BILL,CHARLES,DAVID,EVE,FRED );
   GROUP  = SET OF PEOPLE ;

VAR
   BLUEEYES,BROWNEYES,
   MALE,FEMALE,BOYS,
   MEN,GIRL,LADY : GROUP ;


PROCEDURE OUTNAME ( NAME : PEOPLE);

BEGIN
   CASE NAME OF
      ANN     : WRITE ('ANN ');
      BILL    : WRITE ('BILL ');
      CHARLES : WRITE ('CHARLES ');
      DAVID   : WRITE ('DAVID ');
      EVE     : WRITE ('EVE ');
      FRED    : WRITE ('FRED ')
   END;
END;


PROCEDURE SHOW ( PERSONS : GROUP ) ;

   VAR
      NAME : PEOPLE ; DONE : BOOLEAN ;

   BEGIN
      WRITE(' INCLUDES ');
      NAME:=ANN;
      DONE:=FALSE;
      REPEAT
         IF NAME IN PERSONS
```

Listing 16-1. Set Variable Demonstration (Continued).

```
           THEN OUTNAME (NAME);
        IF NAME <> FRED
           THEN NAME:=SUCC(NAME)
           ELSE DONE:=TRUE;
    UNTIL DONE ;
    WRITELN;
  END;

BEGIN

{EXAMPLES OF SET CREATION/ASSIGNMENTS,UNION AND DIFFERENCE }

  MALE  := [ BILL,CHARLES,DAVID,FRED ] ;
  FEMALE:= [ ANN,EVE ] ;
  BOYS  := [ BILL,CHARLES ] ;
  MEN   := MALE - BOYS ;
  GIRL  := [ ANN ] ;
  LADY  := [ EVE ] ;
  BLUEEYES := [ ANN,CHARLES,FRED ] ;
  BROWNEYES:= MALE + FEMALE - BLUEEYES ;

  WRITELN;

  WRITE ('MALE');
  SHOW ( MALE );
  WRITE ('FEMALE');
  SHOW ( FEMALE );
  WRITE ('BOYS');
  SHOW ( BOYS );
  WRITE ('MEN');
  SHOW ( MEN );
  WRITE ('GIRL');
  SHOW ( GIRL );
  WRITE ('LADY');
  SHOW ( LADY );

  WRITELN; { SET INTERSECTION EXAMPLES }

  WRITE ('M.BLUE');
```

Listing 16-1. Set Variable Demonstration (Continued).

```
   SHOW( MALE x BLUEEYES);
   WRITE ('M,BROWN');
   SHOW( MALE x BROWNEYES);
   WRITE ('F,BLUE');
   SHOW( FEMALE x BLUEEYES);
   WRITE ('F,BROWN');
   SHOW( FEMALE x BROWNEYES);

      { SET EQUALITY TEST }

   IF GIRL = FEMALE x BLUEEYES
      THEN WRITE('   IT"S ANN');
END.
```

Chapter 17

Useful Programs

This chapter contains listings and descriptions of several (hopefully) useful programs. I've attempted to show a range of applications. If nothing else, these will generate some ideas for your own programs. These are presented with a dual purpose. First, the programs provide further examples of programming in Pascal. Second, they are somewhat useful as is or with modifications that you can now perform on them.

LOWER-TO UPPERCASE CONVERSION

The first program is a rather simple example of how to convert a text file to all uppercase. Your implementation of Pascal may not have quite the same method of handling files. The method used here is the one explained in the section on I/O and files.

Listing 17-1 is the program. It reads an input file and converts all alphabetical lower case characters (any character from a to z) to uppercase. All other characters are left unchanged. You might use this to convert a text file to send via a modem to someone who has an all uppercase terminal or computer. The mechanism for the conversion is to subtract decimal 64 from the ASCII value of all characters IN ['a'..'z']. This converts the ASCII code to the uppercase equivalent. The operation is quite straightforward except that the subtraction is not done explicitly. The process takes place in two steps. The first subtracts ORD('a') from the lower case character, resulting in the value 0 for a, through 25 for z. Adding the value

ORD ('A'), which is HEX 41 or decimal 65, completes the conversion. This method was used to show how ASCII codes may be manipulated using the characters. The result shows more clearly what is going on, than subtraction of 64.

About now, you are wondering "why on earth would anyone want to do that?" Since that is a reasonable question, let's explore the possibilities. Suppose you have an uppercase-only terminal and you want to create a file of upper and lower case text to output to a text formatter or printer. You could obviously use this program to convert your uppercase input to lowercase. Suppose that we extend this program to look for some symbol before a character to indicate that it is to remain uppercase. You could use | or @, for example, for this "shift" symbol. Since it would then be extremely awkward to have a title in all capitals, we should provide a "shift lock" feature too. We could use "<" for going from lower- to uppercase, and ">" for going from upper to lower. Now if you use an uppercase terminal and your favorite editor to generate a text file containing " THIS IS A TEST OF THE UPPER TO LOWER <PROCEDURE> and run this text through the program, you would get "This is a test of the upper to lower PROCEDURE".

Let's modify the program to honor those symbols and call it UPLOW. (See Listing 17-2.) UPLOW will benefit from one more addition. If we want to print one of the shift symbols (<,>, or @) in the text, of course, they will not print, but will cause the action that they flag. We need some sort of signal that removes the special meaning from these characters so we can print them in our text. Such a character is usually called an escape character. It is not connected necessarily with the escape key on the terminal but has the function of removing special meaning from an ASCII character. We will use backslash (\) for that purpose. Note that backslash will work on itself, and we can print one by using "\" in the text.

Some Pascal compilers have implemented on OTHERWISE for the CASE statement. If none of the cases apply, the statement between the OTHERWISE and the END; (CASE) is executed. With that feature, the IF CH IN . . . is unnecessary as is the IF THEN ELSE that includes the CASE statement. The otherwise would then be used to handle the conversions and the EOLN conditions. The program listing here will work in standard Pascal.

TEXT FORMATTER

The next program, Listing 17-3, is rather more ambitious. Where would string manipulations be more useful than in a text formatting program? Strangely, I saw little need for any of those developed in Chapter 10 in writing this program. The story wouldn't be complete without a rather "sad" tale of the compiler not catching a syntax error. I had most of this program working, and the next evening decided to make a few minor modifications to it. I first had to change it to the narrow format for reproduction here. I split the first line because the parameter list was too long. Later, I accidentally deleted the first line by hitting a wrong key while in the edit mode. I retyped the line and omitted the comma after OUTPUT. When I compiled the whole thing, I got a funny error about 20 lines from the end. I didn't see any reason for it, but changed a statement slightly to one that had the equivalent action. The error message disappeared. The program crashed when run on a test text file that I had made up previously. A couple hours later, I tracked the area of failure down to a line in SPACE_COUNT. Both errors seemed to have something to do with the definition of the constant SPACE. At that point, I decided that SPACE might not be defined properly if there were an error in the preceding two lines, and I saw the missing comma and inserted it. The program then ran as expected!

The problem was that the compiler got in and out of sync as it went through the program and somehow ended up even. Therefore there were no error messages. Yet there was an error in the program source.

The program is a rather simple text formatter. You may generate a text file with any editor and embed the commands in the text. You may also use UPLOW (see above) on a text created on an all-uppercase terminal. There are six commands implemented. A command is detected by the formatter by the fact that the first character on a line is a comma. The next character is interpreted as a command (see the CASE statement near the end of the program). Each case has a corresponding PROCEDURE or a simple statement to cause the proper action at that point in the text. The commands that are implemented are as follows:

,C—Causes the next line to be centered in the line width. The line is assumed to be narrower than the line width. Before the centered line is printed, the contents of the line buffer is output. Otherwise the previous text would be lost.

,R—Causes the text in the following line to be placed at the right end of the line width. The line buffer is first emptied as with the ,C command above.

,S—Causes a blank line.

,P—Paragraph. This causes printing of the remaining text in the line buffer, a blank line, and an indent in the next line. The indent is controlled by a constant in the Pascal program, called PAR_INDENT.

,N—Puts the formatter in the NO FILL mode.

,F—Turns the FILL mode on.

The paragraph operation requires a bit more explanation. A paragraph command first causes the remaining text in the line buffer to be printed out without added fill spaces. It then skips a line and starts the new paragraph with the text indented by PAR_INDENT at the start of each paragraph by putting spaces in the first locations in the array LINE, and setting CUR_LENGTH to PAR_INDENT.

The program prompts for the desired width of the text and the left margin size. You could change it to have a command, W nn, where nn is a width specification. You could also add a ,L nn for a left margin set.

Constants are provided for setting a top and bottom page margin. It is currently 5 lines for both. Lines of text are counted, and the margin lines are added at the appropriate point. After the last character of the text has been output, a form feed command is issued, again for convenience when outputting to a printer. A page number is centered at the bottom of each page but the last. You could have the program ask whether page numbers are required and set a Boolean flag to enable numbering if so.

The CASE statement labels have been set up to accept either upper- or lowercase commands, which is a nice feature when typing the text in. The program uses a singly dimensioned array of characters called LINE for all the character manipulations. It reads text from the source file, and fills LINE to the specified length, LIN_LEN. If the FILL mode is enabled, it then counts characters back to the last space, and outputs the line to the last character before the last space, inserting extra spaces as required in the text to fill each line. It then moves the partial word left over at the end of the line to the start of the array, and again fills the array. If FILL mode is off, lines of text are simply passed from the source file to the output file. When FILL is off, line length is not checked, and a line may be longer than the LIN_LEN value.

When an EOLN is detected and the fill mode is on, a command is checked for (by looking for the next character to be a comma), and if none is found, a space is inserted and the LINE array is filled from the next line of text. If a command is detected, it is read and interpreted with proper skipping over of the command and reading of the next character of text for filling LINE again after the command is interpreted. The command interpreter section checks for a command on the next line after a command also.

There is one feature implemented here that I would call "cute." I don't know how some other text formatters solve the problem, but I will describe it briefly and then indicate the solution. Suppose a line has eight words and seven spaces. Now suppose that there is a long word that didn't fit the end of the line, so that 11 spaces must be added between words. The ideal situation would be to distribute the extra spaces as evenly as possible over the seven places where they may be added. In this case, the program must insert two extra spaces in four places, and one extra space in three. The example program uses FILL_COUNT for the number to be inserted (11 in the example) and WORD_COUNT for the number of places where they may be inserted. Of course, you could insert the spaces in the string array, moving all subsequent characters "to the right", but this would take considerable time. A simple calculation N := FILL_COUNT DIV WORD_COUNT will calculate a number of spaces to be added for the first position. Now if FILL_COUNT is reduced by the number N, and WORD_COUNT by 1, the calculation will yield the correct number of spaces to be added at each space position in the line.

The number for each space would be as follows:

WORD_COUNT	FILL_COUNT	CALCULATION	N
7	11	11 DIV7	1
6	10	10 DIV 6	1
5	9	9 DIV 5	1
4	8	8 DIV 4	2
3	6	6 DIV 3	2
2	4	4 DIV 2	2
1	2	2 DIV 1	2

This results in the larger spaces always being toward the right end of the lines, and it makes the lines look "left heavy." I accidentally found a calculation that reverses this order. The first part of the calculation is identical, i.e., N := FILL_COUNT DIV WORD_COUNT. Now by adding another test, namely, IF FILL_COUNT MOD WORD_COUNT < > 0 THEN N := N + 1; the following values of N result. Both FILL_COUNT and WORD_COUNT are treated the same as previously.

WORD_COUNT	FILL_COUNT	CALCULATION	N
7	11	11 DIV 7+1	2
6	9	9 DIV 6+1	2
5	7	7 DIV 5+1	2
4	5	5 DIV 4+1	2
3	3	3 DIV 3	1
2	2	2 DIV 2	1
1	1	1 DIV 1	1

The result of this calculation is to put the extra spaces at the left end of the line. Most all text formatters that work with ordinary fixed spacing printers alternately insert the extra spaces at the left and right ends of the line. I don't know if any use this same calculation for arriving at the space arrangement. To alternate between the two calculations, the first FILL COUNT DIV WORD COUNT is done, and then the test IF ODD (LINE COUNT) is added. If the test results in TRUE, the MOD is test is done and N is incremented if the result is not zero. You may recall that the FUNCTION ODD returns TRUE if the integer parameter is an odd number and FALSE if it is an even. Try the formatter without this refinement, and you will see that it does not result in nearly as nice an appearance of the output text.

It is a feature of the Pascal implementation that I use, that if a file name is specified for the output, the justified text goes to a text file that can be listed later. If a device number is specified the text goes straight to a device such as a printer. If the parameter is left blank on the command line, output defaults to the terminal, and it is possible to see how the text will look in its final form without wasting paper to print it.

You might consider this useful as it stands for text, or use it as a basis for developing more and more features. If you run this program on a text file and output to your terminal, you will notice that it is a bit slow. That is the reason that most text processors are written in assembler. However, unless you have a very fast printer, you will find that this processor can keep ahead of your printer very nicely.

I think a few words are in order here about the complexity of a word formatter such as this. The operations are all basically simple. There are many special cases, however. What happens if there is a command on the first line? If ,C and ,R commands always dump the line buffer before fetching the next line for centering or right justification, what happens if the preceding line happened to be a command that has already dumped the buffer? Is the last line handled properly on detection of end of file? Are all the variables initialized properly? What happens if a paragraph happens to fall at a page boundary? Does the program take care of both the paging and the paragraphing without loss of information? Are there conditions that get the line count out of sync so the text on the next page is lower or higher? Is there an invalid sequence of commands? Does it make sense to use a ,C command when not in the fill mode? If not, what happens? What happens if the user inserts two spaces between words, or between sentences? If you will try that, you might see no problem, except that both spaces receive added fill spaces and make a large gap. However, if the double space after a sentence happens to fall at the end of a line, you will find that one space is included at the start of the next line, and it is expanded by the fill spaces too.

All these problems were encountered in the writing of this program. I will leave the solution of that last one to you. You will note that the program backspaces from the end of the line array to the first space, and then once more, to the last character of the previous word. The problem, of course is the assumption that there is only one space. A REPEAT UNTIL loop will solve the problem simply. Watch out, however, because there is another place in the program that must be changed from a single character move to a REPEAT loop.

What I am trying to say here is that some of the program looks overly complicated, with a great number of IF conditions. Since this formatter just sort of grew, it is certain that it could be better organized. Be careful, however. Removing or changing some of the code will not result in obvious errors, but perhaps you will be removing a test for a special case such as one of those mentioned above. Had I started out with a specification for a text formatter that had to implement certain well-defined features, the program would have ended up better structured. Since this was sort of an experiment in "exploratory programming," the results are a little less well organized. Figures 17-1 through 17-3 show a text processed first by UPLOW and then by the text formatter.

It has been my experience in programming for machine controls, that not only is the specification usually rather vague, but it soon becomes clear that the customer doesn't know exactly what the program needs to do, but only what he considers the appropriate end result. "Make my machine so it can produce these parts from those blanks". Working from such vaguely defined requirements always leads to a period of discovering what the problems are and

```
,C
<UPPER LOWER CASE PROCESSOR TEST>
,S
,F
,P
@THIS IS A TEST OF THE UPPER LOWER CASE
PROCESSOR.  @IT IS TO CAPITALIZE
ANY LETTER PRECEEDED BY AN '\@' AND TO
HAVE A SHIFT LOCK CHARACTER ( '\<' TO
SET TO UPPER, AND '\>' TO SET TO LOWER).
@THESE SYMBOLS ARE PRINTABLE BY PRECEDING
THEM WITH A BACKSLASH '\\'.
@THIS IS A FAIRLY SIMPLE PROGRAM.  @HAVING
DONE IT ONCE IN @ASSEMBLER, @I
CAN TESTIFY THAT IT IS NOT STRAIGHTFORWARD
WHEN DONE THAT WAY.  @THIS WILL
BE A TEST FILE THAT CAN BE RUN THROUGH THE
TEXT FORMATTER PRESENTED LATER.
```

Fig. 17-1. Input of text.

learning about the application. There is no substitute in those cases (in my opinion) for what I call "exploratory programming." There are many experts in computer science that would call that operation "premature coding" and argue violently that one must not code a single line of Pascal until the whole problem is thoroughly understood and worked out in a flowchart or a pseudo language on paper first. I strongly maintain that flow charts done before coding and debug are usually a fair start, but that by completion of debugging, they will have to be redone to reflect accurately the final program. Pascal allows exploratory programming by virtue of the ability to write a reasonably sized portion of a larger program as a PROCEDURE, and then to test it thoroughly without incorporating it into the whole.

STRING FUNCTIONS USING RECORDS

We will move on and take a second look at string functions. If you tried some programs that use the functions of Chapter 10, you probably decided that they were rather slow. Some languages handle strings rather efficiently by making the first couple of bytes

```
,C
UPPER LOWER CASE PROCESSOR TEST
,S
,f
,P
This is a test of the upper lower case
processor. It is to capitalize
any letter preceeded by an '@' and to
have a shift lock character ('<' to
set to upper, and '>' to set to lower).
These symbols are printable by preceding
them with a backslash '\'.
This is a fairly simple program. Having
done it once in Assembler, I
can testify that it is not straightforward
when done that way. This will
be a test file that can be run through the
text formatter presented later.
```

Fig. 17-2. Text after UPLOW run.

of the string hold the string length. FORTH in particular uses this technique. When a string is input, the length, when EOLN is detected, is equal to the array index value minus 1. See Listing 10-1.

```
            UPPER LOWER CASE PROCESSOR TEST


        This  is  a test of the upper lower case
processor.  It is to capitalize  any  letter
preceeded  by an '@' and to have a shift lock
character  ('<' to set to upper,  and  '>' to
set  to  lower).  These symbols are printable
by preceding them with a backslash '\'.  This
is  a  fairly`simple program.  Having done it
once in Assembler, I can testify that  it  is
not   straightforward  when  done  that  way.
This will be a test  file  that  can  be  run
through the text formatter presented later.
```

Fig. 17-3. Final output of text.

By saving this length count, the functions that use LEN ( ) may be speeded up considerably. One of the better books on Pascal has some example programs showing how to implement the functions we have implemented here. (I found it after I had written mine). The authors have actually used an array of INTEGER for the string. The first byte is the length, and all characters input are converted to integers to be put into the integer array.

```
N := 1;
REPEAT
    READ (CH);
    STRING [N] := ORD (CH); (CONVERTS TO INTEGER)
    N := N+1;
UNTIL EOLN;
STRING [0] := N-1;
```

In other words, the length is tucked away in the 0 subscript location of the array. The price paid for carrying the length and using an array of integer is that a 32 character string takes 66 locations, since INTEGER variables are 16 bits and CHAR are 8. That may not be true in all the implementations for larger computers, but it is universal in 8 bit microcomputers.

I have shown the string functions of Chapter 10 to Nigel Bennee of Lucidata Ltd., Cambridge England, whose implementation of Pascal I have used for all the example programs in this book. Nigel's response was to ask me why I hadn't used a RECORD for the string.

```
TYPE
    TEX = ARRAY [1..STRLEN] OF CHAR;
    STRING = RECORD
        LENGTH : INTEGER;
    TEXT   : TEX
END;
```

Listing 17-4 is the redone string functions less the VAL and STR functions that are really not needed in Pascal. Their normal use is to allow better formatting of numbers in BASIC. Pascal has formatting capabilities that make such functions unnecessary. The remainder of the string functions in their revised form are shown. The program doesn't really shrink a great deal (except for the LEN function). Since the implementation has a limitation that doesn't allow passing of a VAR pointer to a RECORD, I had to change RSTRNG to a FUNCTION, which slightly complicates its call. Also, in order to output a string, now it becomes necessary to use

WRITELN (STR. TEXT);. In other words, the field .TEXT must be specified in the WRITE or WRITELIN statement.

The major advantage is that all the functions that called LEN previously to get that parameter, no longer have to do that. They simply use the length field of the appropriate string. Of course, when a string of a different length is generated as a result of a string function, that function must update the length field accordingly. Overall, these functions should run considerably faster than the originals.

RECTANGULAR POLAR CONVERSIONS

Listing 17-5 illustrates two useful math functions that are included on all of the scientific calculators. These are the conversions from polar to rectangular coordinates and the inverse. Standard mathematical notation for rectangular coordinate systems use X for the horizontal axis and Y for the vertical. Polar notation uses R for radius and Theta for angle. The Greek letter theta is normally used, but it is not in the ASCII character set. Since this notation is very standard, the program has used lowercase variable names for the formal parameters in the FUNCTIONS and uppercase for the global variables in the test program. PI is declared as a constant for convenience.

The FUNCTION NORMALIZE is perhaps superfluous, since the SIN and COS functions in the Pascal runtime package would normally take care of this, but it is included here to illustrate how the angle can be reduced to a value between 0 and 2 PI radians.

The PROCEDURE POLAR receives four parameters, the X and Y value to be converted to polar, and VAR pointers for the results R and Theta. The ARCTAN function is ambiguous with regard to the quadrant of the result, but the sign of X and Y supply enough information to sort out the quadrants correctly. The series of IF THEN statements assign the proper value to the angle Theta. Tests are also made, and proper results returned for the value of zero for X or Y. The value of R is simply the square root of the sum of the squares of X and Y. The inverse conversion is almost trivial. The test program may be used to verify the proper operation of the FUNCTIONS.

MORTGAGE PAYMENT SCHEDULE

How about a change of pace? Have you ever gone through the traumatic experience of buying a house? It is nice to be able to calculate your payments and generate a payment schedule. This program does that and keeps track of the total interest paid as the payments progress. I've used the feature of one of my Pascal compilers that allows communication with the printer. Yours may not quite work just the same way. The file PR is associated with my line printer. You might want to improve on this one by adding paging. Mortgage schedules might be as long as 360 lines for a 30-year mortgage. At 60 lines per page, that is six pages or so plus the initial printout of the input data and the payment amount. The only "fancy" here is the calculation of the payment. This is a standard formula found in the text books. (See Listing 17-6.)

Pascal doesn't have a standard FUNCTION for X^Y. In BASIC, the last line of that Payment calculation would be (1+INT_FRAC-TION)^NUM_PAYMENTS))))). The FUNCTION PWR does this calculation. VALUE^EXPONENT is calculated by the expression EXP (LN (VALUE)*EXPONENT);. You may remember that you multiply two numbers using logarithms by adding the log values and taking the antilog. To raise a number to an exponent, you multiply the log value by the exponent and then take the "antilog." EXP is the inverse function of LN, or the antilog function.

LETTER FREQUENCY AGAIN

In Chapter 2 on Variables, a program fragment was used to illustrate the use of a CHAR variable as an array index. At the time I wrote that chapter, I remembered having seen such a program somewhere. Later I noticed that it was included in the demonstration programs from Lucidata that are part of their Pascal package. Lucidata has given me permission to use their demonstration programs in this efforts, and I have modified their program simply to produce a formatted output. As it is presented, you may type in text until you terminate the input mode by typing a backslash. Note that the program is using the character input mode, and it won't echo a linefeed when you type a carriage return. You have to type both. It wouldn't be difficult to test each input character for a CR, and output a WRITENLN, however. This program is shown in Listing 17-7.

The program generates a table of frequency of letter usage in the text that you enter. As it is written, it only counts uppercase letters, so you must input uppercase only. You now know how to convert lower- to uppercase, and you could modify this program to accept either and convert all to uppercase. You could also modify this program to read the text from a file and terminate on end of file.

RANDOM NUMBERS, PROBABILITY AND PI

Listing 17-8 represents another example program from Lucidata. It is primarily intended to be a demonstration of how REAL variables are used, but in addition, it is a nice illustration of the generation of random numbers and the use of random numbers to determine probability. The program calculates an approximation to the value of PI. It does this on the basis of probability. Suppose we had a square board whose side was one unit long. Now suppose we draw a circle (or rather a quarter of one) with center at one corner of the square, and with a radius of one unit also. The area of the square is 1.0 square units, and the area of the quarter circle is PI/4, (approximately 0.7854). If we throw darts at the board and they have equal probability of hitting anywhere on the board, we should expect after a large number of throws, that .7854 * NUMBER_OF_THROWS would fall inside the circle.

The program REALS generates random numbers from 0 to 1 for the values of X and Y on the unit square board. It then calculates whether each point is within the unit circle. (It is, if SQR(X) + SQR(Y) is less than one.) It then calculates the approximation to PI to be the number of hits inside the circle divided by the number of "darts thrown" times 4.

The demonstration is undoubtedly as much a test of the randomness of the random number generator as it is an approximation to PI. It does generate an approximation. If you get tired of getting the same answer all the time, change the program to allow you to input the seed for the random number generator.

GRAPHS

Now, back to a few more original programs. Listing 17-9 is a graphics program that you can run if you have an 80 character by 24 line terminal that has the ability to place the cursor by a command. My ADM-3A terminal requires an escape (decimal 27) followed by an equal sign, followed by the cursor line plus decimal 32, followed by the cursor column plus 32. Lines are measured from the top of the screen (1 to 24), and columns are measured from the left (1 to 80). This sequence of four characters will place the cursor anywhere on the screen. Your terminal will most likely require a different sequence. Some terminals require output of column before line. At any rate, if you will insert the proper characters in the SETCURSOR PROCEDURE, you will be able to try this.

The PROCEDURE DRAWLINE is passed the starting and ending X and Y coordinates relative to the screen, and it calculates the cursor positions required to print a row of asterisks (*), to generate the best possible line between those two points. The procedure is somewhat complicated by the fact that a FOR loop in Pascal needs to know in advance if the index will be incremented or decremented. That is, TO or DOWNTO must be used respectively for the two cases. In order to get around that, two separate loops are used to move X, and two to move Y. One of the loops for each axis is used for any one case depending on whether the end point for that axis is larger or smaller than the starting point. The calculations are also somewhat different depending on whether the X or Y distance is larger. The axis that is moving the larger distance is used as the index of the loop, and the independent variable in the calculation of the position for the other axis.

PROCEDURE BOX is a procedure to draw a rectangle with its two major diagonals. You will see that 80 by 24 is hardly high resolution for graphics, but the principles may be used for developing procedures for a much higher resolution application. The idea of course is to develop the tools such as DRAWLINE and to use them to build more complex procedures. Try writing a procedure to draw a circle given the radius or diameter, and a coordinate for the center. The formula for the circle, given the center coordinates X0 and Y0, is $Y = +/- \text{SQRT} (\text{SQR}(R) - \text{SQR} (X-X0)) + Y0$. The $+/-$ denotes plus or minus. That is, both values are used. For a given X, there are two values of Y for a circle. You may be puzzled that your circle looks roughly elliptical. Remember that characters on your terminal are not square. That is, the vertical dimension is larger than the horizontal. You can insert a correction factor in the calculation of Y in the above and get a nearly round circle. Start with $Y = +/- 0.6 *$ SQRT . . . . etc.

CONCLUSION

It is my hope that the set of programs presented in this chapter will be of more help than a great number of words about programming. Some of them have been a bit more system and/or implementation dependent than programs presented earlier. By now, you should have sufficient understanding of Pascal to be able to read the manual for your implementation and sort out the information on file handling, output to devices other than your terminal etc.

Listing 17-1. Uppercase Conversion.

```pascal
PROGRAM UPPER (INPUT, OUTPUT,
              INFILE, OUTFILE);

{ CONVERT MIXED CASE TEXT FILE TO UPPER CASE
  ONLY.  DOES NOT ALTER ANY ASCII VALUES
  EXCEPT LOWER CASE LETTERS. }

VAR
   CH : CHAR;
   INFILE, OUTFILE : FILE OF CHAR;

BEGIN
   RESET (INFILE);
   REWRITE (OUTFILE);
   READ (INFILE, CH);
   WHILE NOT EOF (INFILE) DO
   BEGIN
      IF CH IN ['a'..'z']
         THEN CH := CHR ( ORD (CH)
                  - ORD ('a') + ORD ('A'));
         IF EOLN (INFILE)
            THEN WRITELN (OUTFILE)
            ELSE WRITE (OUTFILE, CH);
         READ (INFILE, CH);
   END;
END.
```

Listing 17-2. Upper- to Mixed-Case Conversion.

```
PROGRAM UPLOW (INPUT, OUTPUT,
               INFILE, OUTFILE);

{ CONVERT UPPER CASE TEXT FILE TO MIXED CASE
  KEEPING CHARACTER AFTER '@' IN UPPER,
  AND USING '<' AS A SHIFT UPPER LOCK
  AND '>' AS SHIFT LOWER LOCK.
  '\' IS AN "ESCAPE" CHARACTER THAT
  ALLOWS INCLUSION OF @, <, OR > IN
  THE TEXT. }

TYPE
   LOCKS = (UPPER, LOWER);

VAR
   CH : CHAR;

   INFILE, OUTFILE : FILE OF CHAR;

   ESCAPE,
   KEEP_UPPER : BOOLEAN;

   LOCK : LOCKS;

BEGIN

   RESET (INFILE);
   REWRITE (OUTFILE);
   READ (INFILE, CH);
   KEEP_UPPER := FALSE;
   LOCK := LOWER;
   ESCAPE := FALSE;

   WHILE NOT EOF (INFILE) DO
   BEGIN

     IF (CH IN ['A'..'Z'])
        AND (NOT KEEP_UPPER)
        AND (LOCK = LOWER)
           THEN CH := CHR ( ORD (CH)
```

Listing 17-2. Upper- to Mixed-Case Conversion (Continued).

```
                      - ORD ('A') + ORD ('a'));

    IF EOLN (INFILE)
      THEN WRITELN (OUTFILE)
      ELSE
        IF (CH IN ['<', '>', '@', '\'])
           AND NOT ESCAPE
          THEN
             CASE CH OF
              '@' : KEEP_UPPER := TRUE;
              '>' : LOCK := LOWER;
              '<' : LOCK := UPPER;
              '\' : ESCAPE := TRUE
             END { CASE CH }
          ELSE BEGIN
                  WRITE (OUTFILE, CH);
                  KEEP_UPPER := FALSE;
                  ESCAPE := FALSE;
               END;
      READ (INFILE, CH);
    END;
END.
```

Listing 17-3. Text Formatter.

```
PROGRAM JUSTIFY (INPUT, OUTPUT,
                 INFILE, OUTFILE);

CONST
   SPACE = CHR (32);
   FORM_FEED = CHR(12);
   PAGE_LENGTH = 66;
   VERT_MARGIN = 5;
   PAR_INDENT = 5;

TYPE
   LINES = ARRAY [1..80] OF CHAR;

VAR
   CH,CH2 : CHAR;
   LINE   : LINES;

   INDEX,
   LINES_PER_PAGE,
   FILL_COUNT,
   LINE_COUNT,
   WORD_COUNT,
   CUR_LENGTH,
   LEFT_MARGIN,
   PAGE_NUM,
   LIN_LEN            : INTEGER;

   INFILE, OUTFILE  : FILE OF CHAR;

   EMPTY,
   FIRST_LINE,
   FILL,
   PARFLAG : BOOLEAN;


PROCEDURE TAB (NUMBER : INTEGER);

VAR
   N : INTEGER;
```

198

Listing 17-3. Text Formatter (Continued).

```
BEGIN
   FOR N := 1 TO NUMBER DO
       WRITE (OUTFILE, SPACE);
END;




PROCEDURE SKIP;

VAR
   N : INTEGER;

BEGIN
   FOR N := 1 TO VERT_MARGIN DO
       WRITELN (OUTFILE)
END;


PROCEDURE COUNT_LINE;

VAR
   N : INTEGER;

BEGIN
   LINE_COUNT := LINE_COUNT + 1;
   IF LINE_COUNT = LINES_PER_PAGE THEN
   BEGIN
     WRITELN (OUTFILE);
     WRITELN (OUTFILE);
     TAB (LEFT_MARGIN +  LIN_LEN DIV 2 - 2);
     WRITELN ('-',PAGE_NUM : 2,'-');
     FOR N := 1 TO VERT_MARGIN - 3 DO
        WRITELN (OUTFILE);
     PAGE_NUM := PAGE_NUM + 1;
     SKIP;
     LINE_COUNT := 0;
   END;
END;
```

Listing 17-3. Text Formatter (Continued).

```
PROCEDURE GETALINE;

BEGIN
  WHILE (CUR_LENGTH < LIN_LEN)
        AND (NOT EOEN(INFILE)) DO
  BEGIN
     CUR_LENGTH := CUR_LENGTH + 1;
     LINE [CUR_LENGTH] := CH;
     READ (INFILE, CH);
  END;
END;

PROCEDURE SPACE_COUNT;

VAR
   INDEX : INTEGER;

BEGIN
   WHILE (LINE [CUR_LENGTH] <> SPACE) DO
      CUR_LENGTH := CUR_LENGTH - 1;
 { BACK OVER LAST SPACE }
   WHILE (LINE [CUR_LENGTH] = SPACE) DO
      CUR_LENGTH := CUR_LENGTH - 1;
 { BACK UP TO PREV. NON SPACE }
   FILL_COUNT := LIN_LEN - CUR_LENGTH;
   WORD_COUNT := 0;
   IF PARFLAG THEN INDEX := PAR_INDENT + 1
      ELSE INDEX := 1;
   FOR INDEX := INDEX TO CUR_LENGTH DO
      IF LINE [INDEX] = SPACE
          THEN WORD_COUNT := WORD_COUNT + 1;
END;

PROCEDURE PUTALINE;

VAR
   K,
   N,
```

200

Listing 17-3. Text Formatter (Continued).

```
   INDEX : INTEGER;

BEGIN
 IF NOT EMPTY
  THEN BEGIN
   TAB (LEFT_MARGIN);
   FOR INDEX := 1 TO CUR_LENGTH DO
   BEGIN
      WRITE (OUTFILE, LINE [INDEX]);
      IF (LINE [INDEX] = SPACE)
         AND (FILL_COUNT <> 0)
         AND ( (NOT PARFLAG)
         OR (INDEX > PAR_INDENT))
      THEN
      BEGIN
         N := FILL_COUNT DIV WORD_COUNT;
         IF ODD (LINE_COUNT) THEN
            IF FILL_COUNT MOD WORD_COUNT <> 0
               THEN N := N + 1;
         TAB (N);
         FILL_COUNT := FILL_COUNT - N;
         WORD_COUNT := WORD_COUNT - 1;
      END;
   END; { FOR INDEX }
   WRITELN (OUTFILE); { CR AT THE END }
   PARFLAG := FALSE;
   COUNT_LINE;
 END; { IF NOT EMPTY }
 EMPTY := FALSE;
END; { PUTALINE }

PROCEDURE FIX_END;

VAR
   INDEX : INTEGER;

BEGIN
   INDEX := 1;
   CUR_LENGTH := CUR_LENGTH + 1;
   WHILE LINE [CUR_LENGTH] = SPACE
```

201

Listing 17-3. Text Formatter (Continued).

```
      DO CUR_LENGTH := CUR_LENGTH + 1;
        { MOVE PAST ALL SPACES }
   FOR CUR_LENGTH := CUR_LENGTH
           TO LIN_LEN DO
   BEGIN
      LINE [INDEX] := LINE [CUR_LENGTH];
      INDEX := INDEX + 1;
   END;
   CUR_LENGTH := INDEX - 1;
END;

PROCEDURE PARAGRAPH;

VAR
   N : INTEGER;

BEGIN
   WRITELN (OUTFILE);
   COUNT_LINE;
  { BLANK LINE FOR PARAGRAPH }
   FOR N := 1 TO PAR_INDENT DO
       LINE [N] := SPACE;
   CUR_LENGTH := PAR_INDENT;
   PARFLAG := TRUE;
END; { PARAGRAPH }

PROCEDURE MOVE_TEXT (COMMAND : CHAR);

VAR
   INDEX : INTEGER;

BEGIN
   CUR_LENGTH := 0;
   GETALINE;
   FILL_COUNT := (LIN_LEN - CUR_LENGTH);
   IF (COMMAND = 'C') OR (COMMAND = 'c')
     THEN FILL_COUNT := FILL_COUNT DIV 2;
   TAB (FILL_COUNT);
   FILL_COUNT := 0;
   PUTALINE;
```

202

Listing 17-3. Text Formatter (Continued).

```
    EMPTY := TRUE;
END;

PROCEDURE BLANKLINE;

BEGIN
   WRITELN (OUTFILE);
   COUNT_LINE;
   CUR_LENGTH := 0
END;

PROCEDURE DO_COMMAND;

BEGIN
   FILL_COUNT := 0;
   IF NOT FIRST_LINE
     THEN PUTALINE; { OUTPUT PARTIAL LINE }
   REPEAT
     READ (INFILE, CH2);{ COMMAND ID }
     READ (INFILE, CH); { THROW AWAY EOLN }
     READ (INFILE, CH);
                 { NEXT CHAR FOR PROCESSING }
     CASE CH2 OF
        'P','p'            : PARAGRAPH;
        'C','c','R','r'    : MOVE_TEXT (CH2);
        'S','s'            : BLANKLINE;
        'N','n'            : FILL:= FALSE;
        'F','f'            : FILL:= TRUE
     END; { CASE }
     IF NOT PARFLAG
        THEN CUR_LENGTH := 0;
   UNTIL CH <> ',';
   FIRST_LINE := FALSE;
END; { DO_COMMAND }

{ MAIN PROGRAM }

BEGIN

{ OPEN FILES }
```

203

Listing 17-3. Text Formatter (Continued).

```
   RESET (INFILE);
   REWRITE (OUTFILE);

{ INITIALIZE VARIABLES }
   FIRST_LINE := TRUE;
   LINES_PER_PAGE := PAGE_LENGTH
               - 2 x VERT_MARGIN;
   READ (INFILE, CH);
   CUR_LENGTH := 0;
   LINE_COUNT := 0;
   PARFLAG := FALSE;
   FILL_COUNT := 0;
   FILL := FALSE;
   PAGE_NUM := 1;

{ GET LINE LENGTH }

   WRITELN;
   WRITE ('Desired line length? ');
   READ (LIN_LEN);
   WRITELN;

   WRITE ('Left margin? ');
   READ (LEFT_MARGIN);
   WRITELN;
   SKIP;

{ GET A LINE OF TEXT }
   WHILE NOT EOF (INFILE) DO
   BEGIN
      IF (CH = ',') AND FIRST_LINE
         THEN DO_COMMAND
         ELSE FIRST_LINE := FALSE;
            { CASE OF COMMAND ON FIRST LINE}
      GETALINE;
      IF (CUR_LENGTH <> LIN_LEN)
         AND (NOT EOF (INFILE))
         THEN BEGIN
            CUR_LENGTH := CUR_LENGTH + 1;
```

Listing 17-3. Text Formatter (Continued).

```
          LINE [CUR_LENGTH] := CH;
          READ (INFILE, CH);
          IF CH = ','
             THEN DO_COMMAND
        END; { IF CUR_LENGTH <> }

    IF (CUR_LENGTH = LIN_LEN) AND FILL
       THEN BEGIN
             SPACE_COUNT;
             PUTALINE;
             FIX_END
          END;
    IF (NOT FILL) AND (CUR_LENGTH <>0)
       THEN BEGIN
           PUTALINE;
           CUR_LENGTH := 0
        END;

    IF EOF (INFILE)
       THEN BEGIN
          PUTALINE;
          WRITE (OUTFILE, FORM_FEED);
       END;
  END; { WHILE NOT EOF (INFILE) }
END.
```

Listing 17-4. Strings Using Records.

```
PROGRAM STRINGS (INPUT,OUTPUT);

CONST
   STRLEN = 32; { LENGTH OF STRING VARIABLES}
   NULL = CHR(0);
   BACKSP = CHR(8);

TYPE
   TEXT = ARRAY [1..STRLEN] OF CHAR;
   STRING = RECORD
               L : INTEGER; { LENGTH }
               T : TEXT { TEXT OF STRING }
            END;

VAR A,B,C : STRING ;
    N : INTEGER ;
    CH : CHAR ;
    RESULT : REAL;


FUNCTION RSTRNG : STRING;

{ READ A STRING FROM TERMINAL. }

VAR
   N : INTEGER ; { LOOP INDEX }
   CH : CHAR ;
   X : STRING;

BEGIN
   FOR N := 1 TO STRLEN DO X.T [N] := NULL;
              { FILL WITH NULLS FIRST }
   N := 1 ;
   REPEAT
      READ (CH) ;
      IF (CH = BACKSP) AND (N > 1)
         THEN BEGIN
                 N := N - 1;
                 X.T [N] := NULL;
              END
```

Listing 17-4. Strings Using Records (Continued).

```
        ELSE IF NOT EOLN THEN X.T [N] := CH;
      {EOLN WOULD ADD A SPACE OTHERWISE}
      IF (CH <> BACKSP) AND (NOT EOLN)
          THEN N := N + 1 ;
   UNTIL EOLN OR (N > STRLEN);
   X.L := N-1;
   RSTRNG := X;
END;



FUNCTION LEN (X : STRING) : INTEGER;

{ RETURNS LENGTH OF STRING }

BEGIN
   LEN := X.L
END;




FUNCTION MID (X : STRING;
        FIRST, NUMBER : INTEGER ) : STRING ;

{ RETURNS A STRING CONTAINING 'NUMBER'
      CHARACTERS STARTING AT 'FIRST' }

VAR N,M : INTEGER;
    Y : STRING ;

BEGIN
   FOR N := 1 TO STRLEN
     DO Y.T [N] := NULL; { FILL WITH NULLS }
   FOR N := 1 TO NUMBER DO
     IF FIRST + N - 1 <= STRLEN
       THEN Y.T [N] := X.T [FIRST + N - 1] ;
       Y.L := NUMBER;
   MID := Y ;
END;
```

Listing 17-4. Strings Using Records (Continued).

```
FUNCTION LEFT (X : STRING;
               NUMBER : INTEGER) : STRING ;

{ RETURNS A STRING CONTAINING THE LEFTMOST
  'NUMBER' CHARACTERS OF STRING. LEFT IS
  SAME AS MID, STARTING AT FIRST CHARACTER }

BEGIN
  LEFT := MID (X,1,NUMBER);
END;




FUNCTION RIGHT (X : STRING;
                NUMBER : INTEGER) : STRING ;

{ RETURNS THE RIGHTMOST 'NUMBER' CHARACTERS
  OF STRING }

BEGIN
   IF LEN (X) > NUMBER THEN
   RIGHT := MID (X,X.L - NUMBER + 1, NUMBER)
   ELSE RIGHT := X ;
END;




FUNCTION INSTR (X,Y : STRING) : INTEGER ;

{ RETURNS THE STRING POSITION (INDEX) OF
  THE FIRST CHARACTER OF STRING Y
  IF IT IS FOUND WITHIN STRING X,
  ELSE RETURNS ZERO }

VAR
   K,N : INTEGER ;
BEGIN
   K := 0; N := 1;
```

Listing 17-4. Strings Using Records (Continued).

```
   REPEAT
      IF MID(X,N,Y.L) = Y THEN K:= N ;
      N := N + 1;
   UNTIL (K <> 0) OR ( N = STRLEN - Y.L);
   INSTR := K ;
END;



FUNCTION CAT (X,Y : STRING) : STRING ;

{ CONCATENATE TWO STRINGS.  TOTAL LENGTH
  MUST NOT EXCEED STRLEN. SPACES ARE KEPT
  DURING CONCATENATION PROCESS }


VAR
   N,K : INTEGER ; { INDEX FOR LOOP }

BEGIN
   K := X.L;
   FOR N := 1 TO Y.L DO X.T [N+K] := Y.T [N];
   X.L := N+K;
   CAT := X;
END;



{ MAIN PROGRAM TO TEST STRING FUNCTIONS }

BEGIN
   REPEAT
      WRITELN ('INPUT A STRING LESS THAN',
               STRLEN : 3,' CHARACTERS LONG');
      A := RSTRNG;
      WRITELN ;
      WRITELN (LEN (A) : 4);

      WRITE ('MID (A,3,4) =');
      B := MID (A,3,4);
      WRITELN (B.T) ;
```

209

Listing 17-4. Strings Using Records (Continued).

```
     WRITE ('LEFT (A,5) =');
     B := LEFT (A,5);
     WRITELN (B,T) ;

     WRITE ('RIGHT (A,5) =') ;
     B := RIGHT (A,5);
     WRITELN (B,T) ;

     WRITE ('INSTRING FUNCTION: ');
     WRITELN('INPUT SUBSTRING FOR SEARCH ');
     B := RSTRNG;
     WRITELN ;
     N := INSTR (A,B);
     WRITELN ('INSTR =',N:3);
     WRITELN ;

     C := CAT (A,B);
     WRITELN ('CONCATENATED ',C,T);
     C := CAT(A,CAT(B,B));
     WRITELN('NESTED CAT ',C,T);

  { NOTE THAT THE ABOVE CAUSES A RECURSIVE
    CALL TO CAT AND THAT A LITERAL STRING
    MUST BE STRLEN CHARACTERS LONG.
    TRAILING BLANKS WILL BE
    THROWN AWAY WHEN CONCATENATED }

  UNTIL FALSE OR (CH = CHR(27)) ;
END.
```

Listing 17-5. Rectangular Polar Conversions.

```
PROGRAM COORD (INPUT, OUTPUT);

{ PERFORM POLAR TO RECTANGULAR AND
  RECTANGULAR TO POLAR COORDINATE
  CONVERSIONS }

CONST
  PI = 3.14159265;

VAR
  R,
  THETA,
  X,
  Y    : REAL;

FUNCTION NORMALIZE (ANGLE : REAL) : REAL;

BEGIN
  WHILE ANGLE > 2*PI DO
    ANGLE := ANGLE - 2*PI;

  WHILE ANGLE < 0 DO
    ANGLE := ANGLE + 2*PI;

  NORMALIZE := ANGLE;
END;



PROCEDURE POLAR (x, y : REAL; VAR r, theta : REAL);

BEGIN
  IF x <> 0
  THEN BEGIN
    theta := ARCTAN (ABS(y)/ABS(x));

    IF (x<0) AND (y>0) { FIRST QUADRANT }
      THEN theta := PI - theta;

    IF (x<0) AND (y<0) { SECOND QUADRANT }
```

211

Listing 17-5. Rectangular Polar Conversions (Continued).

```
      THEN theta := PI + theta;

    IF (x>0) AND (y<0) { THIRD QUADRANT }
      THEN theta := 2*PI - theta;
  END
  ELSE BEGIN
    IF y > 0
      THEN theta := PI/2;

    IF y < 0
      THEN theta := 3 * PI/2;

    IF y = 0
      THEN theta := 0;
  END;

  r := SQRT (SQR (x) + SQR (y));
END;


PROCEDURE RECTANGULAR (r, theta : REAL; VAR x, y : REAL);

BEGIN
  theta := NORMALIZE (theta);
  x := r * COS (theta);
  y := r * SIN (theta);
END;


{ PROGRAM TO TEST CONVERSIONS }

BEGIN
  REPEAT
    WRITE ('INPUT X ');
    READ (X);
    WRITELN;

    WRITE ('INPUT Y ');
    READ (Y);
    WRITELN;
```

212

Listing 17-5. Rectangular Polar Conversions (Continued).

```
      WRITELN;
      POLAR (X, Y, R, THETA);
      WRITELN ('POLAR FORM ');
      WRITELN ('R ',R:10:6,
               ' THETA ',THETA:10:6);

      WRITE('INPUT R ');
      READ (R);
      WRITELN;

      WRITE ('INPUT THETA ');
      READ (THETA);
      WRITELN;

      WRITELN;
      RECTANGULAR (R,THETA,X,Y);
      WRITELN;
      WRITELN ('RECTANGULAR COORDINATES ');
      WRITELN ('X ',X:10:6,' Y ',Y:10:6);
      WRITELN;
   UNTIL R = 0;
END.
```

Listing 17-6. Mortgage Payment Schedule.

```
PROGRAM MORTGAGE (INPUT, OUTPUT, PR);

VAR
   PRINCIPAL,         { THE BEGINNING AMOUNT }
   BALANCE,           { OWED AFTER CURRENT PAYMENT }
   PAYMENT,           { PAYMENT PER PAYMENT PERIOD }
   PRIN_PERIOD,       { PRINCIPAL PAID THIS PERIOD}
   INT_FRACTION,      { INTEREST RATE PER PERIOD}
   INT_PERIOD,        { CURRENT PERIOD INTEREST }
   TOTAL_INTEREST,    { TOTAL OVER MORTGAGE }
   INT_RATE: REAL;    { ANNUAL INTEREST RATE %}

   PAYMENT_NBR,       { PAYMENT NUMBER }
   NUM_PAYMENTS,      { TOTAL NUMBER OF PAYMENTS}
   PAY_PER_YR,        { NUMBER PAYMENTS PER YEAR}
   NUM_OF_YEARS : INTEGER;{TERM OF MORTGAGE}

   PR : FILE OF CHAR;



FUNCTION PWR (VALUE : REAL; EXPONENT : INTEGER) : REAL

BEGIN
   PWR := EXP (LN (VALUE) x EXPONENT);
END;



BEGIN
   WRITELN ('Mortgage Loan Payment Schedule');
   WRITELN;

   WRITE ('ENTER PRINCIPAL AMOUNT ');
   READ (PRINCIPAL);
   WRITELN;

   WRITE ('ENTER ANNUAL INTEREST RATE ');
   READ (INT_RATE);
   WRITELN;
```

Listing 17-6. Mortgage Payment Schedule (Continued).

```
WRITE ('ENTER NUMBER OF PAYMENTS PER YEAR ');
READ (PAY_PER_YEAR);
WRITELN;

WRITE ('NUMBER OF YEARS ');
READ (NUM_OF_YEARS);
WRITELN;

WRITELN (PR); WRITELN (PR); WRITELN (PR);
WRITELN (PR, 'Mortgage Loan Payment Schedule');

WRITELN (PR); WRITELN (PR);

WRITELN (PR,'AMOUNT $',PRINCIPAL :9:2);
WRITELN (PR,'ANNUAL INTEREST RATE ',INT_RATE :6:3);

NUM_PAYMENTS:=NUM_OF_YEARS x PAY_PER_YEAR;
WRITELN (PR,'NUMBER OF PAYMENTS',NUM_PAYMENTS:4);

INT_FRACTION := INT_RATE / (100 x PAY_PER_YEAR);

PAYMENT := PRINCIPAL
          x (INT_FRACTION / (1-(1/((PWR
          (1+INT_FRACT,NUM_PAYMENTS)))))));

WRITELN (PR, 'PAYMENT IS $',PAYMENT :8:2);
WRITELN (PR); WRITELN (PR);
WRITELN ('NUMBER','PRINCIPAL':16,
         'INTEREST':16,
         'BALANCE':16,
         'TOTAL INTEREST':20);
WRITELN;

BALANCE := PRINCIPAL;
TOTAL_INTEREST := 0;

FOR PAYMENT_NBR := 1 TO NUM_PAYMENTS DO
BEGIN
   INT_PERIOD := BALANCE x INT_FRACTION;
```

215

Listing 17-6. Mortgage Payment Schedule (Continued).

```
      PRIN_PERIOD := PAYMENT - INT_PERIOD;
      BALANCE := BALANCE - PRIN_PERIOD;
      TOTAL_INTEREST := TOTAL_INTEREST + INT_PERIOD;
    WRITELN (PAYMENT_NBR : 4, PRIN_PERIOD : 18 : 2,
             INT_PERIOD : 16 : 2, BALANCE : 16 : 2,
             TOTAL_INTEREST : 20 : 2);
  END;
END.
```

Listing 17-7. Character as Array Index.

```
PROGRAM CHARINDX ;

  { A PROGRAM TO DEMONSTRATE
    THE USE OF CHARACTERS AS ARRAY SUBSCRIPTS
    AND AS FOR LOOP CONTROL VARIABLES }

VAR
    CH : CHAR ;
    CHARRAY : ARRAY [ 'A'..'Z' ] OF INTEGER ;
    COUNT : INTEGER;

BEGIN
    COUNT := 0;
    FOR CH:='A' TO 'Z' DO CHARRAY [CH] := 0;
    WRITELN('TYPE IN A SERIES OF CHARACTERS');
    WRITELN ('TYPE A '\' TO END INPUT PHASE');

    REPEAT
       READ (CH);
       IF CH IN [ 'A'..'Z' ] THEN
       CHARRAY [CH] := CHARRAY [CH] + 1;
    UNTIL CH = '\';

    WRITELN;
    WRITELN ('THESE CHARACTERS WERE ENTERED');
    WRITELN ('WITH THE FREQUENCY SHOWN');
    WRITELN;

    FOR CH:='A' TO 'Z' DO
       IF CHARRAY [CH] > 0
          THEN BEGIN
                  WRITE (CH:5, CHARRAY [CH] :4);
                  COUNT := COUNT + 1;
                  IF COUNT MOD 8=0 THEN WRITELN;
               END; { IF CHARRAY [CH] > 0 }
END.
```

Listing 17-8. Approximation of PI.

```
PROGRAM REALDEMO ;

{ A PROGRAM TO DEMONSTRATE
  THE USE OF REAL ( FLOATING-POINT ) NUMBER
  THE PROGRAM PRODUCES AN APPROXIMATION
  TO PI BY COUNTING THE NUMBER OF TIMES
  THAT A RANDOMLY SELECTED POINT
  FALLS WITHIN A QUADRANT INSCRIBED
  WITHIN A SQUARE OF SIDE LENGTH 1.0 }

CONST
   PI = 3.14159265 ; INC = 100 ;

VAR
   ITERS,INSIDE,I,J : INTEGER ;

   APPROXPI,ERROR,PERCENT,
   R,X,Y,SEED            : REAL ;


FUNCTION RAND : REAL ;

   CONST
     MULT = 149 ; DENOM = 10007 ;

   VAR
     TIMES : REAL ;

   BEGIN
     SEED:=SEEDxMULT ;
     IF SEED > DENOM THEN
     BEGIN
        TIMES:=TRUNC(SEED/DENOM);
  { THE REAL REPRESENTATION OF
     THE INTEGER VALUE }
        SEED:=SEED-TIMESxDENOM ;
     END;

{ WITH THE ABOVE VALUES OF MULT AND DENOM,
  SEED CAN TAKE VALUES FROM 125 TO 9983 }
```

Listing 17-8. Approximation of PI (Continued).

```
      RAND:=(SEED-125)/9858;
   END;

BEGIN
   ITERS:=20; { NO OF LINES OF OUTPUT }
   WRITELN;
   WRITELN(' TRIES  INSIDE',
           'APPROX PI':15,'ERROR':15,
           'PERCENT':15);
   INSIDE:=0;
   SEED:=4999; { INITIALIZE RANDOM NUMBER }

   FOR I:=1 TO ITERS DO
   BEGIN
      FOR J:=1 TO INC DO
      BEGIN
         X:=RAND ;
         Y:=RAND ;
         R:=SQR(X) + SQR(Y) ;
         IF R <= 1.0 THEN INSIDE:=INSIDE+1;
      END;
      APPROXPI:=INSIDE/(25.0 x I);
   { 25 = INC / 4 QUADRANTS }
      ERROR:=APPROXPI-PI;
      PERCENT:=ABS (ERROR x 100/PI);
      WRITELN (I x INC, INSIDE:8,
               APPROXPI:15:9, ERROR:15:9,
               PERCENT:15:9);
   END;
END.
```

Listing 17-9. Simple Graphics.

```
PROGRAM GRAPHICS;

VAR
   LINE,COLUMN : INTEGER;
   CH : CHAR;
   X,Y,X1,Y1 : REAL;

PROCEDURE SETCURSOR (LINE,COLUMN : INTEGER);

BEGIN
   WRITE ( CHR(27), CHR(61),
           CHR(LINE+32), CHR(COLUMN+32));
END;

PROCEDURE DRAWLINE (X,Y,X1,Y1 : REAL);

VAR
   A,B : INTEGER;

BEGIN
   IF ABS(X1-X) > ABS(Y1-Y) THEN
   BEGIN
      A:=ROUND (X); B:=ROUND (X1);
      IF X1 > X THEN
      BEGIN
         FOR COLUMN := A TO B DO
         BEGIN
            LINE := ROUND (Y + (Y1-Y)
                    / (X1-X) x (COLUMN-A));
            SETCURSOR (LINE, COLUMN);
            WRITE ('x')
         END;
      END
      ELSE
      BEGIN
         FOR COLUMN := B TO A DO
         BEGIN
            LINE := ROUND (Y1 + (Y-Y1)
                    / (X-X1) x (COLUMN-B));
            SETCURSOR (LINE, COLUMN);
```

220

Listing 17-9. Simple Graphics (Continued).

```
                WRITE ('x')
          END;
        END;
    END
    ELSE
    BEGIN
      A:=ROUND (Y); B:=ROUND (Y1);
      IF Y1 > Y THEN
      BEGIN
        FOR LINE := A TO B DO
        BEGIN
          COLUMN := ROUND (X+ (X-X1)
                    / (Y-Y1) x (LINE-A));
          SETCURSOR (LINE, COLUMN);
          WRITE ('x')
        END;
      END
      ELSE
      BEGIN
        FOR LINE := B TO A DO
        BEGIN
          COLUMN := ROUND (X1 + (X-X1)
                    / (Y-Y1) x (LINE-B));
          SETCURSOR (LINE,COLUMN);
          WRITE ('x')
        END;
      END;
    END;
END;

PROCEDURE BOX;

BEGIN
   DRAWLINE (1.0, 1.0, 79.0, 1.0);
   DRAWLINE (79.0, 1.0, 79.0, 22.0);
   DRAWLINE (79.0, 22.0, 2.0, 22.0);
   DRAWLINE (1.0, 22.0, 1.0, 1.0);
   DRAWLINE (1.0, 1.0, 79.0, 22.0);
   DRAWLINE (1.0, 22.0, 79.0, 1.0)
END;
```

221

Listing 17-9. Simple Graphics (Continued).

```
{ BEGIN TEST PROGRAM HERE }

BEGIN
   CH := 'Y';
   WHILE CH = 'Y' DO
   BEGIN
      WRITE (CHR (26));
      BOX;
      SETCURSOR (5, 30);
      WRITELN ('THIS IS A TEST');

      SETCURSOR (21, 35);
      WRITE ('REPEAT ');
      READ (CH)
   END;
END.
```

Chapter 18

Miscellaneous Topics

This text has covered a little more than I had in mind at the outset of this writing project. During the time it took to put it together, implementations of Pascal came along that had more of the standard features included, so they have been included here. What has been left out? Really very little.

OTHER FILE TYPES

Files may be declared to be FILE OF INTEGER or FILE OF REAL, in which case the numbers are represented as they are internally in Pascal rather than as ASCII characters. All the conversions are done automatically by the code generated by the compiler. You may wonder why these have been implemented. A nine-digit floating point number may be represented in binary form by five bytes. Therefore more data may be put on a disk if it is stored in its binary format. The advantage of the FILE OF CHAR is that the file may be examined by a DOS LIST or EXAMINE utility.

PACKED ARRAYS

In systems where the data path is wider than 8 bits (16 for example), Pascal includes a data type called PACKED ARRAY. When an array of characters is declared as a PACKED ARRAY in a 16 bit system, it is possible to get two characters into each 16 bit word memory location. This too is transparent to the user. Using a packed array is more memory efficient at the expense of the overhead of packing and unpacking information in the array. Since I have been dealing with 8-bit processors, I have not mentioned packed arrays previously in this text.

PROCEDURAL POINTERS

We've discussed passing parameters to PROCEDURES and FUNCTIONS and indicated that you may pass the value of a variable (a VALUE PARAMETER) or a pointer to the location of the variable. In addition to these, Standard Pascal allows functional and procedural parameters by means of which you may pass a procedure a function or another procedure. I know of no implementations for microcomputers that have these. If yours does, they are a natural extension of value and variable parameters, and will not be difficult to understand.

LIMITATIONS OF PASCAL

Perhaps if you have gotten this far it is time to go back and read the first couple of chapters and see if you agree with my observations about the similarities and differences between Pascal and BASIC. You will, I'm certain, agree that Pascal is a larger language and one that is more complex. Probably, you will agree that programs written in Pascal are easier to follow than those written in BASIC (unless the BASIC is exceptionally well documented with comments explaining the variable assignments, etc.). Possibly you will agree with my long-term conclusion that Pascal is annoyingly difficult to fool. Sometimes you have to go on a three-mile detour to do something that you would think could and should be possible to do in a straightforward manner.

Pascal lacks a very few features. One is the ability to initialize an array in such a way as to make a table. For example, in a simple game such as tic-tac-toe, there is usually a table of valid moves for each pattern on the board. In Pascal you simply have to write a procedure to assign the desired values to the array elements, and call the procedure at the start of the execution of the program. Some other languages allow a simple specification of initial values for variables including arrays.

A STRANGE STATEMENT

There is one strange syntax in Pascal that appears in an example in the Glossary but nowhere else. A Boolean variable may be assigned the value of a Boolean expression as in:

SWITCH := (A>B);

Of course the more usual syntax would be:

IF A>B THEN SWITCH := TRUE ELSE SWITCH := FALSE;

Generally speaking, in Pascal if two variables are of the same type, including ARRAYS of the same dimensions and containing the same data type, and RECORDS, the entire contents of one may be assigned to the other by a simple assignment statement. Generally also, arrays may be passed as parameters to procedures, but in some implementations, only pointers to arrays may be passed (VAR pointers).

LARGE PROGRAMS

Due to the size of this book, most of the example programs are rather short. What do you do when the program is very long? I've recently had the responsibility for a 35-page Pascal program that, in the final application program, is just a procedure and a set of subprocedures in a much larger program. When a program is very large, generally more than one person must work on it. It is most desirable to sit down and decide early in the effort just what variables require access by all the procedures of the program. These should become the global variables. A global variable should not be added without discussion and agreement between all the programmers. Any variable that can be local to one or a group of procedures should not be made global. Program efficiency and memory usage are both enhanced by limiting the number of global variables. More importantly, the various parts of the program are linked together by a minimum number of interactive links, that is, variables that may be accessed by more than one programmer's part of the program.

Even if the program is an order of magnitude smaller than these large efforts, the same techniques should be followed. After initial division of the problem, each PROCEDURE that is written should be thoroughly checked using a dummy main program. Small parts of the program should be appended together early to test for such things as misspelled global variables. It is efficient to have the global variable declarations in one disk file to which is always appended the program section under test. In that way, all the program sections will have been debugged with the same global variable list. Obviously, Pascal is designed to encourage this sort of approach to a program. Variable type declarations are an important part of Pascal, and careful selection of types will greatly reduce the chance of bugs as the program develops.

Another method of easing program development is the liberal

use of declared constants. Pascal checks and flags any attempt to change the value of a constant by assigning a different value to it. Other languages that don't have constants require the assignment of constant values to variables. An accidental assignment of a different value to one of those variables within a program will go undetected except as it causes wrong results. There is a second reason for use of as many constants as possible. It is vastly easier to change the values of a list of constants at the beginning of a program than to have to go through the entire source and change literal values in assignment statements or expressions when the program requirements change. Writing your program to be as general as possible, and to allow for expansions and changes with minimum rewriting, is a desirable goal.

Take the time to format and comment your program the first time through. Remember to change the comments when changes are made, so that they explain the program rather than simply mislead someone reading it because they are no longer correct. Try to standardize the way you format each type of statement so that ,for example, an IF THEN ELSE is always structured the same way and is instantly recognizable.

The thoughtful choice of variable names goes a long way toward making your program readable to someone else, or to you, a year later. It also helps to reduce the necessity for comments. For example, declaring a constant Q=3.14159265; would require the comment (PI) after it. Naming the constant PI in the first place is obviously better. CIRCUMFERENCE := PI * DIAMETER; requires no comment at all, but the same thing coded as C := P*D; means very little.

Remember that a large program is nothing more than a collection of small programs all designed to work together. Sometimes a difficult programming problem will yield if you find some part of it that you know how to do, and do it first. Perhaps in the process of doing that part, you will see another part that can be done. You can consider such efforts as valuable in getting familiar with the problem. If another better approach comes to mind later, you must weight the relative merits of the new approach as opposed to the time already spent on the original approach. Sometimes a new idea is so obviously better that there is no choice. At other times, the improvement in performance to be gained is outweighed by the cost in hours of rewriting the program.

I've added a little corollary to Murphy's Law, that is stated "The best idea for the solution to the problem at hand will be thought of the day after the project has been shipped." I find this to be particularly true in the development of software. Murphy's Law, just in case everyone hasn't run across it, in it's simplest form is just the observation that "If anything can go wrong, it will."

Appendices

Appendix A

Syntax Summary

This section presents a concise summary of the syntax of Pascal with examples of BASIC statements where applicable. The BASIC statements follow the Pascal in each example. Rather than include the syntax diagrams that are part of virtually every book written on Pascal, I felt it would be more helpful to include examples of the syntax of the various statements and structures.

STATEMENTS
Assignment:

```
X := 10;     10 LET X=10 (LET IS OPTIONAL)
X := A;      20 X=A
X := 2*A+17; 30 X=2*A+17
```

Array Assignment:
(Two arrays previously declared to be of the same size and contain the same variable type)

```
A := B;   10 FOR N = 1 TO 10
          20 A (N) = B(N)
          30 NEXT N
```

SETS
Set assignment:
```
A := [RED,BLUE,CYAN];
```

Set intersection (and):
A := B * C;
Set union (or):
A := B + C;
Multiple statements on a line:
X := A; Y := 12;   10 X=A : Y=12
(SOME VERSIONS USE ∖)
Compound statements:

```
BEGIN                NO GENERAL EQUIVALENT.
   X := 12;          MAY BE APPROXIMATED USING
   Y := 33;          GUSUB NNN, WHERE NNN IS A
   Z := X DIV Y      MULTI STATEMENT SUBROUTINE.
END;                 OR BY BRANCHING WITH GOTO.
```

LOOP CONTROL

For-Next:

```
FOR X := 1 TO 10 DO  10 FOR X=1 TO 10
BEGIN                20 STATEMENT
    STATEMENT;       30 STATEMENT
    STATEMENT        40 NEXT X
END;                 (THIS IS THE CLOSEST THING
                     TO A COMPOUND STATEMENT
                     IN BASIC)
```

FOR X := 1 TO 10 DO STATEMENT;
(NOTE BEGIN AND END NOT REQUIRED
FOR A SIMPLE STATEMENT)

While do:

```
A := 1; B=0;         10 A=1 : B=0
WHILE A < 10 DO      20 IF A < 10 THEN 30 ELSE 100
BEGIN                30 B=B+A
   B := B + A;       40 A=A+1
   A := A + 1        100 REM NEXT PART OF PROGRAM
```

END;
WHILE A < 10 DO A := A + 1;
(NOTE THAT IF A>=10 IN THESE EXAMPLES,
THE LOOP IS NOT EXECUTED AT ALL)

Repeat until:

A := 1; B := 0;   10 A=1 : B=0

```
REPEAT              20 B = B+A
   B := B + A;       30 A = A+1
   A := A + 1        40 IF A < 10 THEN 20

UNTIL A > 9;
REPEAT A := A + 1 UNTIL A > 9;
(NOTE THAT THIS LOOP WILL BE EXECUTED ONCE
EVEN IF A > 9 ON ENTRY)
```

BRANCH CONTROL

If then else:
```
IF A < B                  10 IF A <B THEN GOSUB 100
THEN                      ELSE GOSUB 200
   BEGIN                  (ON ONE LINE)
      STATEMENT;
      STATEMENT;          100 STATEMENT
      STATEMENT;          110 STATEMENT
   END                    120 STATEMENT : RETURN
ELSE
   BEGIN                  200 STATEMENT
      STATEMENT;          210 STATEMENT
      STATEMENT;          220 STATEMENT
      STATEMENT           230 RETURN
   END;                   (APPROXIMATES COMPOUND
                          STATEMENT)
```

(ALTERNATE FORM FOR BASIC USING GOTO)

```
                      10 IF A < B THEN 100
(THIS IS THE "ELSE")  20 STATEMENT
                      30 STATEMENT
                      40 STATEMENT
                      50 GOTO 200
                      100 STATEMENT
(THIS IS THE "THEN")  110 STATEMENT
                      120 STATEMENT
                      200 REM CONTINUE PROG.
```

```
IF (A<B) AND          10 IF A<B AND
 (C>D) THEN..          C>D THEN..
```

(PASCAL REQUIRES BOOLEAN EXPRESSIONS TO BE
PARENTHESIZED)

IF A IN ['1'..'9','A'..'F'] THEN..   10 IF A>'0' AND A<'@'
OR A>'@' AND A<'G' THEN..
(ONE LINE)

Case statement:

CASE A OF   10 ON A GOTO (OR GOSUB)
   1:STATEMENT;   100,200,300
   2:STATEMENT;
   3:STATEMENT (NO SEMI-
     COLON HERE)
END;

CASE CH OF   10 IF CH='A' THEN A=1
   'A':STATEMENT;   20 IF CH='S' THEN A=2
   'S':STATEMENT;   30 IF CH='Q' THEN A=3
   'Q':STATEMENT   40 ON A GOTO 100,200,300
END;

STATEMENTS MAY BE PROCEDURE CALLS,
SIMPLE, OR COMPOUND STATEMENTS.

SUBROUTINES AND FUNCTIONS

Subroutine:

PROCEDURE ADD (X,Y : INTEGER;   10 Z = X+Y
   VAR Z:INTEGER);   20 RETURN
BEGIN
   Z := X+Y
END;
FUNCTION ADD (X,Y : INTEGER)   10 DEF FNA (X) = X+Y
   : INTEGER;
BEGIN
   ADD := X+Y
END;

Calling a subroutine or function:

ADD (A,B,C);   10 X=3 : Y=4
                       20 GOSUB 100

(RESULT RETURNED IN C) 30 REM Z CONTAINS RESULT
C := ADD(A,B);   10 X=3 : Y=4
                       20 Z = FNA (X)

234

Variable Declarations:

VAR
    A,B,C : INTEGER;   10 DEFINT A,B,C
D,E,F : REAL;   NONE REQUIRED
G : ARRAY [1..10] OF INTEGER;   20 DEF A(10)

Type declarations:

TYPE
    STRING10 = ARRAY [1..10] OF CHAR;
    COLORS = (RED, GREEN, BLUE, CYAN, MAGENTA,
                YELLOW);
    NAMES = RECORD
        FIRST : STRING10;
        INIT : CHAR;
        LAST : STRING10;
THERE IS NO EQUIVALENT TO THE TYPE DECLARATION
IN BASIC.

Accessing a RECORD:

VAR
    NAME : NAMES;
    LASTNAME : STRING10;
    NAMEARRAY : ARRAY [1..100] OF NAMES: (AN ARRAY
    OF RECORDS)
    NAMEFILE : FILE OF NAMES;
BEGIN
    WRITELN (NAME.FIRST);
    LASTNAME := NAME. LAST; (ASSIGNS PART OF A RE-
    CORD TO AN ARRAY)
    NAME := NAMEARRAY [22]; (ASSIGN A WHOLE RE-
    CORD TO ANOTHER)
    READ NAMEFILE, NAME); ("   "   "   "   "   )
    WITH NAME DO
    BEGIN
        FIRST := 'RONALD   ';
        INIT := 'W';
        LAST := 'ANDERSON '
    END;
END;

Constants:

CONST	
A = 17;	10 A=17
PI = 3.14159265;	20 PI = 3.14159265
Q = 'STRING CONSTANT';	30 Q\$ = 'STRING CONSTANT'
(THESE MAY NOT BE CHANGED WITHIN THE PROGRAM)	(USE VARIABLES, WHICH MAY BE CHANGED ACCIDENTALLY WITHIN THE PROGRAM)

Program heading:
PROGRAM PROGNAME (INPUT, OUTPUT, FILE1, FILE2);

Pascal Extensions

If you have any version of Pascal running, you are aware that there are some things that your Pascal can do that haven't yet been mentioned. These extensions usually fall into the areas of the "shortcomings" of Pascal, namely dealing with hardware interfaces, string manipulations, and interface to assembler code. Sometimes additional data TYPES are predeclared, such as BYTE, HEX, etc. Let's look at how some of the Pascal implementations handle these in turn.

HARDWARE INTERFACES

Program Listings B-1 and B-2 show how two different implementations handle placing variables at an absolute address. The programs produce identical results. Listing B-1 is a program that runs in Lucidata 6809 Pascal. It accesses the ACIA (Asynchronous Communications Interface Adaptor) that communicates with the terminal directly. Address $E004 in my system is the control register for the ACIA. A 1 in bit 0 indicates that a character has been received and is in the receiver buffer. The next consecutive address, $E005, is the receive data buffer, which contains the last character received. Reading the data buffer clears the status bit in the control register. The program reads the ACIA directly by assigning the variable STATUS to address $E004 and the variable CH to address $E005.

Lucidata has an extension data type called BYTE, which is, of course, a single byte as opposed to the two-byte INTEGER data type. You assign consecutive absolute addresses to variables in Lucidata Pascal by the use of a "pragmat." There are several pragmat functions in this Pascal to allow turning the listing on and off at various points in the program, etc. All the pragmats are initiated by a character sequence that looks like a comment. That is, the special "compiler instructions" are embedded in a comment. These instructions are much like assembler pseudo operations that enable paging in a listing, etc. Lucidata accepts either braces '(' or the delimiter pair '(*' for comments. Since braces are standard, I have used them throughout this text. Unfortunately, Lucidata only accepts the double delimiters for a pragmat. (*$ADDRESS =$E004*) switches variable assignments from the data stack to the absolute address $E004. I should mention that Motorola used the dollar sign preceding a hexadecimal value as a signal to their assembler that the value is Hex and not Decimal. The convention has "stuck" with much of the software written for the 6800 and 6809. Once the variables are switched to absolute, they are assigned consecutive memory locations until the switch is "turned off" by the pragmat (*$STACK). At that point, variables are again assigned on the data stack.

The program reads a character from the terminal and then prints out its ASCII value in Decimal and Hex. The function HEX accepts a decimal number from 0 to 15 and returns an ASCII character equivalent to the Hex digit that represents that number. Since ASCII values are less than 8 bits long, the decimal value DIV 16 yields the high order Hex digit value, and the decimal value MOD 16 yields the low order Hex digit value. The function HEX then converts the value to the ASCII Hex digit.

The main program asks for a character. The empty REPEAT UNTIL loop tests the value of STATUS with the Pascal function ODD. Remember that the flag for a character is bit 0, so if ODD is true, a character is present. The function of the loop is to wait for a character, and no action other than the test is required. Since CH was declared at the address of the data register, CH already contains the character. Lucidata, at this point did something I didn't ask it to do. I tried using a WRITE (CHR (13)); which should have sent only a carriage return, so that the result would overwrite the prompt "CHARACTER?". I got a linefeed too, though no WRITELN was present. In order to overwrite the prompt, I had to use a loop to issue 11 backspace characters to my terminal. WRITE (CH) echos the character. ORD (CH) returns the decimal value of the ASCII code, and the next two lines write the Hex value of the high and low order Hex digits respectively. Input of DELETE or RUB character (decimal 127) terminates the loop and ends the program execution.

The second version, Listing B-2, runs in OmegaSoft Pascal. OmegaSoft allows absolute addressing for variables by adding "@$E004" etc. after the variable declaration. OmegaSoft doesn't have BYTE variables, but CHAR are a single byte in length, and the complication is very slight in the test of the STATUS of the control register, requiring the use of the ORD function to convert the character to an integer value. OmegaSoft didn't give me a carriage return that I didn't ask for, and I simply overwrote the prompt by WRITE (CHR(13));. The remainder of the program is identical with the Lucidata version.

EXTERNAL PROCEDURES AND STRING EXTENSIONS

You will notice that as soon as we got into extensions, we had to start talking about specific implementations of Pascal. Listing B-3 is the program that I used to format all the program listings in this book. It turns out that I used two extensions of Lucidata Pascal in it. You may remember that one can output an array of characters (VAR LINE : ARRAY [1..40] OF CHAR;) by using WRITELN (LINE);. Lucidata has added an extension that seems only to work if the array is declared as a type:

```
TYPE
    STRING40 = ARRAY [1..40] OF CHAR;
VAR
    LINE : STRING40;
BEGIN
.
.
READ (LINE);
.
```

This extension will read characters and put them into the array LINE until a carriage return is encountered. It seems then to fill the remainder of the array with spaces rather than nulls. Another problem is that it doesn't recognize backspace, and therefore doesn't allow corrections. That is of no concern reading a line at a time from a file, but it prohibits any corrections in the TITLE information that is input. The extension therefore is not very useful. The fact that it fills the remainder of the string with spaces means that the printer has to go through the motions of printing every line as a full width line. It would therefore be better to write your own line input procedure to accept backspaces and fill with nulls. The procedure we wrote for STRING input would do fine.

The second extension used in this program is the EXTERNAL linkage that allows calling a subroutine written in assembler. PROCEDURE PINIT; declares a procedure name, and EXTERNAL $CCC0; defines the address of the subroutine. If parameters are to be passed to the external procedure, these are defined in the PROCEDURE declaration just as they are in other procedures. The parameters are passed in various registers and on the stack, and the assembler routine must get them and operate on them. It may or may not return a result. The method of passing parameters and returning a result is straightforward and explained in the manual, but it applies only to that particular implementation (and the 6809 processor). This code was included in FORMAT because, though the Print routine resides in System memory and remains there once used, the data port for the printer becomes uninitialized when the computer is reset, which happens frequently while debugging a program. Lucidata Pascal doesn't automatically initialize the port, and it is simpler to include the subroutine call in the program than to overlay the runtime package (which in this case has provision for running device initialization subroutines when started). Another problem with doing the device initialization automatically is that if the print routine is not in memory, a jump to the initialization routine would result in the program going west immediately.

OmegaSoft handles external routines in a slightly different manner. It is a native code compiler that generates source code for a relocatable assembler. The absolute address of the external is not therefore specified. Just the word EXTERNAL; is used. You then generate an assembler source file:

```
NAM PRINTER
*
    XDEF PINIT
PINIT EQU $CCC0
    END
```

Having thus defined an address for Pinit, you assemble this file and link it along with the runtime package and your user program. Should you want to write a procedure or function in assembler, the parameters are all passed simply and cleanly on the 6809 User Stack. You read them relative to the stack pointer, do the procedure, remove the original parameters from the stack and RTS (6809 code for ReTurn from Subroutine). If you write a function, you push the result onto the User Stack after removing the original parameters, and RTS.

OmegaSoft Pascal has implemented many string functions. You can declare a string variable of desired length by:

VAR

    LINE : STRING[40];

Several of the string functions of BASIC have been implemented, though we've shown them to be of limited necessity in Pascal. Whether you use extensions extensively or not depends on your goal. In writing this text, my goal was to present only things that were standard in Pascal, at least until the start of this chapter. If you want your program to be "portable," that is, usable by someone with a different processor, operating system and Pascal compiler, you should stick to the standard features only. If you have only one Pascal compiler and are writing programs for your own use or to run specific hardware, by all means use all the extensions that are available.

Listing B-1. Variable at Absolute Address Lucidata Version.

```
PROGRAM ABS2 (INPUT, OUTPUT);

{ ABSOLUTE VARIABLE ADDRESSES IN
  LUCIDATA PASCAL }

VAR
 (x$ADDRESS = $E004 x)
   STATUS : BYTE;
   CH : CHAR;
 (x$STACK x)
   N : INTEGER;

FUNCTION HEX (NUMBER : INTEGER) : CHAR;

BEGIN
   IF NUMBER IN [0..9]
      THEN HEX := CHR (NUMBER + 48);
   IF NUMBER IN [10..15]
      THEN HEX := CHR (NUMBER + 55);
END;

BEGIN
  REPEAT
    WRITE ('CHARACTER ?');
    REPEAT
    UNTIL ODD (STATUS);
    FOR N := 1 TO 11 DO WRITE (CHR(8));
    WRITE (CH); { ECHO CHARACTER }
    WRITE ('DECIMAL':12, ORD(CH):4);
    WRITE ('HEX':8, HEX (ORD (CH) DIV 16):3);
    WRITELN (HEX (ORD (CH) MOD 16));
  UNTIL ORD (CH) = 127;
END.
```

Listing B-2. Variable at Absolute Address OmegaSoft Version.

```
PROGRAM ABS3 (INPUT, OUTPUT);

{ ILLUSTRATING USE OF ABSOLUTE ADDRESSES
  IN OMEGASOFT 6809 PASCAL }

VAR
   STATUS : CHAR @ $E004;
   CH : CHAR @ $E005;


FUNCTION HEX (NUMBER : INTEGER) : CHAR;

BEGIN
   IF NUMBER IN [0..9]
      THEN HEX := CHR (NUMBER + 48);
   IF NUMBER IN [10..15]
      THEN HEX := CHR (NUMBER + 55);
END;

BEGIN
  REPEAT
    WRITE ('CHARACTER ?');
    REPEAT
    UNTIL ODD (ORD(STATUS));
    WRITE (CHR (13)); { RETURN ONLY }
    WRITE (CH); { ECHO CHARACTER }
    WRITE ('DECIMAL':12, ORD(CH):4);
    WRITE ('HEX':8, HEX (ORD (CH) DIV 16):3);
    WRITELN (HEX (ORD (CH) MOD 16));
  UNTIL ORD (CH) = 127;
END.
```

Listing B-3. External Procedures.

```
PROGRAM FORMAT (INPUT, OUTPUT, DATA, PRINTER);


TYPE
   STRING60 = ARRAY [1..60] OF CHAR;
   STRING45 = ARRAY [1..45] OF CHAR;

VAR
   PAGE,L          : INTEGER;
   LINE            : STRING60;
   TITLE           : STRING45;
   PRINTER, DATA   : FILE OF CHAR;


PROCEDURE PINIT;

   EXTERNAL $CCC0;   { INITIALIZE PRINTER PORT }


BEGIN
   RESET (DATA);
   PAGE := 1;
   WRITE ('TITLE? ');
   READ (TITLE);
   WRITELN;
   PINIT;
   READ (DATA, LINE);
   REPEAT
      FOR L := 1 TO 12 DO WRITELN (PRINTER);

      WRITELN
         (PRINTER, '                              ',
                    TITLE, 'PAGE':12, PAGE :3);
      WRITELN (PRINTER);

      L := 1;

      WHILE (L <= 40) AND NOT EOF (DATA) DO
      BEGIN
```

244

```
          WRITE
          (PRINTER,'                          ');
          WRITELN (PRINTER, LINE);
          READ (DATA, LINE);
          L := L+1;
       END;

       FOR L := 1 TO 12 DO WRITELN (PRINTER);
       PAGE := PAGE + 1;
    UNTIL EOF (DATA);
    WRITE (PRINTER, CHR(12));        { FORMFEED LAST PAGE }
END.
```

Appendix C

Answers to Problems

In the game of REVERSE, you will find that if you win a game, answer 'Y' to the prompt TRY AGAIN? and then reverse 0, the program will respond:

YOU WON IN 0 TRIES!

The problem is that if HOWMANY is not IN [2..N], CHECK FOR WIN is not called and WON remains TRUE from the previously won game. Therefore the statement IF WON THEN WRITELN ('YOU WON IN . . . . . . etc. is executed. Tries have been cleared to 0. The cure is to place WON := FALSE; after TRIES := 0; in the main program in the portion identified by comment as the outer loop

Listing C-1. Prime Numbers by Sieve Method (8-3).

```
PROGRAM PRIMESIV (INPUT,OUTPUT);

{ PROGRAM TO FIND PRIME NUMBERS BY SIEVE OF ERASTOSTHENES
  METHOD }

VAR
   MAX,           { LIMIT OF PRIMES }
   PRIMPTR,       { POINTER TO PRIME WHOSE
                    MULTIPLES ARE BEING ZEROED }
   J, N,          { INDEX VARIABLES }
   INTERVAL,      { BETWEEN PRIMES BEING ZEROED }
   COUNT,         { OF PRIMES }
   HALFMAX,       { HALF OF MAX }
   SEARCHLIM      { LIMIT OF MULTIPLES SEARCH }
                : INTEGER;

   PRIME : ARRAY [1..150000] OF BOOLEAN;

FUNCTION SQRT (NUMBER : INTEGER) : INTEGER;

CONST
   INIT = 4;

VAR
   RESULT,
   GUESS  : INTEGER;

BEGIN
   RESULT := INIT;
   GUESS := 0;

   WHILE ABS (GUESS - RESULT) > 1 DO
   BEGIN
      GUESS := (RESULT + GUESS) DIV 2;
      RESULT := NUMBER DIV GUESS;
   END;
   SQRT := GUESS;
END;

BEGIN
```

Listing C-1. Prime Numbers by Sieve Method (8-3) (Continued).

```
WRITELN;
WRITE ('MAXIMUM NUMBER? ');
READ (MAX);
WRITELN ('FINDING PRIMES TO ', MAX : 6);
WRITELN;

      { INITIALIZE VARIABLES }

HALFMAX := MAX DIV 2;
SEARCHLIM := SQRT (MAX) + 1;
INTERVAL := 3;
PRIMPTR := 2;

  { INITIALIZE ARRAY OF ODD NUMBERS }

FOR N := 1 TO HALFMAX DO PRIME [N] := TRUE;
          { JUST FLAG, NOT VALUE }

 { MAIN LOOP }
WHILE INTERVAL < SEARCHLIM DO
BEGIN
   J := INTERVAL+ (INTERVAL+1) DIV 2;

    { FINDS FIRST MULTIPLE OF PRIME WHOSE MULTIPLES
      ARE TO BE CANCELLED }

   WHILE J <= HALFMAX DO
   BEGIN
     PRIME [J] := FALSE;
     J := J + INTERVAL;
   END; { WHILE J }

   PRIMPTR := PRIMPTR + 1;

   WHILE PRIME [PRIMPTR] = FALSE
      DO PRIMPTR := PRIMPTR + 1;
       { FINDS NEXT VALID PRIME }

   INTERVAL := PRIMPTR x 2 - 1;
END; { WHILE INTERVAL }
```

249

Listing C-1. Prime Numbers by Sieve Method (8-3) (Continued).

```
    COUNT := 2;
    WRITE ('      1      2');
    FOR N := 2 TO HALFMAX DO
    BEGIN
        IF PRIME [N] THEN
        BEGIN
            WRITE (N * 2 -1 : 7);
            COUNT := COUNT + 1;
            IF COUNT MOD 10 = 0 THEN WRITELN;
        END;
    END; { FOR N }
    WRITELN;
    WRITELN;
    WRITELN ('THERE WERE', COUNT : 6, ' PRIMES.');
END.
```

Listing C-2. Main Sort Program (11-1).

```
PROGRAM SORTEST (INPUT, OUTPUT, DATA);

CONST
   NUMBER = 100;

VAR
   LIST : ARRAY [1..NUMBER] OF INTEGER;
   DATA : FILE OF CHAR;
   SWAPS,                    { COUNT SWAPS OR MOVES }
   COMPARES : INTEGER;       { COUNT COMPARISONS }
   N : INTEGER;              {INDEX VARIABLE }

PROCEDURE SORT (FIRST, LAST : INTEGER);

{ PROCEDURE TO BE INSERTED HERE FOR VARIOUS SORT
     ALGORITHMS }

BEGIN
END;

{ MAIN PROGRAM }

BEGIN
   RESET (DATA);
   FOR N := 1 TO NUMBER DO
      READ (DATA, LIST [N]);          { GET THE LIST TO SORT }
   SWAPS := 0; COMPARES := 0;

   SORT (1,NUMBER);
   FOR N := 1 TO NUMBER DO
   BEGIN
      WRITE (LIST [N] : 7);
      IF N MOD 10 = 0 THEN WRITELN;
   END;
   WRITELN;
   WRITELN ('COMPARES ',COMPARES : 6);
   WRITELN ('SWAPS    ',SWAPS : 6);
END.
```

Listing C-3. Bubble Sort Procedure (11-2).

```
PROCEDURE SORT (FIRST, LAST : INTEGER);

VAR
   DONE : BOOLEAN;
   LASTITEM : INTEGER;
           { POINTER TO THE LAST ITEM TO BE COMPARED }

PROCEDURE SWAP (ITEM : INTEGER);

VAR
   TEMP : INTEGER;

BEGIN
   TEMP := LIST [ITEM];
   LIST [ITEM] := LIST [ITEM + 1];
   LIST [ITEM + 1] := TEMP;
   SWAPS := SWAPS + 1;
   DONE := FALSE;
END;

BEGIN { BUBBLE SORT }
   WRITELN;
   WRITELN ('SORTING BY BUBBLE SORT METHOD');
   WRITELN;
   LASTITEM := NUMBER - 1;
   REPEAT
      DONE := TRUE;
      FOR N := 1 TO LASTITEM DO
      BEGIN
         IF LIST [N] > LIST [N+1]
            THEN SWAP (N);
         COMPARES := COMPARES + 1;
      END; { FOR N := 1 TO LASTITEM }
      LASTITEM := LASTITEM - 1;
   UNTIL DONE;
END; { SORT }
```

Listing C-4. Insertion Sort Procedure (11-3).

```
PROCEDURE SORT (FIRST, LAST : INTEGER);

VAR
    CURITEM,        { VALUE OF CURENT ITEM FOR COMPARISON }
    LASTOUT,        { POINTER TO LAST ITEM IN OUTPUT LIST }
    INITEM,         { POINTER TO CURRENT ITEM IN INPUT LIST }
    INSPTR : INTEGER;
                    { POINTER TO PLACE FOR INSERTION OF CURRENT
                      ITEM IN OUTPUT LIST}

{ NOTE, THE OUTPUT LIST STARTS AT THE TOP
  OF THE ARRAY AND GROWS TO REPLACE
  ITEMS REMOVED FROM THE INPUT LIST }

PROCEDURE FINDPLACE ;

  { FIND PLACE FOR INSERTION }

BEGIN
    INSPTR := 0;

    REPEAT
      INSPTR := INSPTR + 1;
      COMPARES := COMPARES + 1;
    UNTIL (CURITEM < LIST [INSPTR])
          OR (INSPTR = INITEM);

END; { EXIT WITH INSPTR POINTING AT PLACE
        TO INSERT CURITEM AFTER MOVING ALL
        OTHER ITEMS IN OUTPUT LIST DOWN }

PROCEDURE INSERT;

BEGIN
    IF INSPTR <> INITEM THEN
    BEGIN
      FOR N := LASTOUT DOWNTO INSPTR DO
      BEGIN
        LIST [N+1] := LIST [N];
                    { MOVE THE ITEMS TO MAKE ROOM }
```

Listing C-4. Insertion Sort Procedure (11-3) (Continued).

```
        SWAPS := SWAPS + 1;
    END;
    LIST [INSPTR] := CURITEM;
                { INSERT THE CURRENT ITEM IN ITS PLACE }
    SWAPS := SWAPS + 1;
                    { MOVED CURRENT ITEM TOO }
  END; { ELSE ITEM IN PROPER PLACE ALREADY }
END;


BEGIN { SORT BY INSERTION }
   LASTOUT := FIRST; { INITIALIZE VARIABLES }
   INITEM := FIRST + 1;
   COMPARES := 0;   SWAPS := 0;

   WRITELN;
   WRITELN ('SORTING BY INSERTION');
   WRITELN;

   REPEAT
      CURITEM := LIST [INITEM];
      FINDPLACE;
      INSERT;
      LASTOUT := LASTOUT + 1;
      INITEM := LASTOUT + 1;
   UNTIL LASTOUT = LAST;
END; { INSERTION SORT PROCEDURE }
```

Listing C-5. Insertion Sort with Binary Search Procedure (11-4).

```
PROCEDURE SORT (FIRST, LAST : INTEGER);

VAR
   CURITEM,       { VALUE OF CURENT ITEM FOR COMPARISON }
   LASTOUT,       { POINTER TO LAST ITEM IN OUTPUT LIST }
   INITEM,        { POINTER TO CURRENT ITEM IN INPUT LIST }
   INSPTR : INTEGER; { POINTER TO PLACE FOR INSERTION OF
                       CURRENT ITEM IN OUTPUT LIST }

{ NOTE, THE OUTPUT LIST STARTS AT THE TOP OF
  THE ARRAY AND GROWS TO REPLACE
  ITEMS REMOVED FROM THE INPUT LIST }

PROCEDURE FINDPLACE ;

  { FIND PLACE FOR INSERTION }

VAR
   INTVAL : INTEGER; { SEARCH INTERVAL }
   FOUND : BOOLEAN ; { FLAG FOR DONE }

BEGIN
   FOUND := FALSE;

   IF LASTOUT > 2
     THEN INTVAL := LASTOUT DIV 2
     ELSE INTVAL := 1;

   INSPTR := INTVAL;

   REPEAT
     IF INTVAL > 1
       THEN INTVAL := INTVAL DIV 2;

     IF CURITEM > LIST [INSPTR]
       THEN INSPTR := INSPTR + INTVAL
       ELSE
       BEGIN
         { TEST SPECIAL CASES OF INSERT AT
           TOP OR BOTTOM OF LIST }
```

```
          IF (INSPTR = INITEM) OR (INSPTR = 1)
            THEN FOUND := TRUE
            ELSE BEGIN
                    IF CURITEM >= LIST [INSPTR - 1]
                      THEN FOUND := TRUE
                      ELSE INSPTR := INSPTR - INTVAL;
                   COMPARES := COMPARES + 1;
                 END;
        END;
     COMPARES := COMPARES + 1;
   UNTIL FOUND;
END; { EXIT WITH INSPTR POINTING AT PLACE
       TO INSERT CURITEM AFTER MOVING ALL
       OTHER ITEMS IN OUTPUT LIST DOWN }

PROCEDURE INSERT;

BEGIN
   IF INSPTR <> INITEM THEN
   BEGIN
     FOR N := LASTOUT DOWNTO INSPTR DO
     BEGIN
        LIST [N+1] := LIST [N];
                       { MOVE THE ITEMS TO MAKE ROOM }
        SWAPS := SWAPS + 1;
     END;
     LIST [INSPTR] := CURITEM;
    { INSERT THE CURRENT ITEM IN ITS PLACE }
     SWAPS := SWAPS + 1; { MOVED CURRENT ITEM TOO }
   END; { ELSE ITEM IN PROPER PLACE ALREADY }
END;


BEGIN
   RESET (DATA);
   FOR N := 1 TO NUMBER
     DO READ (DATA,LIST [N]); {GET LIST}

   LASTOUT := FIRST; { INITIALIZE VARIABLES}
```

256

```
INITEM := FIRST+1;
COMPARES := 0;    SWAPS := 0;

WRITELN;
WRITELN ('INSERTION SORT WITH BINARY SEARCH');
WRITELN;

REPEAT
   CURITEM := LIST [INITEM];
   FINDPLACE;
   INSERT;
   LASTOUT := LASTOUT + 1;
   INITEM := LASTOUT + 1;
UNTIL LASTOUT = LAST;
END;
```

Listing C-6. Shell-Metzner Sort Procedure (11-5).

```
PROCEDURE SORT (FIRST, LAST:INTEGER);

CONST
   FIRSTINT = 47;

VAR
   INTERVAL,     { INTERVAL BETWEEN ITEMS TO BE COMPARED }
   INDEX,        { POINTER, HOLDS PLACE WHEN SWAP
                   POINTERS BACK UP }
   ITEM1 : INTEGER;
                   { POINTER FOR FIRST ITEM FOR COMPARISON }

   SWAPPED : BOOLEAN; { SWAPPED DATA }

PROCEDURE SWAP;

VAR
   TEMP : INTEGER; { FOR SAVING ONE VALUE DURING SWAP }
BEGIN
   TEMP := LIST [ITEM1];
   LIST [ITEM1] := LIST [ITEM1 + INTERVAL];
   LIST [ITEM1+INTERVAL] := TEMP;
   SWAPPED := TRUE;
   SWAPS := SWAPS + 1;
END;


BEGIN

   { INITIALIZE VARIABLES }
   INTERVAL := FIRSTINT ;
   INDEX := FIRST;
   ITEM1 := FIRST;
   SWAPS := 0;
   COMPARES := 0;

   WRITELN;
   WRITELN ('SORTING BY SHELL METZNER SORT');
   WRITELN;
```

Listing C-6. Shell-Metzner Sort Procedure (11-5) (Continued).

```
REPEAT
    SWAPPED := FALSE;
    COMPARES := COMPARES + 1;
    IF LIST [ITEM1] > LIST [ITEM1+INTERVAL]
      THEN BEGIN
       SWAP;
       ITEM1 := ITEM1 - INTERVAL;
      END;
    IF (NOT SWAPPED) OR (ITEM1 < 1)
      THEN BEGIN
       INDEX := INDEX + 1;
       IF INDEX > (LAST - INTERVAL)
         THEN BEGIN
          INTERVAL := INTERVAL DIV 2;
          INDEX := 1;
         END;
       ITEM1 := INDEX;
      END;
  UNTIL INTERVAL = 0;
END; { SHELL SORT }
```

Listing C-7. Quicksort Procedure (11-6).

```
PROCEDURE SORT (FIRST, LAST : INTEGER);

VAR
   I,
   J,
   X : INTEGER;


PROCEDURE SWAP (ITEM1, ITEM2 : INTEGER);

VAR
   TEMP : INTEGER;

BEGIN
   TEMP := LIST [ITEM1];
   LIST [ITEM1] := LIST [ITEM2];
   LIST [ITEM2] := TEMP;

   SWAPS := SWAPS + 1;
END;




BEGIN
   I := FIRST;  J := LAST;
   X := LIST [(FIRST + LAST) DIV 2];

   REPEAT
      WHILE LIST [I] < X DO
      BEGIN
         I := I + 1; COMPARES :=COMPARES + 1;
      END;
      COMPARES := COMPARES + 1;
   { ONE FOR THE COMPARE THAT ENDED THE WHILE}

      WHILE X < LIST [J] DO
      BEGIN
         J := J - 1; COMPARES :=COMPARES + 1;
      END;
```

Listing C-7. Quicksort Procedure (11-6) (Continued).

```
      COMPARES := COMPARES + 1;

      IF I <= J THEN
      BEGIN
         SWAP (I,J);
         I := I + 1;
         J := J - 1;
      END;
   UNTIL I > J;

   IF FIRST < J THEN SORT (FIRST,J);
   IF I < LAST THEN SORT (I,LAST);
END; { QUICKSORT PROCEDURE }
```

Listing C-8. Improved Write Record Program (12-1).

```
PROGRAM RECTEST (INPUT, OUTPUT, DATA);

CONST
   CLRSCRN = CHR (26); { CHARACTER CONSTANT :

TYPE
   STRING = ARRAY [1..15] OF CHAR;
   NAMES = RECORD
               LAST : STRING;
               FIRST : STRING;
               INITIAL : CHAR
           END;

VAR
   CH : CHAR;
   NAME : NAMES;
   DATA : FILE OF NAMES;

PROCEDURE RSTRNG (VAR X : STRING);

VAR
   N : INTEGER; { LOOP INDEX }

BEGIN
   FOR N := 1 TO 15 DO X [N] := CHR (0);
                   { FILL WITH NULLS }
   N := 1;
   REPEAT
     READ (CH);
     IF (N>1) AND (CH = CHR(8))
         THEN N := N - 2
         ELSE IF NOT EOLN THEN X [N] := CH;
     N := N + 1;
   UNTIL EOLN OR (N > 15);
END;

BEGIN
   REWRITE (DATA);
   WRITE (CLRSCRN);
   WRITE ('INPUT DATA AS PROMPTED. ');
```

Listing C-8. Improved Write Record Program (12-1) (Continued).

```
    WRITELN (' TO QUIT, ENTER RETURN');
    WRITE (' ONLY FOR LAST NAME. ');
    WRITELN (' (HIT RETURN TO CONTINUE.');
    READ (CH);
    REPEAT
       WRITE (CLRSCRN);
       WRITE ('INPUT FIRST NAME ');
       RSTRNG (NAME.FIRST);
       WRITELN;
       WRITE ('INPUT MIDDLE INITIAL ');
       READ (NAME.INITIAL);
       WRITELN;
       WRITE ('INPUT LAST NAME ');
       RSTRNG (NAME.LAST);
       WRITELN;
       IF NAME.LAST [1] = CHR (0)
                   { THIS STATEMENT ADDED }
           THEN NAME.LAST := 'ZZZZZZZZZZZZZZZ';
       WRITE (DATA, NAME);
    UNTIL NAME.LAST = 'ZZZZZZZZZZZZZZZ'
END.
```

Listing C-9. Improved Read Record Program (12-2).

```
PROGRAM RECREAD (INPUT, OUTPUT, DATA);

CONST
   STRLEN = 15;

TYPE
   STRING = ARRAY [1..STRLEN] OF CHAR;
   NAMES = RECORD
               LAST : STRING;
               FIRST : STRING;
               INITIAL : CHAR
            END;

VAR
   NAME : NAMES;
   DATA : FILE OF NAMES;


PROCEDURE WSTRING (STRNG : STRING);

VAR
   N : INTEGER;

BEGIN
   N := 1;
   REPEAT
      WRITE (STRNG [N]);
      N := N + 1;
   UNTIL (STRNG [N - 1] = CHR(0))
        OR (N = STRLEN+1);
   WRITE (' '); { WRITE ONE SPACE AFTER STRING }
END; { WSTRING }


BEGIN
   RESET (DATA);
   WRITE (CHR(26)); { CLEAR SCREEN AND HOME CURSOR }
   READ (DATA, NAME);
   WHILE NAME.LAST <> 'ZZZZZZZZZZZZZZZ'
   DO BEGIN
```

Listing C-9. Improved Read Record Program (12-2) (Continued).

```
        WSTRING ( NAME.FIRST);
        WRITE (NAME.INITIAL,'. ');
        WSTRING (NAME.LAST);
        WRITELN;
        READ (DATA, NAME)
    END;
END.
```

Listing C-10. Improved Print Labels (13-2).

```
PROGRAM PLABEL (INPUT, OUTPUT, DATA, PRINTER);

CONST
   NULL = CHR(0);

TYPE
   STRING32 = ARRAY [1..32] OF CHAR;
   STRING15 = ARRAY [1..15] OF CHAR;
   STRING12 = ARRAY [1..12] OF CHAR;
   STRING7  = ARRAY [1..7] OF CHAR;
   STRING2  = ARRAY [1..2] OF CHAR;
   STRING1  = ARRAY [1..1] OF CHAR;

   NAMES = RECORD
            PREFIX     : STRING2;
            FIRST      : STRING12;
            INITIAL    : STRING1;
            LAST       : STRING15;
            STREET     : STRING32;
            ADDITIONAL : STRING32;
            CITY       : STRING15;
            STATE      : STRING2;
            ZIP        : STRING7;
            PHONE      : STRING12
          END;


VAR
   NAME : NAMES;
   DATA : FILE OF NAMES;
   N : INTEGER ; { LOOP INDEX }
   PRINTER : FILF OF CHAR;

BEGIN
   RESET (DATA);
   READ (DATA,NAME);
   WHILE NOT EOF (DATA) DO
   BEGIN

       IF NAME.PREFIX [1] = 'R'
```

Listing C-10. Improved Print Labels (13-2) (Continued).

```
            THEN WRITE (PRINTER, 'MRS. ');

      IF NAME.PREFIX [1] = 'D'
         THEN IF NAME.PREFIX [2] = 'R'
                THEN WRITE (PRINTER, 'DR. ')
                ELSE WRITE (PRINTER, 'DR. & MRS. ');

      IF NAME.PREFIX [1] = 'M' THEN
         CASE NAME.PREFIX [2] OF
            'R' : WRITE (PRINTER, 'MR. ');
            'S' : WRITE (PRINTER, 'MS. ');
            'M' : WRITE (PRINTER, 'MR. & MRS. ');
            'I' : WRITE (PRINTER, 'MISS. ')
         END; {CASE PREFIX }

      WRITE (PRINTER,NAME.FIRST,' ');

      IF NAME.INITIAL <> NULL
         THEN WRITE (PRINTER, NAME.INITIAL,'. '):

      WRITELN (PRINTER, NAME.LAST);
      WRITELN (PRINTER, NAME.STREET);

      IF NAME.ADDITIONAL [1] <> NULL
         THEN WRITELN (PRINTER, NAME.ADDITIONAL);

      WRITELN (PRINTER,NAME.CITY,', ',NAME.STATE,'
                      NAME.ZIP);
      WRITELN (PRINTER);
      WRITELN (PRINTER);
      IF NAME.ADDITIONAL [1] = NULL
        THEN WRITELN (PRINTER);
        { 6 LINES TO A ONE INCH LABEL }
      READ (DATA,NAME);
   END;
END.
```

Listing C-11. Improved Print Directory (13-3).

```
PROGRAM PDIR (INPUT, OUTPUT, DATA, PRINTER);

CONST
   NULL = CHR(0);
   FORMFEED = CHR(12);

TYPE
   STRING32 = ARRAY [1..32] OF CHAR;
   STRING15 = ARRAY [1..15] OF CHAR;
   STRING12 = ARRAY [1..12] OF CHAR;
   STRING7  = ARRAY [1..7] OF CHAR;
   STRING2  = ARRAY [1..2] OF CHAR;
   STRING1  = ARRAY [1..1] OF CHAR;

   NAMES = RECORD
           PREFIX     : STRING2;
           FIRST      : STRING12;
           INITIAL    : STRING1;
           LAST       : STRING15;
           STREET     : STRING32;
           ADDITIONAL : STRING32;
           CITY       : STRING15;
           STATE      : STRING2;
           ZIP        : STRING7;
           PHONE      : STRING12
        END;

VAR
   NAME : NAMES;
   DATA : FILE OF NAMES;
   N : INTEGER ; { LOOP INDEX }
   PRINTER : FILE OF CHAR;
   ITEMCOUNT : INTEGER; { FOR PAGE FORMAT }

PROCEDURE THREELINES;

BEGIN
   WRITELN (PRINTER);
   WRITELN (PRINTER);
```

Listing C-11. Improved Print Directory (13-3) (Continued).

```
    WRITELN (PRINTER);
END;


BEGIN
    RESET (DATA);
    READ (DATA,NAME);
    ITEMCOUNT := 1;
    WRITE (PRINTER, FORMFEED);
    THREELINES;
    WHILE NOT EOF (DATA) DO
    BEGIN
        IF NAME.PREFIX [1] = 'R'
            THEN WRITE (PRINTER, 'MRS. ');
        IF NAME.PREFIX [1] = 'D'
            THEN IF NAME.PREFIX [2] = 'R'
                    THEN WRITE (PRINTER, 'DR. ')
                    ELSE WRITE (PRINTER, 'DR. & MRS. ');
        IF NAME.PREFIX [1] = 'M' THEN
            CASE NAME.PREFIX [2] OF
                'R' : WRITE (PRINTER, 'MR. ');
                'S' : WRITE (PRINTER, 'MS. ');
                'M' : WRITE (PRINTER, 'MR. & MRS. ');
                'I' : WRITE (PRINTER, 'MISS. ')
            END; {CASE PREFIX }

        WRITE (PRINTER,NAME.FIRST,' ');

        IF NAME.INITIAL <> NULL
            THEN WRITE (PRINTER, NAME.INITIAL,'. ');

        WRITELN (PRINTER, NAME.LAST,'    ',
                            NAME.STREET);

        WRITELN (PRINTER,NAME.ADDITIONAL,'    ',
                            NAME.CITY,', ',
                            NAME.STATE,' ',
                            NAME.ZIP,'    ',
                            NAME.PHONE);
```

Listing C-11. Improved Print Directory (13-3) (Continued).

```
    WRITELN (PRINTER);

    ITEMCOUNT := ITEMCOUNT + 1;
    IF ITEMCOUNT = 20 THEN
    BEGIN
       WRITE (PRINTER, FORMFEED);
       THREELINES;
       ITEMCOUNT := 1;
    END;
    READ (DATA,NAME);
  END; { WHILE NOT EOF }
END.
```

Listing C-12. Improved Edit a Data File (13-4).

```
PROGRAM CHANGE (INPUT, OUTPUT, INDATA, OUTDATA);

CONST
   CLRSCRN = CHR(26); { CHARACTER CONSTANT }
   NULL = CHR(0);

TYPE
   STRING32 = ARRAY [1..32] OF CHAR;
   STRING15 = ARRAY [1..15] OF CHAR;
   STRING12 = ARRAY [1..12] OF CHAR;
   STRING7  = ARRAY [1..7] OF CHAR;
   STRING2  = ARRAY [1..2] OF CHAR;
   STRING1  = ARRAY [1..1] OF CHAR;

   NAMES = RECORD
            PREFIX     : STRING2;
            FIRST      : STRING12;
            INITIAL    : STRING1;
            LAST       : STRING15;
            STREET     : STRING32;
            ADDITIONAL : STRING32;
            CITY       : STRING15;
            STATE      : STRING2;
            ZIP        : STRING7;
            PHONE      : STRING12
         END;

   SEARCH = RECORD
            FIRST      : STRING12;
            INITIAL    : STRING1;
            LAST       : STRING15
         END;

VAR
   CH         : CHAR;
   NAME       : NAMES;
   INDATA,
   OUTDATA    : FILE OF NAMES;
   INSTR      : STRING32;
   K,N        : INTEGER ; { LOOP INDEX }
```

271

Listing C-12. Improved Edit a Data File (13-4) (Continued).

```
   SEARCHLIST : ARRAY [1..20] OF SEARCH; {LIST OF RECORDS}



PROCEDURE RSTRNG (VAR X : STRING32);


BEGIN
   FOR N := 1 TO 32 DO X [N] := CHR (0);
                   { FILL WITH NULLS }
   N := 1;
   REPEAT
     READ (CH);
     IF (N>1) AND (CH = CHR(8))
        THEN N := N - 2
        ELSE BEGIN
                 IF NOT EOLN
                    THEN X [N] := CH;
               END;
     IF N = 0 THEN X [1] := NULL;
     N := N + 1;
   UNTIL EOLN OR (N > 32);
END;



PROCEDURE GETLIST;

BEGIN

   { INITIALIZE ALL ENTRIES TO FOUND }
   FOR N := 1 TO 20
     DO SEARCHLIST [N].LAST [1] := NULL;
   K := 1;
   REPEAT
     WRITE (CLRSCRN);
     WRITE (NULL); { TERMINAL REQUIRES TIME FOR CLEAR }
     WRITELN ('IDENTIFY RECORD TO BE CHANGED');
```

272

Listing C-12. Improved Edit a Data File (13-4) (Continued).

```
      WRITE ('FIRST NAME                 ');
      RSTRNG (INSTR);
      FOR N := 1 TO 12
        DO SEARCHLIST [K].FIRST [N] := INSTR [N];
      WRITELN;

      WRITE ('INITIAL                   ');
      RSTRNG (INSTR);
      SEARCHLIST [K].INITIAL [1] := INSTR [1];
      WRITELN;

      WRITE ('LAST NAME                 ');
      RSTRNG (INSTR);
      FOR N := 1 TO 15
        DO SEARCHLIST [K].LAST [N] := INSTR [N];
      WRITELN;

      K := K + 1;
   UNTIL (K = 21) OR (SEARCHLIST [K-1].LAST [1] = NULL';
END;

PROCEDURE FINDRECORD;

VAR
   FOUND : BOOLEAN;

BEGIN
   READ (INDATA, NAME);
   FOUND := FALSE;
   WHILE (NOT EOF(INDATA)) AND (NOT FOUND) DO
   BEGIN
      N := 1;
      REPEAT
         FOUND := TRUE;

         IF NAME.LAST <> SEARCHLIST [N].LAST
           THEN FOUND := FALSE;

         IF NAME.FIRST<>SEARCHLIST [N].FIRST
           THEN FOUND := FALSE;
```

273

Listing C-12. Improved Edit a Data File (13-4) (Continued).

```
        IF NAME.INITIAL <> SEARCHLIST [N].INITIAL
            THEN FOUND := FALSE;

        N := N + 1'
      UNTIL FOUND OR (N = K);

      IF FOUND
        THEN SEARCHLIST [N-1].LAST [1] :=NULL;
                    { MARK AS FOUND }
      IF NOT FOUND
         THEN BEGIN
         WRITE (OUTDATA, NAME);{ NOT CHANGED}
         READ (INDATA,NAME);  { GET ANOTHER }
      END; { IF NOT FOUND }
    END; { WHILE NOT EOF }
END; { FINDRECORD }



BEGIN
    RESET (INDATA);
    REWRITE (OUTDATA)'
    GETLIST:

    REPEAT
     FINDRECORD;
     IF NOT EOF (INDATA)
       THEN BEGIN
         WRITE (CLRSCRN);
         WRITE (NAME.PREFIX,' ',
                NAME.FIRST,' ');
         IF NAME.INITIAL <> NULL
           THEN WRITE (NAME.INITIAL,'. ');
         WRITELN (NAME.LAST);
         WRITELN (NAME.STREET);
         WRITELN (NAME.ADDITIONAL);
         WRITELN (NAME.CITY,', ',
                  NAME.STATE,' ',
                  NAME.ZIP);
```

274

Listing C-12. Improved Edit a Data File (13-4) (Continued).

```
WRITELN (NAME,PHONE);
WRITELN;
WRITELN
('IS THIS RECORD TO BE CORRECTED? ');
READ (CH);
WRITELN;
IF CH ='Y'
  THEN BEGIN
  WRITE
    ('DELETE (D) OR CHANGE (C) ');
  READ (CH);
  WRITELN;
  IF CH = 'C' THEN BEGIN
   REPEAT
    WRITELN;
    WRITE
    ('TYPE RETURN TO RETAIN ');
    WRITELN
    ('SAME INFORMATION IN FIELD');

    WRITELN
   ('PREFIX: MR, mRS, MS, MIss, DR,');
    WRITE
('       Mr.& Mrs, Dr.&Mrs        ');
    RSTRNG (INSTR);
    IF INSTR [1] <> NULL
     THEN FOR N := 1 TO 2
     DO NAME,PREFIX [N] := INSTR [N];
    WRITELN;

    WRITE
('INPUT FIRST NAME                ');
    RSTRNG (INSTR);
    IF INSTR [1] <> NULL
     THEN FOR N := 1 TO 12
     DO NAME,FIRST [N] := INSTR [N];
    WRITELN;

    WRITE
('INPUT MIDDLE INITIAL            ');
```

275

Listing C-12. Improved Edit a Data File (13-4) (Continued).

```
    RSTRNG (INSTR);
    IF INSTR [1] <> NULL
     THEN NAME.INITIAL [1] :=
                      INSTR [1];
    WRITELN;

    WRITE
('INPUT LAST NAME                  ');
    RSTRNG (INSTR);
    IF INSTR [1] <> NULL
      THEN FOR N := 1 TO 15
        DO NAME.LAST [N] := INSTR [N];
    WRITELN;

    WRITE
('INPUT STREET ADDRESS             ');
    RSTRNG (INSTR);
    IF INSTR [1] <> NULL
     THEN NAME.STREET := INSTR;
    WRITELN;

    WRITE
('ADDITIONAL ADDRESS (CR IF NONE)  ');
    RSTRNG (INSTR);
    IF INSTR [1] <> NULL
     THEN NAME.ADDITIONAL := INSTR;
    WRITELN;

    WRITE
('CITY                             ');
    RSTRNG (INSTR);
    IF INSTR [1] <> NULL
     THEN FOR N := 1 TO 15
        DO NAME.CITY [N] := INSTR [N];
    WRITELN;

    WRITE
('STATE                            ');
    RSTRNG (INSTR);
    IF INSTR [1] <> NULL
```

276

Listing C-12. Improved Edit a Data File (13-4) (Continued).

```
              THEN FOR N := 1 TO 2
                DO NAME.STATE [N] := INSTR [N];
              WRITELN;

              WRITE
          ('ZIP                              ');
                RSTRNG (INSTR);
                IF INSTR [1] <> NULL
                  THEN FOR N := 1 TO 7
                    DO NAME.ZIP [N] := INSTR [N];
                WRITELN'

              WRITE
          ('PHONE (AAA PPP-NNNN)             ),
                RSTRNG (INSTR);
                IF INSTR [1] <> NULL
                 THEN FOR N := 1 TO 12
                   DO NAME.PHONE [N] := INSTR [N];
                WRITELN;
                WRITE ('OK TO WRITE TO DISK? ');
                READ (CH);
                WRITELN;
              UNTIL CH = 'Y';

              WRITE (OUTDATA, NAME);
            END; { IF CH = 'C' }
          END; {IF CH = 'Y' }
        END; { IF NOT ENDFILE }
      UNTIL EOF (INDATA);
      FOR N := 1 TO 20 DO
      BEGIN
        IF SEARCHLIST [N].LAST [1] <> NULL
          THEN WRITELN (SEARCHLIST [N].FIRST,
            ' ',SEARCHLIST [N].INITIAL,'. ',
                SEARCHLIST [N].LAST,
                ' NOT FOUND xxxxxxx');
      END;
END.
```

Listing C-13. Improved Create or Add to a File (13-5).

```
PROGRAM CREADD (INPUT, OUTPUT, DATA, INDATA);

LABEL
   10;

CONST
   CLRSCRN = CHR(26); { CHARACTER CONSTANT }
   NULL = CHR(0);

TYPE
   STRING32 = ARRAY [1..32] OF CHAR;
   STRING15 = ARRAY [1..15] OF CHAR;
   STRING12 = ARRAY [1..12] OF CHAR;
   STRING7  = ARRAY [1..7] OF CHAR;
   STRING2  = ARRAY [1..2] OF CHAR;
   STRING1  = ARRAY [1..1] OF CHAR;

   NAMES = RECORD
            PREFIX     : STRING2;
            FIRST      : STRING12;
            INITIAL    : STRING1;
            LAST       : STRING15;
            STREET     : STRING32;
            ADDITIONAL : STRING32;
            CITY       : STRING15;
            STATE      : STRING2;
            ZIP        : STRING7;
            PHONE      : STRING12
        END;


VAR
   CH : CHAR;
   NAME : NAMES;
   INDATA,
   DATA : FILE OF NAMES;
   INSTR : STRING32;
   N : INTEGER ; { LOOP INDEX }
```

Listing C-13. Improved Create or Add a File (13-5) (Continued)

```
PROCEDURE RSTRNG (VAR X : STRING32);


BEGIN
   FOR N := 1 TO 32 DO X [N] := CHR (0),
                    { FILL WITH NULLS }
   N := 1;
   REPEAT
      READ (CH);
      IF (N>1) AND (CH = CHR(8))
         THEN N := N - 2
         ELSE BEGIN
                  IF NOT EOLN
                     THEN X [N] := CH;
              END;
      IF N = 0 THEN X [1] := NULL;
      N := N + 1;
   UNTIL EOLN OR (N > 32);
END;

BEGIN
   REWRITE (DATA);
   WRITE (CLRSCRN);
   WRITE ('CREATE A NEW FILE (C) OR ADD ');
   WRITELN ('TO AN OLD ONE (A) ');
   READ (CH);
   IF CH = 'A'
      THEN BEGIN
      RESET (INDATA);
      READ (INDATA,NAME);
      WHILE NOT EOF (INDATA) DO
      BEGIN
         IF NAME.LAST [2] <> NULL
          THEN WRITE (DATA,NAME);
             {PATCH TO REMOVE NULL RECORDS }
          READ (INDATA,NAME);
      END; { WHILE NOT EOF }
   END; {IF CH = 'A' }
```

Listing C-13. Improved Create or Add to a file (13-5) (Continued)

```
WRITE ('INPUT DATA AS PROMPTED. ');
WRITELN ('TO QUIT, ENTER RETURN');
WRITE (' ONLY FOR LAST NAME. ');
WRITELN (' (HIT RETURN TO CONTINUE.)');
READ (CH);

REPEAT
 REPEAT
   WRITE (CLRSCRN);

   WRITELN ('PREFIX: MR, mRS, MS, MIss, DR,');
   WRITE ('        Mr.& Mrs, Dr.&Mrs    ');
   RSTRNG (INSTR);
   FOR N := 1 TO 2
     DO NAME.PREFIX [N] := INSTR [N];
   WRITELN;

   WRITE ('INPUT FIRST NAME           ');
   RSTRNG (INSTR);
   FOR N := 1 TO 12
    DO NAME.FIRST [N] := INSTR [N];
   WRITELN;

   WRITE ('INPUT MIDDLE INITIAL      ');
   RSTRNG (INSTR);
   NAME.INITIAL [1] := INSTR [1];
   WRITELN;

   WRITE ('INPUT LAST NAME           ');
   RSTRNG (INSTR);
   FOR N := 1 TO 15
     DO NAME.LAST [N] := INSTR [N];
   WRITELN;
   IF NAME.LAST [1] = NULL
     THEN GOTO 10;

   WRITE , INPUT STREET ADDRESS      ');
   RSTRNG (NAME.STREET);
   WRITELN;
```

Listing C-13. Improved Create or Add to a File (13-5) (Continued).

```
      WRITE ('ADDITIONAL ADDRESS (CR IF NONE)  ');
      RSTRNG (NAME.ADDITIONAL);
      WRITELN;

      WRITE ('CITY                              ');
      RSTRNG (INSTR);
      FOR N := 1 TO 15
        DO NAME.CITY [N] := INSTR [N];
      WRITELN;

      WRITE ('STATE                             ';
      RSTRNG (INSTR);
      FOR N := 1 TO 2
       DO NAME.STATE [N] := INSTR [N];
      WRITELN;

      WRITE ('ZIP                               ');
      RSTRNG (INSTR);
      FOR N := 1 TO 7
       DO NAME.ZIP [N] := INSTR [N];
      WRITELN;

      WRITE ('PHONE (AAA PPP-NNNN)              ');
      RSTRNG (INSTR);
      FOR N := 1 TO 12
       DO NAME.PHONE [N] := INSTR [N];
      WRITELN;

      WRITE ('OK TO WRITE RECORD TO DISK? ');
      READ (CH);
      WRITELN;
     UNTIL CH = 'Y';
 10: IF NAME.LAST [2] <> NULL
         THEN WRITE (DATA, NAME);
    UNTIL NAME.LAST [2] = NULL;
END.
```

Listing C-14. Improved Sort a Data File (13-6).

```
PROGRAM SORTNAME (INPUT, OUTPUT, INDATA, OUTDATA.

CONST
   CLRSCRN = CHR(26); { CHARACTER CONSTANT }
   NULL = CHR(0);

TYPE
   STRING32 = ARRAY [1..32] OF CHAR;
   STRING15 = ARRAY [1..15] OF CHAR;
   STRING12 = ARRAY [1..12] OF CHAR;
   STRING7  = ARRAY [1..7] OF CHAR;
   STRING2  = ARRAY [1..2] OF CHAR;
   STRING1  = ARRAY [1..1] OF CHAR;


   NAMES = RECORD
             PREFIX     : STRING2;
             FIRST      : STRING12;
             INITIAL    : STRING1;
             LAST       : STRING15;
             STREET     : STRING32;
             ADDITIONAL : STRING32;
             CITY       : STRING15;
             STATE      : STRING2;
             ZIP        : STRING7;
             PHONE      : STRING12
           END;

VAR
   CH          : CHAR;
   NAME        : NAMES;
   INDATA,
   OUTDATA     : FILE OF NAMES;
   INSTR       : STRING32;
   N, NUMITEMS : INTEGER ; { LOOP INDEX }
   TAGS        : ARRAY [1..200] OF INTEGER;
   BIGARRAY    : ARRAY [1..200] OF NAMES;
   ZIP         : BOOLEAN ;
        { SORT MODE LAST NAME IF NOT ZIP }
```

Listing C-14. Improved Sort a Data File (13-6) (Continued).

```
PROCEDURE SORT (FIRST, LAST:INTEGER);

CONST
    FIRSTINT = 255;

VAR
    INTERVAL, { INTERVAL BETWEEN ITEMS TO BE COMPARED }
    INDEX,    { POINTER, HOLDS PLACE WHEN SWAP
                POINTERS BACK UP }
    ITEM1 : INTEGER;
            { POINTER FOR FIRST ITEM FOR COMPARISON }

    TOSWAP,            { FLAG TO SWAP ITEMS   }
    SWAPPED : BOOLEAN;  { FLAG FOR SWAPPED DATA }

PROCEDURE SWAP;

VAR
    TEMP : INTEGER;
        { FOR SAVING ONE VALUE DURING SWAP }
BEGIN
    TEMP := TAGS [ITEM1];
    TAGS [ITEM1] := TAGS [ITEM1+INTERVAL];
    TAGS [ITEM1+INTERVAL] := TEMP;
    SWAPPED := TRUE;
END;

PROCEDURE COMPAREZIP;

VAR
    FIRST,SECOND : CHAR;

BEGIN
    TOSWAP := FALSE;
    N := 1;
    REPEAT
        FIRST :=
                BIGARRAY [TAGS [ITEM1]].ZIP [N];
        SECOND := BIGARRAY
            [TAGS [ITEM1 + INTERVAL]].ZIP [N];
```

Listing C-14. Improved Sort a Data File (13-6) (Continued).

```
      IF FIRST > SECOND THEN TOSWAP := TRUE;
      N := N + 1;
   UNTIL (FIRST <> SECOND) OR (N = 8);
END;


PROCEDURE COMPARENAME;

VAR
   FIRST,SECOND : CHAR;

BEGIN
   TOSWAP := FALSE;
   N := 1;
   REPEAT
      FIRST :=
            BIGARRAY [TAGS [ITEM1]].LAST [N];
      SECOND := BIGARRAY
            [TAGS [ITEM1 + INTERVAL]].LAST [N];
      IF FIRST > SECOND THEN TOSWAP := TRUE;
      N := N + 1;
   UNTIL (FIRST <> SECOND) OR (N = 16);
END;



BEGIN

   { INITIALIZE VARIABLES }
   INTERVAL := FIRSTINT ;
   REPEAT
      INTERVAL := INTERVAL DIV 2;
   UNTIL INTERVAL < LAST;
   INDEX := FIRST;
   ITEM1 := FIRST;

   WRITELN;
   WRITELN ('SORTING BY SHELL METZNER SORT');
   WRITELN;
```

Listing C-14. Improved Sort a Data File (13-6) (Continued)

```
    REPEAT
       SWAPPED := FALSE;

       IF ZIP
          THEN COMPAREZIP
          ELSE COMPARENAME;

       IF TOSWAP THEN
       BEGIN
          SWAP;
          ITEM1 := ITEM1 - INTERVAL;
       END;
       IF (NOT SWAPPED) OR (ITEM1 < 1) THEN
       BEGIN
          INDEX := INDEX + 1;
          IF INDEX > (LAST - INTERVAL) THEN
          BEGIN
             INTERVAL := INTERVAL DIV 2;
             INDEX := 1;
          END;
          ITEM1 := INDEX;
       END;
    UNTIL INTERVAL = 0;
END; { SHELL SORT }

BEGIN
   RESET (INDATA);
   REWRITE (OUTDATA);

   FOR N := 1 TO 200 DO TAGS [N] := N;
                 {INITIALIZE POINTER ARRAY.

   REPEAT
      WRITE
   ('SORT BY LAST NAME (N) OR ZIP CODE (Z)?');
      READ (CH);
      WRITELN
   UNTIL CH IN ['N','Z'];

      IF CH = 'N' THEN ZIP := FALSE;
```

285

Listing C-14. Improved Sort a Data File (13-6) (Continued).

```
    IF CH = 'Z' THEN ZIP := TRUE;

  READ (INDATA, NAME);
  N := 1;
  WHILE NOT EOF (INDATA) DO
  BEGIN
      BIGARRAY [N] := NAME;
      READ (INDATA, NAME);
      N := N + 1;
  END;
  NUMITEMS := N-1;
  SORT (1,NUMITEMS);
  FOR N := 1 TO NUMITEMS DO
  BEGIN
      WRITE (OUTDATA, BIGARRAY [TAGS [N]]);
  END;
END.
```

Appendix D

Basic
RIP

Compilers vs Assemblers

This chapter is a little parenthetical insert to explain a few of the reasons that compilers generate less efficient code than do assemblers. Since I am presently running a 6809 system, the assembler listings here will be 6809 versions. The 6809 has a multiplicity of addressing modes and a register set that needs to be described. There are two index registers, X and Y. Both are 16 bits long. There are two 8 bit accumulators, A and B, which are concatenated to form the D accumulator. In the D configuration, A is the high order and B the low. In addition, there are two stack pointers, S and U. The "system stack" uses the S pointer. All subroutine return addresses are automatically pushed on the system stack. The U stack is the "User" stack. The programmer may use it or ignore it. The processor doesn't use it for any system functions. Indexed addressing may use X, Y, S, or U as the pointer, and it may include a constant offset as in LDD 5,X; a register offset as in LDA B,X. You may also specify a post increment mode as in LDA 0,X+ (or ++ for a double increment), or a pre decrement mode LDB 0,—X.

If you have done assembler programming with any microprocessor, you should be able to follow this discussion. As an example, I am going to use the compiler output from two compilers that generate assembler source code and an assembler version of the same thing. Refer to the Listing 8-3, the Sieve program, for finding prime numbers. The main loop in the program that does all the work is:

```
WHILE J <= HALFMAX DO
BEGIN
    PRIME [J] := FALSE;
    J := J + INTERVAL;
END·
```

LINE AT A TIME COMPILING

The compiler, first of all, will treat each statement by itself. That is, most compilers don't look at the context of the statement. They don't assume that any register contains useful results from a previous calculation. They must assume the worst case. For example, if the compiler has multiple dimensioned array capability, it will handle array references in some standard way that will work for both single and multiple dimensions, though there might be a faster way to access singly dimensioned arrays. That means, of course that the more capable compilers will be less efficient. Naturally an assembler programmer will always try to save results in a register for use in the next section of code, or in a repeat loop. The compiler will generate code in most cases that will look rather "mechanical" compared to assembler coding. One of the compilers that I use generated the following code for the prime number program main loop:

```
* WHILE J <= HALFMAX DO

LBL1    EQU     *
        LDX     J               J IS THE VARIABLE NAME
        PSHU    X
        LDX     HALFMAX
        TFR     X,D             TRANSFER CONTENTS OF
                                    X TO D

        LDX     #0
        CMPD    ,U++
        BLO     *+5
        LDX     #1
        CMPX    #0
        LBEQ    LBL2

*

* PRIME J := 0

LDX     #PRIME
PSHU    X
```

288

```
        LDX    j
        PULU   D
        LEAX   D,X
        PSHU   X
        LDX    #0
        TFR    X,D
        STB    [,U++]      INDIRECT ADDRESSING

*
* J := J + INTERVAL;
        LDX    j
        PSHU   X
        LDX    INTERVAL
        PULU   D
        LEAX   D,X
        STX    J
        LBRA   LBL1
LBL2    EQU    *
```

HAND OPTIMIZATION

This compiler is reasonably efficient, tnough a little hand optimization can reduce the code here by a factor of two or so. Notice the rather awkward handling of comparing the variables J and HALFMAX. The previous section of code calculated the initial value for J and the last instruction on the previous line is STX J. This section starts with LDX J. As I indicated above, the compiler is not "smart enough" to know that the index register X already contains the value of J. Of course, optimization could be done by removing the adjacent STX and LDX instructions. In this case, the last step in the loop is STX J also. This may be removed too. For some unknown reason, this compiler does the compare backwards. That is, it compares halfmax to J rather than the other way around.

The next section of code compiled for PRIME [J] := 0 loads the index register with the base address of the array PRIME. It then gets the index J. The LEAX D,X instruction simply adds D, the index, to X, the base address, and puts the results in X. Since the compiler seems to be obsessed with using X for all operations, it pushes X on the stack, gets the value 0 in X, transfers it to D, and stores it via the B register and an indirect addressing mode instruction in the address that X pushed on the user stack. The code is rather efficient, but the following would do the same thing in a more straightforward manner:

```
LDX     #PRIME
LDD     J
LEAX    D,X
LDB     #0
STB     0,X
```

The final section of code simply increments J by the amount in INTERVAL. The writer of this compiler has chosen to use the LEAX D,X instruction to implement the addition of two INTEGER numbers. We could implement this by:

```
LDX     J
LDD     INTERVAL
LEAX    D,X
STX     J
```

alternately

```
LDD     .
ADDD    INTERVAL
STD     J
```

You should be gaining some understanding as to why the code is inefficient. Actually, as compilers go, this is rather good code. It has implemented 16 bit compares and array index calculations without resorting to a single call to a runtime 16 bit add or 16 bit subtract subroutine!

ASSEMBLER VERSION

Just for comparison, a version of this whole section of code, written in assembler takes advantage of the fact that X contains the initial J value, and that register B may contain the value INTERVAL. The loop can be reduced to the following in an assembler version:

```
CRSLP   CMPX  HLFMAX  X CONTAINS THE VALUE J
        BHI   NXTINT  WHILE J <= HLFMAX
        CLR   0,X     PRIME [J] := 0
        ABX           J := J + INTERVAL
        BRA   CRSLP   END
NXTINT
```

If that seems incredibly short by comparison, remember that the registers had to be set up initially so that they contained the values for J and INTERVAL. If there is a point to be made, it is that the assembler programmer probably used more instructions outside of the loop to set it up, but minimized the execution time within the loop. This was done deliberately because this loop is executed several thousand times in finding the primes to a limit of 10,000. The author of the assembler program realized that INTERVAL would never exceed a value that would fit a single byte and so used the B accumulator. The instruction ABX (Add B to X) is a specialized and much faster instruction than LEAX D,X (LoaD Effective Address X, or in other words increment X by D). A compiler written to recognize all these facts and the context of the line of high level code would be very complex, large, and slow!

ANOTHER COMPILER'S OUTPUT

Now, let's look at another compiler output. This one too, is supposed to generate assembler source code. While it is true that the code generated may be assembled with a 6809 assembler, there is little more to indicate that it is assembler code. The code for these same lines is as follows:

```
* WHILE J <= HALFMAX DO
PF0014          EQU          *
                LDD          BOS-$0098
                PSHU         D
                LDD          BOS-$00A0
                PSHU         D
                LDA          $08
                PSHU         A
                LBSR         OPR05
*BEGIN
*    PRIME [J] := FALSE;
                LDX          #BOS-$0098
                PSHU         X
                LDD          BOS-$0098
                PSHU         D
                LBSR         INT01
                FDB          $0001
                FDB          $3A97
                FDB          $0001
                LDA          #$00
                STA          [0,U++]
*  J := J + INTERVAL;
```

```
                              LDX          #BOS-$0098
                              PSHU         X
                              LDD          BOS-$0098
                              PSHU         D
                              LDD          BOS-$009C
                              PSHU         D
                              LBSR         OPR00
                              PULU         X,D
                              STD          0,X
    ~ END (WHILE J)
                              LBRA         PF0014
    PF0015                    EQU     *
```

While this is still assembler code, you might agree that it is
considerably more abstract than that in the first compiler output.
The assembler code generated is obviously setting up parameters
and constants, and calling runtime package subroutines. Incidentally, in this implementation, all the global variables are on the User
stack of the 6809, and are referenced not by name but by their offset
from the BOS (bottom of stack). The source lines may be included
as comments, but this sort of code generation obviously lends itself
to optimization with a great deal more difficulty than the code in the
first example.

A P-code compiler generates code that is generally not listable
(though some versions have a sort of P-code disassembler) and
therefore not possible to optimize by hand. In general, P-code will
be more compact than the last preceding example. Since the P-code
doesn't execute directly, but must be interpreted, it is slower than
"native code."

CONCLUSION

To summarize, the code generated by a compiler is less efficient because it must treat each statement as a separate entity. It
can't look at the context and make decisions about register alloca-
tions, the use of a single byte for a value that won't exceed 8 bit
representation, for example. The compiler will have predetermined
the use of all the machine's resources, and these will remain fixed
throughout the program. A good assembler programmer will, on the
other hand, try to leave the results of one operation in registers for
the next operation. In my opinion at least, it is this overall approach
control, which the assembler programmer has, that allows his
programs to be so much more efficient than the compiler output.

Perhaps someday when computer memory capabilities become larger and compiler writers can "bootstrap" their compilers by writing them efficiently in higher-level languages, some better "optimizing compilers" will be written. These will look at context, and provide some flexibility in the assignment of registers. They will recognize when results are available in a register and may be left there for use in the next section of code, and they will approach much more closely what can be done by a good assembler programmer

Glossary

Glossary of Pascal Terms

AND—A logical operator. It is used to perform the AND function between two logical expressions as in:

IF (A>B) AND (C>D) THEN ...

ARRAY—A single- or multiple-dimensioned data structure. A single-dimensional array is called a vector. It could be described as a list. Arrays are accessed by a single variable name and a number for each dimension as in TABLE [3,4]. In the case of two-dimensional arrays, you might visualize the dimensions as representing row and column in a table. In Pascal square brackets are used to contain array subscripts. Subscripts may be expressions, constants, or variables of types INTEGER, SCALLAR, or CHAR. Standard Pascal allows arrays of up to seven dimensions, though it is hard to visualize an array of dimensions greater than three. Some implementations limit the maximum to less than seven.

BEGIN—Used as a starting delimiter for a compound statement or a WHILE DO loop.

block—The term for a complete unit of a Pascal program. A program is a block as is a procedure or function. A block has the following structure. Many of the items are optional, but if present must be in this order.

PROGRAM (PARAMETERS)
LABEL

```
CONST
TYPE
VAR
PROCEDURE (OR FUNCTION) (A BLOCK)
BEGIN
END.
```

BOOLEAN—A variable type that has only the two values TRUE and FALSE.

CASE—A reserved word indicating the start of a case statement structure. The case statement is sometimes called an "n way branch". It provides means for taking a number of different courses of action based on a number of conditions. (See Chapter 4.)

```
CASE CH OF
    'A' : APPEND;
    'E' : BEGIN
            WRITELN ('THE END');
            EXIT
          END;
    'F',
    'Z' : FIXIT;
END;
```

CHAR—A type of variable that holds an ASCII character.

CHR—A function that converts an INTEGER to an ASCII character. WRITE (CHR(13));, for example will write a carriage return to the output file. It is used primarily to output control characters.

comment—An explanation of a program statement or section. Comments in Pascal may be enclosed in "curly braces" ( ) or, since these don't appear on all terminal keyboards, with the double delimiters (**). Most implementations of Pascal accept either.

compound statement—A group of simple statements enclosed between BEGIN and END. Compound statements are treated like single statements. They are used in such structures as IF THEN ELSE statements. Where the "object" of the THEN or ELSE may be a compound statement.

conditional—Conditional branching is one form of control of program flow, exemplified by the CASE statement, the IF THEN ELSE, WHILE DO, and REPEAT UNTIL structures.

CONST—The heading of the section of the program or block where the constants are declared.

DIV—The operator for the INTEGER division function. The result is truncated. 4 DIV 3 = 1 and 3 DIV 4 = 0.

DO—Used in FOR DO and WHILE DO constructs. The words FOR DO or WHILE DO bracket the conditions as in:
    FOR N := 1 TO 25 DO ...
    WHILE K < 17 DO ..

DOWNTO—The keyword that indicates a descending count for a FOR DO loop:
    FOR K := 30 DOWNTO 1 DO ...

ELSE—*See* IF THEN ELSE

END—The keyword that terminates a compound statement initiated by a BEGIN. It also terminates a CASE statement and a RECORD type declaration.

FOR—The keyword for a FOR DO loop. The loop may encompass a single statement or a compound one:
    FOR INDEX := 1 TO 17 DO
    BEGIN
        STATEMENT;
        STATEMENT;
        STATEMENT
    END;

    FOR INDEX := 17 DOWNTO 1 DO STATEMENT;
The index variable for a FOR DO loop may be of type INTEGER, CHAR, or SCALAR. A STEP may not be specified.

function—The identifier for a function block. A function returns a result which must be assigned to a variable in the function call
    FUNCTION HALF (NUMBER : INTEGER) : INTEGER;
    BEGIN
        HALF := NUMBER DIV 2;
    END;

(IN PROGRAM BODY)

RESULT := HALF(88); (THE PARAMETER MAY BE A VARIABLE OF EXPRESSION)

HEX—Some implementations of Pascal allow hexadecimal numbers as an aid to manipulating machine hardware address information. These implementations have a variable type HEX that may have hexadecimal integer values within the range of the valid values for INTEGER numbers.

IN—Used as a test to see if a value is included in a list or the value of a SET variable.

IF A IN [1..23] THEN ....

IF CHARACTER IN ['A'..'F'] THEN ...

IF LETTER IN ['A','E','I','O','U'] THEN VOWEL := TRUE;

INTEGER—A variable type that holds a whole (or integer) number value. Microprocessor implementations usually limit the range of values to those represented by 16 bit binary numbers, (-32768 to 32767).

literal—The term used to describe a STRING represented by a number of characters between single quotation marks as in 'This is a literal string' as opposed to a string represented by a variable name, and also distinguishes a literal numerical constant such as 3, as opposed to a symbolic constant or variable.

MARK—Used in connection with dynamic variable allocation to mark the start of allocation so that memory may be deallocated later with RELEASE.

MOD—The function that returns the remainder of an integer divide. 5 MOD 3 yields 2, the remainder of the division.

NEW—Used to create or allocate memory for a RECORD to be pointed at by the variable used as the argument for NEW.

NEW (FIRST);

This statement would allocate memory for a record of the type for which FIRST was declared as a pointer, and set the value of the variable FIRST to be pointing at that record.

NIL—The empty pointer value usually assigned to the pointer in the last RECORD of a linked list to indicate the end of the list.

NOT—The logical negation operator. If Boolean variable A has the value of FALSE, NOT A has the value of TRUE.

ODD—A function in Pascal which returns a Boolean value of TRUE if the parameter is ODD and FALSE if it is even. You could define ODD as:

```
FUNCTION ODD (VALUE : INTEGER) : BOOLEAN;
BEGIN
    ODD := VALUE MOD 2 < > 0;
END;
```

This construction is unusual even for Pascal, but valid. Since ODD is a BOOLEAN variable, and VALUE MOD 2 < > 0 is a Boolean expression.

OPERATOR—A general term for the mathematical operators indicating the four functions (+, −, *, and /), and the logical operators >, <, =, and combinations of these. The logical functions of AND, OR, and NOT are operators as are the integer MOD and DIV.

OR—A logical operator used to perform the logical OR function of two Boolean expressions or variables as in

IF A OR B THEN ...

The resulting expression evaluates TRUE if either of the Boolean expressions joined by the OR is TRUE (or if both are true). Expressions joined by an OR must be parenthesized if they are not just simple variable names, for example, IF (TOP < BOTTOM) OR (NUMBER > 23).

ORD—A function that returns the integer value of a variable or literal of type CHAR or SCALAR. ORD ('A') returns 65, the decimal ASCII value of 'A'. If a TYPE DAYSOFWEEK = (SUN, MON, TUE, WED, THU, FRI, SAT); has been declared, and a variable DAY of that type has the value TUE, ORD (DAY) will return the integer value 2. ORD (SUN) will return 0. The value corresponds to the order of the values listed in the type declaration, starting at zero.

parameter—A parameter is a value or a pointer passed to a BLOCK, usually a FUNCTION or a PROCEDURE. In the statement Y := SIN (X), X is the parameter passed to the function SIN. Parameters are enclosed in parentheses.

POINTER—A type of variable that may point at a RECORD. Pointers are usually associated with linked lists. See Chapter 16.

PRED—A function that returns the predecessor of an ordered variable (INTEGER or SCALAR type). PRED(TUE) would re turn MON. PRED (5) would return 4

program—*See* block.

PROCEDURE— The Pascal word for subroutine. A procedure may be passed parameters and may return them or modify global variables. Procedures are not required to have parameters either input or returned.

READ— A predeclared function used to read input data from a file or the terminal. READ (DATAFILE, X); would read the value of the variable X from a file named DATAFILE. If X were INTEGER, the file would have to be of type INTEGER or CHAR.

READLN— A function that is similar to READ except that after reading, it skips to the start of the next line of the file (i.e. past the next EOLN. READLN is only valid when reading a file of CHAR.

REAL— The variable type that deals with numbers that may have decimal fractions such as PI (3.141592654). The number of significant digits for REAL numbers will vary with the implementation.

RECORD— A variable type that may be defined as a combination of only variable types as sub parts of the RECORD, usually called fields.

```
TYPE
    CUSTOMER = RECORD
            COMPANYNAME : ARRAY [1..32] OF CHAR;
            ADDRESS   : ARRAY ]1..32] OF CHAR;
            CITY   : ARRAY [1..20] OF CHAR;
            STATE   : ARRAY [1..2] OF CHAR;
            ZIP   : ARRAY [1..7] OF CHAR
    END;
```

The record type is CUSTOMER, and the fields are defined as arrays of character of various lengths.

RELEASE— The keyword that releases the memory that has been allocated for a linked list. Memory is released back to the last MARK statement. That is, all RECORDS that have been created by using NEW since the last time MARK was used, are "forgotten"

REPEAT— The keyword that signals the start of a REPEAT UNTIL loop. The REPEAT UNTIL is always executed at least once since the test condition for exiting the loop is at the end.

```
N := 1;
REPEAT
    N := N + 1;
UNTIL N > 9;
```

reserved—A reserved word may not be used as an identifier in a program under any circumstances. Reserved words in Pascal are such words as BEGIN, END, READ, WRITE, REPEAT, UNTIL, FOR, DO, WHILE, TO, DOWNTO, etc. That is, all the words used as keywords. Predeclared function and procedure names are in general not reserved. Functions such as ODD may be redefined in your program.

RESET—The PROCEDURE used to open a file for read. RESET (DATA).

REWRITE—The PROCEDURE used to open a file for write. REWRITE (DATA).

SCALAR—The listed or enumerated data type.

TYPE
    DIRECTION = (LEFT, RIGHT);

VAR
    TURNSIGNAL : DIRECTION;

TURNSIGNAL is a SCALAR variable. It can have only the values LEFT and RIGHT, that were enumerated in the type declaration.

SET—A type of variable that is declared as "SET OF (SCALAR TYPE). The SCALAR type must have been declared previously. For example:

TYPE
    COLORS = (RED, BLUE, GREEN, YELLOW, MAGENTA, CYAN);

VAR
    COLOR : COLORS;
    MIX : SET OF COLORS;

The variable COLOR is a SCALAR TYPE and its value may be any one of the colors listed in the TYPE declaration. The value of MIX, the SET variable may include none, one, several, or all of the colors in the type declaration. That is, MIX may have the value [] (empty), [RED], [BLUE, MAGENTA, GREEN], or any other combination of the values allowed COLOR. See Chapter 17.

statement—A group of keywords, variable names, operators, constants etc. that perform some program action. A statement is ended by a semicolon or one of the terminators END or UNTIL. A statement is to a program what a sentence is to prose.

```
IF A < B
    THEN C := 1
    ELSE C := 2;
‾OR K := 1 TO 17 DO THING [K] := K/(8*PI);
```

A group of statements between the keywords BEGIN and END form a compound statement.

SUCC—(SUCCESSOR). The function that returns the next item of ˙n ordered type such as INTEGER or SCALAR. This function is the inverse of PRED.

```
SUCC (5) = 6
SUCC (TUE) = WED
```

THEN—*See* IF THEN ELSE
TO—*See* FOR DO
TYPE—The heading of the section of the program where variable type declarations are made.

UNTIL—*See* REPEAT.

VAR—VAR has two uses. It is the heading of the program section where the variables are declared, and it serves to indicate in a PROCEDURE parameter list that the value of the parameter is not to be passed to the procedure, but a pointer to the location of the variable, so that the procedure may modify that variable (to return the results of the procedure).

```
PROCEDURE POLAR (X,Y : REAL; VAR RHO, THETA :
REAL);
(PROCEDURE TO CONVERT RECTANGULAR COOR-
DINATES TO POLAR FORM)
BEGIN
END;
```

```
(IN MAIN PROGRAM)
    POLAR (A,B,RADIUS,ANGLE);
```

The value in variables A and B are passed to POLAR, whic‾ modifies the contents of the variables RADIUS and ANGLE to return the result of the conversion.

WHILE—This is the keyword for a WHILE DO loop. This loop differs from the REPEAT UNTIL loop in that the test of the conditions to stay in the loop is made before the loop is executed, and the loop will not be executed even once if the test fails.

```
A := 1;
WHILE A < 9 DO
BEGIN
    A := A + 1;
    B := B + A;
END;
```

WRITE—A procedure to write to an output file or terminal.

WRITE (DATA, 'THIS IS A TEST');

This statement will write 'THIS IS A TEST' to a file identified as DATA, provided the file is open for write, and is a file of CHAR.

WRITELN—A procedure to write to an output file or terminal. This procedure does the same thing as WRITE except that it adds a CR to the end of the line. WRITELN; is a valid statement that causes a linefeed and carriage return on the output device. Writeln is only valid to a FILE OF CHAR.

Basic
RIP

Index

309

Edited by Dennis Thurlow